The Good Citizen

Second Edition

The Good Citizen

How a Younger Generation Is Reshaping American Politics

Second Edition

Russell J. Dalton
University of California, Irvine

Los Angeles | London | New Delhi
Singapore | Washington DC

Los Angeles | London | New Delhi
Singapore | Washington DC

FOR INFORMATION:

CQ Press

An Imprint of SAGE Publications, Inc.

2455 Teller Road

Thousand Oaks, California 91320

E-mail: order@sagepub.com

SAGE Publications Ltd.

1 Oliver's Yard

55 City Road

London EC1Y 1SP

United Kingdom

SAGE Publications India Pvt. Ltd.

B 1/I 1 Mohan Cooperative Industrial Area

Mathura Road, New Delhi 110 044

India

SAGE Publications Asia-Pacific Pte. Ltd.

3 Church Street

#10-04 Samsung Hub

Singapore 049483

Printed in the United States of America

Library of Congress Cataloging-in-Publication Data

Dalton, Russell J.
The good citizen : how a younger generation is reshaping American politics / Russell J. Dalton, University of California, Irvine. — Second edition.

pages cm
Includes bibliographical references and index.

ISBN 978-1-5063-1802-8 (pbk. : alk. paper)

1. Citizenship--United States. 2. Voluntarism—United States. 3. Youth—Political activity—United States. 4. Political culture—United States. I. Title.

JK1759.D179 2016
324.0835'0973—dc23   2015027583

This book is printed on acid-free paper.

Acquisitions Editor: Sarah Calabi

Editorial Assistant: Raquel Christie

Production Editor: Tracy Buyan

Copy Editor: Lynn Weber

Typesetter: C&M Digitals (P) Ltd.

Proofreader: Jeff Bryant

Cover Designer: Gail Buschman

Marketing Manager: Amy Whitaker

17 18 19 10 9 8 7 6 5 4 3 2

CONTENTS

TABLES AND FIGURES

TABLES

FIGURES

PREFACE TO THE SECOND EDITION

In the midst of a period of gloom and doom about democracy in America, the first edition of this book made the contrarian argument that the chorus of experts criticizing the American public—and young people in particular—had overlooked important counterevidence. Previous scholarship had created a conventional wisdom that highlighted the negatives and overlooked the positives—it looked back to the past with excessive admiration and looked forward to the future with guarded pessimism.

The catchphrase for the first edition of *The Good Citizen* was "The good news is . . . the bad news is wrong" (or at least overstated). It argued that changing norms of citizenship were transforming American politics and society. The book described both positive and negative elements of this shift in citizenship norms and tried to provide a more balanced view of contemporary American democracy and its prospects for the future.

This study also had a strong generational theme. Like others, I saw much to admire in "the greatest generation" that lived through the Great Depression and World War II. However, I also saw elements of greatness or potential greatness among American youth. So the first edition discussed the strengths and weaknesses of different generations and rejected the view that to praise senior Americans one must denigrate the young.

Then came the 2008 U.S. presidential elections. I think it is fair to say that the conventional political science research implied that the Obama campaign was doomed from the start. As one of the leading academic specialists on voting said on the eve of the Iowa caucuses, "conventional wisdom has a name for candidates who rely on the youth vote: loser." His skepticism, and that of other election specialists, proved incorrect a week after he gave this quote. Obama amazed most observers by winning the Democratic Party nomination and, even more amazingly, doing this with young voters as a major part of his coalition. Then in November 2008 he won the election as the United States' forty-fourth president and then reelection in 2012. If you read *The Good Citizen* in 2007, you shouldn't have been so surprised by Obama's successful appeal to young Americans. So what is new now?

THE SECOND EDITION

This edition marshals new evidence on Americans' changing norms of citizenship and how this specifically applies to today's youth. In 2014 the General Social Survey (GSS) repeated many of the questions that were analyzed from the 2004 GSS in the first edition of this book. (Eventually the International Social Survey Program [ISSP] will distribute a cross-national replication of their 2004 survey.) Having evidence over time enables us to see if citizen norms are really changing. Moreover, the Great Recession during the intervening period might have challenged some of the conclusions of the first edition. Young people no longer see affluence as assured, partisan polarization has brought many policy issues into question, and there is increasing debate on the tolerance of Americans in this changing political context.

In addition, the 2014 survey allows us to study the Millennial Generation in closer details as they finish schooling and begin their careers and family. We can begin to see whether the distinct patterns of youth in 2004 were a consequence of being young that faded with age or are enduring characteristics of their generation. The 2014 GSS survey also asked new questions that allow us to examine the consequences of citizenship norms in other areas. Having two surveys separated by a decade is more than twice as good as having only one survey.

I also updated the statistical primer to help students in understanding the public opinion results presented throughout the book, especially the interpretation of correlations and similar statistics. This appears as Appendix A.

ACKNOWLEDGMENTS

The first edition of this book was dedicated to my good friend and colleague, Jack Peltason. Jack passed away in March 2015 as I was completing this revision. His commitment to American democracy guided my thinking and will continue to in the future. Jack was an impressive scholar and an even more impressive human being.

This project drew upon the support of many people. I want to thank Marc Howard and the Center for the Democracy and Civil Society (CDACS) at Georgetown University for involving me in a study of American opinions that stimulated the first edition of this book. I am equally indebted to the group of scholars who design and collect the GSS/ISSP surveys; these are extremely valuable resources for social science research.

Many colleagues have commented on various portions of this research in either the first or second editions, and I want to thank them for their advice: Charles Barrilleaux, Catherine Bolzendahl, Hilde Coffé, E. J. Dionne, David Farrell, James Gibson, Miki Caul Kittilson, Kevin Deegan Krause, Carl Schwartz, Tom Smith, Steve Weldon, and Christian Welzel. My planning for the second edition greatly benefited from the thoughtful reviews by Robert Boatright, Patricia Crouse, Terri Fine, Michael Franz, Shamira Gelbman, Tyler Johnson, Arthur Sanders, and Robert Schmuhl.

Students in some of my courses at UC Irvine read and commented on parts of this project and then the first edition of the book. Gianna Linnert provided administrative support on the second edition. I also benefited from the many universities and educational groups that invited me to talk about the first edition; sharing the contrarian findings of the book with students has been one of the most positive experiences in this project.

My UC Irvine colleague Martin Wattenberg was very helpful as I worked on this book, and he wrote a book expressing a much different view (*Is Voting for Young People?*). We did not change each other's minds, but this dialogue and the data Marty shared helped me to develop my thinking. Finally, Ronald Inglehart's research on postmaterial/self-expressive values provides the intellectual base for much of this presentation, so this book is a by-product of his mentorship over decades.

Charisse Kiino helped launch the first edition and is every author's dream of a knowledgeable and supportive editor. Sarah Calabi was an equally supportive editor for the second edition, and Lynn Weber thoughtfully improved my prose. CQ Press is a wonderful team to work with, and they produced a book that I hope students and their instructors will read and debate.

Finally, when I published the first edition it had a young woman on the cover in the famous Rosie the Riveter pose. My wife was flattered, because she assumed that I had chosen the drawing "of her" for the cover of the book. I assured her this was my plan. But since CQ Press decided on a different cover for the new edition, my only salvation is to thank her profusely in print and to dedicate this book to her. She is a testament that youth is a state of mind, as her high score on the Pew Millennial Quiz shows (www.pewresearch.org/quiz/how-millennial-are-you/).

Russell J. Dalton
Irvine, California

ABOUT THE AUTHOR

Russell J. Dalton is a research professor in the Center for the Study of Democracy at the University of California, Irvine. He has received a Fulbright professorship at the University of Mannheim, a Barbra Streisand Center fellowship, a German Marshall Research fellowship, and a POSCO fellowship at the East/West Center. He has written or edited over twenty books and 150 research articles that reflect his scholarly interests in comparative public opinion, political parties, social movements, and empirical democratic theory. He has also recently published two other books with CQ Press: *Citizen Politics: Public Opinion and Political Parties in Advanced Industrial Democracies* (2013) and *The Apartisan American: Dealignment and Changing Electoral Politics* (2012).

To Ginny Dalton

Thank you for the memories

and more in the future

CITIZENSHIP AND THE TRANSFORMATION OF AMERICAN SOCIETY

> Every age since the ancient Greeks fashioned an image of being political based upon citizenship.
>
> Engin Isin, *Being Political*

What does it mean to be a "good citizen" in today's society?

An article on the annual UCLA survey of college freshmen presented an interview with a California university student who had spent his semester break as a volunteer helping to salvage homes flooded by Hurricane Katrina.[1] The young man had organized a group of student volunteers, who then gave up their break to do hard labor in the devastated region far from their campus. He said finding volunteers willing to work "was easier than I expected." Indeed, the gist of the article was that volunteering in 2005 was at its highest percentage in the twenty-five years of the college survey. This experience was repeated as young people came to help with the destruction of Hurricane Sandy in 2012, and the UCLA survey found that volunteering had risen further in the fall 2013 freshman class.[2]

Later I also spoke with another student who had traveled to help with hurricane cleanup. Beyond this experience, he was active on a variety of social and political causes, from problems of development in Africa, to campus politics, to conflict in the Middle East. When I asked about his interest in political parties and elections, however, there was stark lack of interest. Like many of his fellow students, he had not voted in the last election. He had not participated in the presidential campaign, which was his first opportunity to vote. This behavior seems paradoxical considering the effort involved; it's just a short walk from the campus to the nearest polling station but almost a two thousand mile drive to go across country where he had volunteered.

These stories illustrate some of the ways that the patterns of citizenship are changing. Many young people in America—and in other Western democracies—are concerned about their society and others in the world. And they are willing to contribute their time and effort to make a difference. They see a role for themselves and their government in improving the world in which we live. At the same time, they relate to government and society in different ways than their elders. Research in the United States and other affluent democracies shows that today's citizens are the most educated, most cosmopolitan, and most supportive of self-expressive values than any others in the history of democracy.[3] So from both anecdotal and empirical perspectives, most of the social and political changes in the American public over the past half-century would seem to have strengthened the foundations of democracy.

Despite this positive and hopeful view of America, a very different story is often told today in political and academic circles. A recent essay in *The Economist* lists the mounting problems of contemporary democracies and then put the blame for what's gone wrong with democracy directly on its citizens: "The biggest challenge to democracy . . . comes from the voters themselves. Plato's great worry about democracy, that citizens would 'live day to day, indulging the pleasure of the moment', has proved prescient."[4] Similarly, a host of political analysts bemoan what is wrong with America and its citizens.[5] Too few of us are voting, we are disconnected from our fellow citizens and lacking in social capital, we are losing faith in our government, and the nation is in social disarray. The *lack* of good citizenship is the phrase you often hear as an explanation for these disturbing trends.

What you also hear is that the young are the primary source of this decline. Authors from Harvard professor Robert Putman to former television news anchor Tom Brokaw extol the civic values and engagement of the older "greatest generation" with great hyperbole.[6] Putnam along with many others hold that the slow, steady, and ineluctable replacement of older, civic-minded generations by the disaffected Generation X is the most important reason for the erosion of social capital in America.[7] These political experts seemingly agree that young Americans are dropping out of politics, losing faith in government, and even becoming disenchanted with their personal lives.[8] A recent *Time* magazine article on the Millennial Generation began with the following introduction:

> Here are some broad descriptions about the generation known as Millennials: They're narcissistic. They're lazy. They're coddled. They're even a bit delusional. Those aren't just unfounded negative stereotypes about 80 million Americans born roughly between 1980 and 2000. They're backed up by a decade of sociological research.[9]

Perhaps not since Aristotle held that "political science is not a proper study for the young" have youth been so roundly denounced by their elders.

At the same time, other experts are more positive. Ronald Inglehart, for example, says that younger generations are more committed to participatory values and democratic ideals, more concerned with the well-being of others, and more cognitively sophisticated than previous generations in the United States and other affluent democracies.[10] Other analysts discuss a younger generation that is politically engaged, albeit in different ways than their elders.[11] Contemporary research points to the rising levels of volunteerism among the young, ranging from Teach America to the Peace Corps to local community activities. Youth are also more positive toward the political and social diversity of America, more tolerant of others. Thus, *The Economist* recently had a special article on youth that began with a different tag line: "Today's young people are held to be alienated, unhappy, violent failures. They are proving anything but."[12] So the debate continues, and it is an important debate because it portends our country's future.

We have two very different images of American society and politics. One perspective says American democracy is at risk in large part because of the changing values and participation patterns of the young. The other side points to new patterns of citizenship that have emerged among the young, the better educated, and other parts of American society. These opposing views have generated sharp debates about the vitality of our democracy, and they are the subject of this book.

Perhaps the subtitle for this volume should be: "The good news is . . . the bad news is wrong." Indeed, something is changing in American society and politics. But is it correct to conclude, as many do, that if politics is not working as it did in the past, then our entire system of democracy is at risk? To understand what is changing, and its implications for American democracy, it is more helpful first to ask that simple but fundamental question:

What does it mean to be a good citizen in America today?

Take a moment to think of how you would answer. What are the criteria you would use? Voting? Paying taxes? Obeying the law? Volunteer work? Protesting wrongdoing? Being concerned for those in need? Membership in a political party? Trusting government officials?

This book examines how the American public answers this question— and the fact is, people answer it in different ways. I argue that the changing definition of what it means to be a good citizen—what I call the *norms of citizenship*—are the key to understanding what is really going on.

Let me begin by summarizing the social restructuring of American society since the mid-twentieth century (Figure 1.1). Changing living standards, occupational experiences, the entry of women into the labor force, expanding civil rights, and other societal changes are producing two reinforcing effects. First, people possess new skills and resources that enable them to better manage the complexities of politics—people today are better educated, have more information available to them, and enjoy a higher standard of living. This removes some of the restrictions on democratic citizenship that existed in earlier time periods when these skills and resources were less commonly available. Second, social forces are reshaping social and political values. Americans are more assertive and less deferential to authority, and they place more emphasis on participating in the decisions affecting their lives. The expansion of these self-expressive values has a host of political implications.[13]

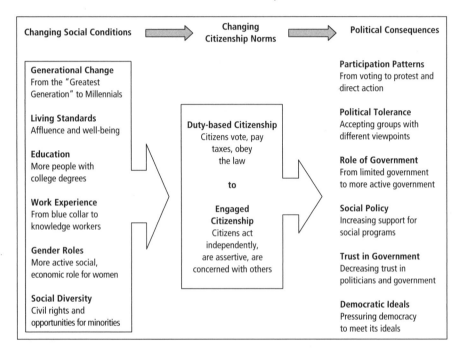

FIGURE 1.1   The Changing American Public

► *Changing social conditions reshape the norms of what it means to be a good citizen, and this affects how citizens act and think about politics.*

The figure suggests that as the characteristics of citizens and society have changed, this reshapes political values including the norms of good citizenship. Citizenship norms essentially define what people think is expected of them as participants in the political system, along with their expectations of government and the political process.

Most definitions of citizenship typically focus on the traditional norms of American citizenship—voting, paying taxes, serving on a jury—and how these seem to be eroding. I call this **duty-based citizenship** because these norms reflect the formal obligations, responsibilities, and rights of citizenship as they have been defined in the past.

However, it is just as important to examine new norms that make up what I call **engaged citizenship**. These norms are emerging among the American public with increasing prominence. Engaged citizenship emphasizes a more assertive role for the citizen and a broader definition of citizenship to include social concerns and the welfare of others. As illustrated by the Katrina volunteers, many Americans believe they are fully engaged in society even if they do not vote or conform to traditional definitions of citizenship. Moreover, the social and political transformation of the United States over the past several decades has systematically shifted the balance between these citizenship norms. Thus a second observation is that duty-based norms are decreasing, especially among the young, but the norms of engaged citizenship are increasing.

Third, Figure 1.1 suggests that changes in citizenship norms affect citizens' political values and behaviors. For instance, duty-based norms of citizenship stimulate turnout in elections and a sense of patriotic allegiance to the elected government, while engaged citizenship may promote other forms of political action, ranging from volunteerism to public protest. These contrasting norms also shape other political values, such as tolerance of others and public policy priorities. Even trust in government itself is influenced by how individuals define their own norms of citizenship.

American politics and the citizenry are changing. Before anyone can deliver a generalized indictment of the American public, we need a full understanding of how citizenship norms are changing and the effects of these changes. It is undeniable that the American public at the beginning of the twenty-first century is different from the American electorate in the mid-twentieth century. However, some of these differences, such as increased political tolerance and acceptance of diversity in society and politics, actually benefit American democracy. Other generational differences are just different—they're not a threat to American democracy unless these changes are ignored or resisted. A full examination of citizenship norms and their consequences will provide a more complex, and potentially more optimistic, picture of the challenges and opportunities facing American democracy today.

In addition, we need to place the American experience in a broader cross-national context. Many scholars who study American politics *only* study American politics. This leads to an introspective view of what is presumably unique about the American experience and how patterns of citizenship may, or may not be, idiosyncratic to the United States. American politics is the last great field of area study research in which one nation is examined by itself. Many trends apparent in American norms of citizenship and political activity are common to other affluent democracies. Other patterns may be distinctly American. Only by broadening the field of comparison can we see the similarities and the differences.

The shift in the norms of citizenship does not mean that American democracy does not face challenges in responding to new citizen demands and new patterns of action. Indeed, the vitality of democracy is that it must, and usually does, respond to such challenges, and this in turn strengthens the democratic process. But it is my contention that political reforms must reflect a true understanding of the American public and its values. By accurately recognizing the current challenges, and responding to them rather than making dire claims about political decay, American democracy can continue to evolve and develop. The fact remains that we cannot return to the politics of the 1950s, and we probably should not want to. However, we can improve the democratic process if we first understand how Americans and their world are really changing.

THE SOCIAL TRANSFORMATION OF AMERICA

On a cab ride from Ann Arbor to the Detroit airport the cab driver told me the story of the American dream as his life story. Now, driving a cab is not a fun job; it requires long hours, uncertainty, and brings in typically modest income. The cab driver had grown up in the Detroit area. His relatives worked in the auto plants, and he drove a cab as a second job to make ends meet. We started talking about politics, and when he learned I was a university professor, he told me of his children. His son had graduated from the University of Michigan and had begun a successful business career. He was even prouder of his daughter, who was finishing law school. "All this on a cab driver's salary," he said with great pride in his children.

If you live in America, you have heard this story many times. It is the story of American society. The past five decades have seen this story repeated over and over again because this has been a period of exceptional social and political change.[14] There was a tremendous increase in the average standard of living as the American economy expanded. The postwar baby boom generation reaped these benefits and, like the cab driver's children, were often the first in their family to attend college.

In addition, a rights revolution empowered a large share of the public that had been limited to the periphery of politics. The civil rights movement of the 1960s and 1970s ended centuries of official governmental acceptance of racial discrimination. The women's movement of the 1970s and 1980s transformed gender roles that had roots in social relations since the beginning of human history. (In the 1950s and early 1960s it was unlikely that the cab driver's daughter would have attended law school regardless of her abilities.) America became an even more socially and ethnically diverse nation, building on its immigrant past. Today, the definition of equal rights is expanding to include homosexuals through the legalization of gay marriage and protection from other forms of discrimination.

In *The Rise of the Creative Class*, Richard Florida discusses how a time traveler from 1950 would view life in the United States if he or she was transported to 1900, and then again to 2000.[15] Florida suggests that *technological change* would appear greater between 1900 and 1950, as people moved from horse-and-buggy times all the way to the space age. But *cultural change* would seem greater between 1950 and 2000, as America went from a closed social structure with limited standards of living to a very affluent society that gives nearly equal status to women, blacks, and other minorities. Similarly, I am fairly certain that if Dwight D. Eisenhower and Adlai Stevenson returned to observe the 2012 U.S. presidential election, they would not recognize it as the same electorate and politics as they encountered in their 1952 and 1956 campaigns for the Oval Office.

In the same respect, many of our scholarly images of American public opinion and political behavior are shaped by an older view of our political system. The landmark studies of Angus Campbell, Philip Converse, Warren Miller, and Donald Stokes remain unrivaled in their theoretical and empirical richness in describing the American public.[16] However, they examined the electorate of the 1950s. At an intellectual level, we may be aware of how the American public and politics have changed since 1952, but since these changes accumulate slowly over time, it is easy to overlook their total impact. The electorate of 1956, for instance, was only marginally different from the electorate of 1952; and the electorate of 2012 is only marginally different from that of 2008. As gradual changes accumulate over five or six decades, however, this produces a major transformation in the socioeconomic conditions of the American public—conditions that are directly related to citizenship norms. None of the trends described below is likely to surprise you. But you may be struck by the size of the total change across a long span of time.

Perhaps the clearest evidence of change, and the carrier of new experiences and new norms, is the generational turnover of the American public. The public of the 1950s largely came of age during the Great Depression or before and had lived through one or both world wars—experiences that had a strong influence on images of citizenship and politics. We can see how rapidly the process of demographic change reshapes the public by following the changing generational composition of the public from 1952 to the present in Figure 1.2. In the 1952 electorate, 85 percent of Americans had grown up before the outbreak of World War II (born before 1926). This includes the "greatest generation" (born between 1895 and 1926) heralded by Tom Brokaw and other recent authors. Each year, with mounting frequency, some of this generation leave the electorate and are replaced by new citizens. In 1968, in the midst of the flower-power decade of the 1960s, the "greatest generation" still composed 60 percent of the populace. By 2012, this generation has all but left the electorate. In their place, a third of the contemporary public in 2012 are post–World War II Baby Boomers, a quarter is the Flower Generation of the 1960s and early 1970s, and another quarter are the Eighties generation who followed. Generation X came of age at the end of the twentieth century and comprises about a fifth of the adult public. Most recently, a new Millennial Generation—born in 1982 or later—is entering adulthood; about a fifth of the adult public were Millennials in 2012.[17]

The steady march of generations across time has important implications for citizenship norms. Anyone born before 1926 was raised in a much different political context, where people were expected to be dutiful, parents taught their children to be obedient, political skills were limited, and social realities were dramatically different from contemporary

---

FIGURE 1.2   **Generational Change**

▶ *With the passage of time, the older "Greatest Generation" that experienced WWII is leaving the electorate to be replaced by Boomers, the 1960s generation, and now Gen X and Millennials.*

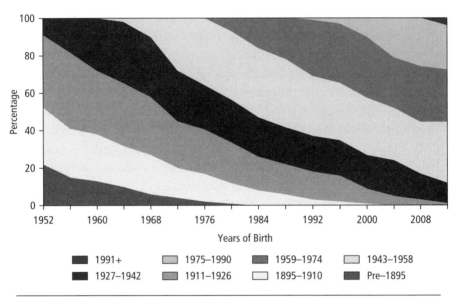

	1991+		1975–1990		1959–1974		1943–1958
	1927–1942		1911–1926		1895–1910		Pre–1895

Source: American National Election Study (ANES) Cumulative File, 1952–2008; 2012 ANES.

life. These Americans carry the living memories of the Great Depression, four-term president Franklin Delano Roosevelt, and World War II and its aftermath—and so they also embody the norms of citizenship shaped by these experiences.

The Baby Boomers experienced a very different kind of life as American social and economic stability was reestablished after the war. In further contrast, the 1960s generation experienced a nation in the midst of traumatic social change—the end of segregation, women's liberation, and the expansion of civil and human rights around the world. The curriculum of schools changed to reinforce these developments, and surveys show that parents also began emphasizing initiative and independence in rearing their children.[18] And most recently, Generation X and the Millennial

Generation are growing up in an era when individualism appears dominant, and both affluence and consumerism seem overdeveloped (even if unequally shared).[19] If nothing else changed, we would expect that political norms would react to this new social context.

Citizenship norms also reflect the personal characteristics of the people. Over the past several decades, the politically relevant skills and resources of the average American have increased dramatically. One of the best indicators of this trend is educational achievement. Advanced industrial societies require more educated and technically sophisticated citizens, and modern affluence has expanded educational opportunities. University enrollments grew dramatically during the latter half of the twentieth century. By the 1990s, graduate degrees were almost as common as bachelor's degrees were in mid-century.

These trends have steadily raised the educational level of the American public (Figure 1.3). For instance, two-fifths of American adults in 1952 had a primary education or less, and another fifth had only some high school. In the presidential election that year, the Eisenhower and Stevenson campaigns faced a citizenry with limited formal education, modest income levels, and relatively modest political sophistication. It might not be surprising that these individuals would have a limited definition of the appropriate role of a citizen. By 2012, the educational composition of the American public had changed dramatically. Barely a tenth have less than a high school degree, and more than three-fifths have at least some college education—and many of these have earned one or more degrees. The contemporary American public has a level of formal schooling that would have been unimaginable in the 1950s.

There is no direct, one-to-one relationship between years of schooling and political sophistication. Nonetheless, education tends to heighten a person's level of political knowledge and interest.[20] Educational levels affect the modes of political decision making that people use, and rising educational levels increase the breadth of political interests.[21] A doubling of the public's educational level may not double the level of political sophistication and engagement, but a significant increase should and does occur. The public today is the most educated in the history of American democracy, and this contributes to a more expansive and engaged image of citizenship.

FIGURE 1.3   Educational Change

▶ *Citizens with less than a high school education were a majority of the public in the 1950s, and now a majority have attended college.*

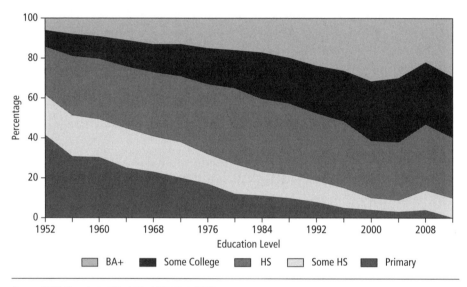

Source: ANES Cumulative File, 1952–2008; 2012 ANES.

Even more provocatively, social scientists have found that the average person's IQ has risen over the past century in the U.S. and other affluent democracies.[22] The average American in 2012 had an IQ that was 18 points higher than the average American in 1952. This is a very large increase such that the average person in 2012 scores at what was the 85th percentile in 1952! We are getting smarter according to this evidence, which should make it easier for people to follow politics, participate in the process, and understand the complex issues we face. This rise in IQ is due to many factors, such as improving living standards, improving health, and the lessening of negative environmental conditions, but a major factor is the expansion of education and the development of a scientific way of thinking about the world.

Social modernization has also transformed the structure of the economy from one based on industrial production and manufacturing (and farming) to one dominated by the services and the information sectors. Instead of the traditional blue-collar union worker, who manufactured goods and things, the paragon of today's workforce is the "knowledge worker" whose career is based on the creation, manipulation, and application of information.[23] Business managers, lawyers, accountants, teachers, computer programmers, designers, database managers, and media professionals all represent different examples of knowledge workers. If one takes a sociological view of the world, where life experiences shape political values, this shift in occupation patterns should affect citizenship norms. The traditional blue-collar employee works in a hierarchical organization where following orders, routine, and structure are guiding principles. Knowledge workers, in contrast, are supposed to be creative, adaptive, and technologically adept, which presumably produces a different image of what one's role should be in society. Richard Florida calls them the "creative class" and links their careers to values of individuality, diversity, openness, and meritocracy.[24]

These trends are a well-known aspect of American society, but we often overlook the amount of change they have fomented in politics over the past six decades. Figure 1.4 plots the broad employment patterns of American men from 1952 until 2012. (We'll track only males at this point to separate out the shift in the social position of women that is examined below.) In the 1950s, most of the labor force was employed in working-class occupations, and another sixth had jobs in farming. The category of professionals and managers, which is an indirect measure for knowledge workers (the actual number of knowledge workers is significantly larger) was small by comparison. Barely a quarter of the labor force held such jobs in the 1950s.

Slowly but steadily, labor patterns shifted. By 2012, blue-collar workers and professionals/knowledge workers are at rough parity, and the proportions of service and clerical workers have increased (some of whom should also be classified as knowledge workers). Florida uses a slightly more restrictive definition of the creative class but similarly argues that their proportion of the labor force has doubled since 1950.[25] Again, if

FIGURE 1.4   **Changing Occupations of Men**

▶ *Fewer American males are employed in blue-collar or agricultural occupations, while professional and service employment has increased.*

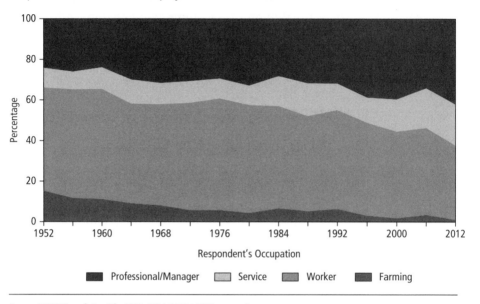

Respondent's Occupation

■ Professional/Manager   ▨ Service   ▨ Worker   ▨ Farming

Source: ANES Cumulative File, 1952–2004; 2012 ANES; men only.

nothing else had changed, we would expect that the political outlook of the modern knowledge worker would be much different than in previous generations.

The social transformation of the American public has no better illustration than the changing social status of women. At the time Angus Campbell and colleagues published *The American Voter* in 1960, women held a restricted role in society and politics. American women had limited economic and political power, and most women were homemakers and mothers. One of the coauthors of *The American Voter* noted that their interviewers regularly encountered women who thought the interviewer should return when her husband was home to answer the survey questions, since politics was the man's domain.

The women's movement changed these social roles in a relatively brief span of time. Women steadily moved into the workplace, entered universities, and became more engaged in the political process. Employment patterns illustrate the changes. Figure 1.5 tracks the percentage of women who were housemakers, in paid employment, or another status across the past five decades.[26] In 1952, two-thirds of women described themselves as homemakers. The image of June Cleaver, the stay-at-home-mom on the popular TV show *Leave It to Beaver,* was not an inaccurate portrayal of the middle-class American woman of that era. By 2012, however, two-thirds of women were employed and only a sixth described themselves as homemakers. The professional woman is now a staple of American society and culture. The freedom and anxieties of the upwardly mobile women in the TV programs *Girls* or *The Good Wife* are more typical of the contemporary age.

The changing social status of women also affects their citizenship traits. For instance, women's educational levels have risen even more rapidly than men's. By 2012, the educational attainment of young men and women was essentially equal, with slightly more women attending college. As women enter the workforce, this should stimulate political participation; no longer is politics a male preserve. For instance, although women are still underrepresented in politics, the growth in the number of women officeholders during the last half of the twentieth century is quite dramatic.[27] Rather than being mere spectators or supporters of their husbands, women are now politically engaged and create their own political identities. Though gender inequity and issues of upward professional mobility remain, this transformation in the social position of half the public has clear political implications.

Race is another major source of political transformation within the American electorate. In the 1950s, the American National Election Studies found that about two-thirds of African Americans said they were not registered to vote, and few actually voted. By law or tradition, many of these Americans were excluded from the most basic rights of citizenship. The civil rights movement and the transformation of politics in the South finally incorporated African Americans into the electorate.[28] African Americans' voting participation surged with Barack Obama's candidacy in 2008 and 2012, but black and white Americans already voted at

| FIGURE 1.5 | Working Women |

▶ *The percentage of women who describe themselves as housewives has dropped*
dramatically as most women have entered the active labor force.

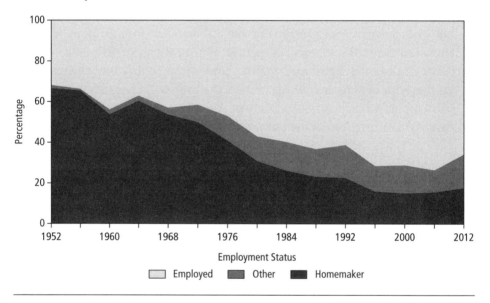

Employment Status

☐ Employed   ▥ Other   ■ Homemaker

Source: ANES Cumulative File, 1952–2004; 2012 ANES; women only, retirees not included.

roughly equal rates in the presidential elections of 2000 and 2004. In other words, almost a tenth of the public was excluded from citizenship in the mid-twentieth century, and these individuals are now both included and more active. Moreover, Hispanic and Asian Americans are also entering the electorate in increasing numbers, transforming the complexion of American politics. If Adlai Stevenson could witness the Democratic National Convention in 2008 and 2012, he would surely be amazed at the change in the party that nominated him for president in both 1952 and 1956.

Though historically seismic, these generational, educational, gender, and racial changes are not the only ingredients of the social transformation of the United States into an advanced industrial society.[29] The average living standard of Americans has more than tripled over this period as well, closely linked to changes in the structure of the economy and rising levels of skills and knowledge. Michael Shermer summarizes some of the most striking changes in living standards:

> We also have more material goods—SUVs, DVDs, PCs, TVs, designer clothes, name-brand jewelry, home appliances and gadgets of all kinds. The homes in which we keep all our goodies have doubled in size in just the last half a century, from about 1,100 square feet in the 1950s to more than 2,200 square feet today. And 95 percent of these homes have central heating, compared with just 15 percent a century ago, and 78 percent have air conditioners, compared with the numbers of our grandparents' generation—zip.[30]

In addition, the growth of the mass media and now the Internet has created an information environment that is radically different from that of the 1950s. Information is now instantaneous, and it's available from a wide variety of sources. The advancement of transportation technologies has shrunk the size of the nation and the world and increased the breadth of our life experiences.[31] These social changes inevitably increase the skills and resources that are useful in being an active democratic citizen.

These trends accompany changes in the forms of social organization and interaction. Structured forms of organization, such as political parties run by backroom "bosses" and tightly run political machines, have given way to voluntary associations and ad hoc advocacy groups, which in turn become less formal and more spontaneous in organization. Communities are becoming less bounded by geographical proximity—think of your Facebook friends. Individuals are involved in increasingly complex and competing social networks that divide their loyalties. Institutional ties are becoming more fluid; hardly anyone expects to work a lifetime for one employer anymore.

None of these trends is surprising to analysts of American society, but too often we overlook the magnitude of these changes cumulated over decades. In fact, these trends are altering the norms of citizenship and the nature of American politics. They have taken place in a slow and relatively silent process over several decades, but they now reflect the new reality of political life.

THE PLOT OF THIS BOOK

This study uses public opinion surveys to examine citizenship norms in America. Its goal is to make this information accessible to anyone interested in American politics, even if he or she is not well versed in statistics and research methodologies. The basic theme is quite straightforward: The modernization of American society has transformed the norms of citizenship, and this is affecting the political values and actions of the public—often in positive ways that previous research has overlooked.

The book has three sections. The first section describes citizenship norms in theory and reality. The idea of citizenship has a long history in political research and an equally long list of meanings and uses. Chapter 2 summarizes the key principles of citizenship in contemporary political thought, then introduces a battery of citizenship norms developed through an international collaboration of scholars. These questions appeared in the 2004 and 2014 General Social Surveys (GSS) of the American public as well as in the International Social Survey Program (ISSP), which includes other nations. These surveys are the central evidence for this study.[32] In addition, the Center for Democracy and Civil Society (CDACS) at Georgetown University included similar questions in its 2005 Citizenship, Involvement, and Democracy Survey; at points we provide evidence from this survey as well.[33]

These surveys identify two clusters of citizenship norms—duty-based and engaged citizenship—that organize the analysis in this volume. The first, citizen duty, reflects traditional norms of the citizen as loyal to, and supportive of, the political system. The second cluster typifies the new, challenging values found among younger Americans. We describe which groups of people lean toward these two rival definitions of good citizenship.

The second section (Chapters 4–7) considers some of the potential consequences of changing norms of citizenship. We are limited to the topics included in the General Social Surveys, but this fortunately provides a wealth of evidence on important political attitudes and activities. Chapter 4 challenges the idea that political participation is broadly declining; it presents new evidence that Americans are engaged in different ways than in the past. Except for voting participation, more

Americans participate in politics than ever before, especially direct, policy-focused, and individualized forms of activity. Changing norms of citizenship affect the choice of political activities.

Chapter 5 examines the link between citizenship norms and political tolerance. Popular political discourse suggests that Americans have become polarized on ideological grounds, divided into red and blue states and comparable states of mind, intolerant toward those who are different. In fact, political tolerance has increased markedly over the past several decades, and this tolerance is concentrated among the young and better educated. These findings provide a much more positive image of how the American public has changed its political values over the past several generations.

Chapter 6 examines the implications of citizenship norms on the making of public policy—what policies people favor at both national and local levels. Long-term trends show that people have actually expanded their policy expectations of government over the past several decades, despite the efforts by some public officials to roll back the scope of government action. Moreover, citizenship norms are clearly linked to these expectations. The norms of citizen duty are linked to a restrictive image of the government's policy role. Engaged citizens, meanwhile, see the need for greater government activity, especially activity in distinct policy domains. Citizenship norms shape our expectations of government and what it should provide.

Some of the loudest voices in the crisis-of-democracy literature have focused on the decline of trust in government and political institutions since the late 1960s as an ominous sign for our nation. Chapter 7 tracks these trends and analyzes the relationship between citizenship and political support. Again, changing citizenship norms are related to these sentiments, but in complex ways. The engaged citizen is less trustful of politicians when compared with duty-based citizens, but engaged citizens are also more supportive of democratic principles and democratic values. This suggests that changing citizenship norms are pressuring democracy to meet its ideals—and challenging politicians and institutions that fall short of these ideals.

While these analyses largely focus on the American experience, Chapter 8 places the U.S. findings in cross-national context. Using data from the 2004 International Social Survey Program, I compare the patterns of citizenship norms of Americans and Europeans and their consequences. This shows what is distinct about the American experience and what is part of a common process affecting other affluent democracies.

The conclusion considers the implications of the findings for the democratic process in America. We cannot recreate the halcyon politics of a generation ago—nor should we necessarily want to. New patterns of citizenship call for new processes and new institutions that will reflect the values of the contemporary American public.

CONCLUSION

In many ways this book presents an unconventional view of the American public. Many of my colleagues in political science are skeptical of positive claims about the American public—and they are especially skeptical that any good can come from the young. Instead, they warn that democracy is at risk and that American youth are a primary reason.

I respect my colleagues' views and have benefited from their writings—*but this book tells the rest of the story.* Politics in the United States and other affluent societies is changing in ways that hold the potential for strengthening and broadening the democratic process. The old patterns are eroding—as in norms of duty-based voting and deference toward authority—but there are positive and negative implications of these trends if we look for both. The new norms of engaged citizenship come with their own potential advantages and problems. America has become more democratic since the mid-twentieth century, even if progress is still incomplete. Understanding the current state of American political consciousness is the purpose of this book. If we do not become preoccupied with the patterns of democracy in the past but look toward the potential for our democracy in the future, we can better understand the American public and take advantage of the potential for further progress.

THE MEANING AND
MEASUREMENT OF CITIZENSHIP

> We are bound by ideals that move us beyond our backgrounds, lift us above our interests and teach us what it means to be citizens. Every child must be taught these ideals. Every citizen must uphold them. . . . I ask you to be citizens. Citizens, not spectators. Citizens, not subjects. Responsible citizens, building communities of service and a nation of character.

If you were quizzed on who is quoted above, there are many possibilities. People often suggest this was something President Obama could have said, or maybe President Kennedy. A student in one of my classes even suggested President Eisenhower. In fact, it was George W. Bush at his inauguration in 2001, who was encouraged to talk about citizenship by political science advisors. This ambiguity reflects that fact citizenship is presumably a good thing, so more citizenship must be even better.

However, the exact meaning of citizenship is open to multiple interpretations. This idea has a history dating from the first democratic polity, and theorists—republicans, liberals, neoliberals, communitarians, social-democrats, and others—differ substantially in their definitions of citizenship. Moreover, which of these meanings applies in the United States, or any other single nation, is also a matter of much debate.

This chapter begins by summarizing previous writings on the meaning of citizenship. I don't discuss the full philosophical history of the concept, because this would fill a volume and many such studies are available.[1] Instead, I try to identify the key elements of citizenship discussed in the contemporary debates. Then, we shift our attention to two surveys of Americans' citizenship norms from questions asked in the 2004 and 2014 General Social Surveys. These surveys determine how Americans themselves define what is important to being a good citizen and suggest possible changes over time.

CITIZENSHIP IN THEORY

What makes for a good citizen? There is no single, clear answer. As a reference point, one might use examples from American popular culture. A recent book provides examples of how citizenship was portrayed in civic texts, scouting handbooks, and other historical memorabilia from the 1940s until the 1960s.[2] There are all the expected examples, such as respecting authority and obeying the laws, but also some unexpected ones. I didn't know that "eating meat," "having a good posture," and "not poisoning my neighbor's dog" were key definitions of citizenship. Such answers suggest that we should look deeper for definitions of good citizenship to guide our analyses.

Citizenship is a concept with a long history in political science. Its origins can be traced back to debates between Aristotle and Plato over how a citizen of Athens should act. Through the millennia, the term has acquired multiple meanings. This may, in part, reflect the importance of the idea of citizenship, so that scholars and political analysts compete to define its meaning.[3]

It is important to identify what we are *not studying*. Sometimes citizenship is used to describe a legal status as a citizen of a nation. This book is not concerned with this specific legal definition of citizenship: who is a citizen, how one becomes a citizen, the legal rights of citizenship. Similarly, a legal approach to citizenship sometimes examines the rights guaranteed to an individual as a function of citizenship. Again, this is an important topic, but it is not the topic of this study. Citizenship is also used to describe identity with a nation, feelings of patriotism and national pride; this is only partially related to our interests here. These legal elements of citizenship are indirectly tied to the topics examined here, but they are relevant to this discussion only to the extent that citizens define legal rights or responsibilities as part of their expectations of citizenship.

How, then, might citizenship be defined? I begin with an open definition of citizenship: The term refers to what people feel is expected of them as "good" citizens. Reflecting Almond and Verba's description of a political culture as a shared set of social norms,[4] this study defines citizenship as a shared set of expectations about the citizen's role in politics. I believe that images of the citizen's role are central to defining a nation's culture because they tell citizens what is expected of them and what they expect of themselves. As this book will show, these expectations shape other elements of the political process.

This does not mean that individuals approve of these norms or that their personal values are consistent with these norms. The interaction between these norms and behavior is, in fact, an important research question to consider. For instance, someone might say that tolerance is an important norm for a democratic citizen—but then not be tolerant in his or her own political beliefs or actions.

One approach to defining citizenship norms starts with Aristotle's observation that citizenship balances two contending roles: Citizens are "all who share in the civic life *of ruling* and *being ruled* in turn."[5] This simple, insightful observation underlies much of the theoretical literature about citizenship to the present.

First, **public participation** in politics is broadly considered a defining element of democratic citizenship.[6] The United States was founded on the principal of citizen participation in political decision making, even if this participation was initially limited by the constitutional structure. The principle of citizen participation remains a defining element of American democracy, and Tocqueville argued that it was a distinctive element of the political culture (see Chapter 4).

Because of this emphasis on participation, the current debate on citizenship centers on the notion that political involvement is decreasing. On the one hand, some analysts argue that decreasing participation in elections and other forms of political activity are eroding the foundations of the democratic process.[7] Thus, citizenship norms themselves are weakening. Other analysts maintain that the social transformation of American society has increased the ability of the average citizen to be politically engaged.[8] This counterposition maintains that Americans are turning to other forms of political engagement besides traditional electoral politics, and this is expanding and empowering the public's influence.[9]

Thus, a central issue in the debate about democratic citizenship involves the question of how much citizens believe they should participate. There is little consensus on how much participation, and in what forms, is beneficial for democracy. There is even less agreement on how much participation actually occurs today.

The other part of the Aristotelian equation for citizenship is the acceptance of **the authority of the state**. Autocratic governments emphasize the obedience of the subject to the state as the prime criterion of citizenship, and democracies also stress the importance of state sovereignty. Indeed, accepting the legitimacy of the state and the rule of law is often the implied first principle of democratic citizenship, since without the rule of law meaningful political discourse and discussion cannot exist.

Political philosophy is replete with those who stress the acceptance of state sovereignty—from Bodin to Hobbes to Hamilton—even before the participatory elements of democracy. Similarly, the U.S. government presents itself in these terms to its new citizens. The U.S. Immigration and Citizenship Service's booklet for prospective citizens first describes the Constitution's importance as presenting the principle that "everyone must follow the law."[10] Several pages later comes a discussion of the rights provided in the Constitution's Bill of Rights, which is paired with a discussion of the duties and responsibilities of citizenship: voting, serving in the army, and paying taxes.[11] The centrality of obedience is quite clear in what the United States tells its new citizens.

This dichotomy between ruling and being ruled is central to the definition of citizenship. Both are necessary in the modern democratic state, and the proper balance between these principles is central element to the philosophical literature on citizenship. One objective of this study is to learn how the American public views these principles.

Another element of citizenship involves our relation to others in the polity. T. H. Marshall described this as **social citizenship**.[12] The expansion of civil and political rights generated attention to a new category of social rights, such as offering social services, providing for those in need, and taking heed of the general welfare of others.[13] Citizenship thus includes an ethical and moral responsibility to others in the polity, and beyond. The framework of distributive justice provides a theoretical base for equality as a basis of citizenship. Unless individuals have sufficient resources to meet their basic social needs, democratic principles of political equality and participation are meaningless. Although initially identified with the European welfare state and social democratic critiques of capitalism, this idea of citizenship has been embraced by liberal interests in America.[14]

Social citizenship also potentially reaches beyond the nation-state. Contemporary discussions of equality and distributive justice are often embedded in a framework of global human rights and responsibilities. Thus, a socially concerned citizen cares about those less fortunate at home as well as issues of global inequality and the conditions of the global community. Many scholars now treat citizenship as part of a global community, with global interests and responsibilities.[15]

This study focuses on these different aspects of citizenship. Democratic citizenship requires a mix of all these elements, and one can easily point to examples of the detrimental effects when one element—state authority, say—is given too much emphasis over the others. Yet analysts continually assert that all these aspects of citizenship are declining in contemporary America.[16] These claims of eroding citizenship norms are what gives such urgency to the study of citizenship—and what prompted Bush to call for a renewal of citizenship in his 2001 Inaugural Address. If the norms of citizenship are what bind Americans to their polity and each other, then a broad decline would have fundamental implications for society and politics.

The philosophical debate about contemporary citizenship is much richer and more extensive than I have briefly outlined here. Each theoretical tradition posits that a different mix of traits defines contemporary norms of citizenship or that a different mix of these norms is desirable. However, this debate has lacked one component: What do the citizens themselves think of citizenship? How do Americans weigh the various elements of citizenship? Let's consult the American public in the next section.

WHAT IS A "GOOD" CITIZEN?

As politics has visibly changed in affluent democracies, a number of research projects have examined the norms of citizenship.[17] The most authoritative sources are now the 2004 and 2014 surveys by the International Social Survey Program (ISSP).[18] The ISSP developed a battery of questions to assess citizenship norms—and then replicated this survey in several dozen nations. In the United States, the 2004 and 2014 General Social Surveys included this ISSP battery and asked Americans to describe what it means to be a good citizen:

> There are different opinions as to what it takes to be a good citizen. As far as you are concerned personally, on a scale of 1 to 7, where 1 is not at all important and 7 is very important, how important is it to . . .[19]

The GSS surveys asked about the perceived norms of good citizenship rather than personal adherence to each behavior. Both surveys asked about norms that theoretically represented the four categories theorized in recent survey research on citizenship (Table 2.1).

Participation is a prime criterion for defining the democratic citizen and his or her role within the political process, and it is central to the philosophical literature on democracy. Both surveys thus ask about the importance of always voting in elections. In addition, these studies ask about the importance of participation beyond voting: being active in social or political organizations (participating in civil society) and choosing products for political, ethical, or environmental reasons even if they cost more. This does not include all the diverse forms of political action (see Chapter 4), although it provides a range of opportunities. Moreover, the survey does not ask if the respondent participates in these activities—the questions simply ask whether they recognize such norms as existing in American society.

A second category, related to the idea of participation, taps what is called **autonomy**.[20] Autonomy implies that good citizens should be sufficiently informed about government to exercise a participatory role. The good citizen should participate in democratic deliberation and discuss politics with other citizens and, ideally, understand the views of

TABLE 2.1	Categories of Citizenship	

Concept	General Social Survey 2004	General Social Survey 2014
Participation	Always vote in elections	Always vote in elections
	Be active in social or political associations	Be active in social or political associations
	Choose products for political, ethical, or environmental reasons	Choose products for political, ethical or environmental reasons
Autonomy	Try to understand reasoning of people with other opinions	Try to understand reasoning of people with other opinions
	Keep watch on actions of government	Keep watch on actions of government
Social order	Always obey laws and regulations	Always obey laws and regulations
	Never try to evade taxes	Never try to evade taxes
	Being willing to serve in the military in a time of need	
Solidarity	Support people in America who are worse off than yourself	Support people in America who are worse off than yourself
	Help people in rest of the world who are worse off than yourself	Help people in rest of the world who are worse off than yourself

Source: 2004 and 2014 General Social Surveys.

others. Other researchers have described such items as representing critical and deliberative aspects of citizenship.[21] The surveys measure these orientations with a question on keeping watch on the government and with another question on understanding the reasoning of people with other opinions.

Social order represents the acceptance of state authority as part of citizenship. The GSS asks two items on obeying the law: never trying to avoid taxes and always obeying laws and regulations. In addition, the 2004 GSS asked about willingness to serve in the military. The 2014 GSS dropped the military service item because members of the ISSP planning committee felt the relevance of military service varied too widely across the nations in the international project.[22]

Finally, **solidarity** is a fourth category that taps the idea of social citizenship. This idea represents a long tradition in European social democracy or Christian socialism—that a concern for others should be included within the definition of citizenship.[23] The GSS thus asks about the importance of helping others in America who are worse off or helping people in the rest of the world who are worse off.

THE TWO FACES OF CITIZENSHIP

Although the choice of citizen items in the survey was theoretically derived in terms of four criteria, an initial question is whether people actually conceive of citizenship in these same terms. In short, is the empirical evidence from public opinion consistent with our theoretical expectations? The chapter appendix describes the statistical methods used to empirically identify the framework that Americans actually use in conceptualizing citizenship. While there is a distinct philosophical logic to the four separate categories of citizenship norms in Table 2.1, the American public perceives citizenship in terms of a simpler structure. Answers to the survey questions reflect two broad frames that organize Americans' thinking about citizenship.

I used a statistical analysis method to identify the commonality among the separate questions in the GSS surveys (see the chapter appendix). One aspect of citizenship includes what I describe as the principle of **citizen duty**. The two social order items—obeying the law and paying taxes—are strongly connected (unfortunately the military service item was not asked in 2014). Respondents in the 2004 GSS survey, and to a lesser extent those in the 2014 survey, also link voting turnout and social order. The fusion of these two different sets of norms suggests that some forms of participation—such as voting—are motivated by the same sense of duty that encourages individuals to be law-abiding citizens.

Duty-based citizenship thus reflects primarily traditional notions of republican citizenship as the responsibilities of a citizen-subject. The good citizen pays taxes, follows the legitimate laws of government, and contributes to the national need such as service in the military. Indeed, previous studies of voting turnout indicates that feelings of citizen duty are a strong stimulus of voting.[24] Allegiance to the state and voting are linked together. For instance, the U.S. Citizenship and Immigration Service begins its description of the duties and responsibilities of citizens as follows: "the right to vote is a duty as well as a privilege."[25] Thus, the clustering of participation and order norms into a single pattern of duty-based citizenship has a strong foundation in prior empirical research and democratic theory:

Duty-based Citizenship	Engaged Citizenship
• Obey the law	• Keep watch on government
• Never evade taxes	• Understand others
• Vote in elections	• Active in association
• (Serve in military)	• Choose products
	• Help worse-off in U.S.
	• Help worse-off in world

The other aspect, **engaged citizenship**, spans several forms of citizenship. It includes participation, but that participation is centered in non-electoral activities such as being active in civil society groups and buying products for political or ethical reasons. This dimension also incorporates the autonomy norm—that one should keep watch on government and try to understand the opinions of others. Engaged citizens also possess a moral or empathetic element of citizenship, and both solidarity items of helping others (at home and abroad) are strongly related to the underlying factor. This is significant because analysts typically maintain that concern about the community is an element of traditional citizenship values; these surveys suggest that it falls most heavily in the engaged citizenship cluster. Overall, this second group of survey questions suggests a pattern of the socially engaged citizen: one who is aware of others, is willing to act on his or her principles, and is willing to challenge political elites.

The replication of these two basic dimensions across two General Social Surveys survey reinforces the validity of these patterns. These two dimensions of citizenship are not contradictory (since all items are positively related), but they reflect different emphases in the role of a democratic citizen. Both clusters involve a norm of participation, although in different styles of political action. Both define citizenship as a mixture of responsibilities and rights, but different responsibilities and different rights. Although both dimensions are linked to democratic theory, neither completely matches the mix of norms posited in previous philosophical models.

If citizen duty captures the traditional model of democratic citizenship, then it leads to a set of predictions about the causes and consequences of these norms. For instance, duty norms are seemingly the citizenship norms of the "Greatest Generation" that analysts now see as waning in America. Previous research suggests that respect for authority and the rule of law is stronger among older Americans and weaker among the young.[26] Similarly, the emphasis on voting may be strongest among older generations socialized during a period when this was considered a primary duty of citizenship.[27] One also expects that duty-based citizenship should promote distinct forms of political participation, images of government, and other attitudes and behavior, themes explored in more detail below.

In comparison, engaged citizenship partially overlaps with the liberal or communitarian models of citizenship. These norms stress the rights and social responsibilities of citizenship. Instead of seeing political participation primarily as a duty to vote, engaged citizenship prompts individuals to be involved in a wider repertoire of activities that give them direct voice in the decisions affecting their lives. This evokes the values implicit in Benjamin Barber's idea of "strong democracy."[28] Independently, Lance Bennet and his colleagues have described similar contrast between dutiful citizens and actualizing citizens—alternative terms for the same value clusters observed here.[29] Engaged citizenship also overlaps with the patterns of postmaterial or self-expressive values that Inglehart has described in affluent societies.[30] Postmaterialists emphasize participatory norms, a tendency to challenge elites, and more interest in noneconomic social issues. Engaged citizenship includes a responsibility to others in society. Such feelings of social responsibility have a long tradition in European social democratic and Christian social traditions, and they are present in American political norms.

This dichotomy in citizenship norms—duty-based citizenship versus engaged citizenship—provides the foundation for the research presented in this book. The recognition of these norms should be sufficient to shape citizen attitudes and behavior—if these are meaningful norms. Much of the rest of the volume is devoted to articulating and then testing these distinctions.

THE DISTRIBUTION OF CITIZENSHIP NORMS

Having mapped the clustering of citizenship values that Americans see, let's now look at which norms receive the most and least support from the public.

Figure 2.1 presents the average importance score given to each norm for the two waves of the General Social Survey. Although I have emphasized the distinct clusters of citizenship norms, these data make it clear that all these norms are accepted by most Americans. On the 7-point scale used in the GSS, all the items score well above the midpoint of the scale (3.5), and several are heavily skewed with means above 6.0. Thus, it is not that Americans accept one set of norms and reject others—rather all these norms are recognized as important, with some more important to different individuals.

The items on the left of the figure are the norms most closely identified with duty-based citizenship. Nearly all Americans agree that these are

| FIGURE 2.1 | The Importance of Citizenship Norms |

▶ *The importance Americans attach to each of the different aspects of citizenship; the higher the bar the more important the item is.*

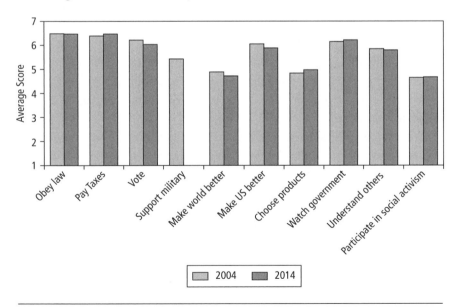

Source: 2004 and 2014 General Social Survey.

Note: Figure entries are mean scores on the 7-point importance scale: 1 = *not at all important* to 7 = *very important.*

important elements of citizenship. Using the 2004 survey as an example, obeying the law receives the highest importance rating (mean = 6.5) of any of these ten items, closely followed by paying taxes (6.4) and always voting (6.2). The sense of duty is thus deeply embedded in Americans' notions of citizenship.

The items on the right of the figure are more closely linked to engaged citizenship. Although we have described these as emerging norms, these are also ranked as important by most Americans. In 2004 the solidarity norm of helping those worse off in America receives a relatively high rating (6.0), as does the norm of understanding others (5.8). The norms of engagement receive less attention from the public, but the differences in importance between both sets of norms are fairly modest.

If citizenship norms heavily reflect the politics of the day, we might expect substantial change between the 2004 and 2014 surveys because this was a decade of substantial political and economic change. The first survey was taken not long after the September 11 terrorist attacks, the overthrow of Saddam Hussein's Iraqi government, and George W. Bush's election as president. The 2014 survey, on the other hand, was done after the U.S. had left Iraq, when America was still recuperating from the Great Recession and Barack Obama was president. Other forces were at work as well. The Tea Party reinvigorated the conservative movement and perhaps a sense of duty among conservatives, while Obama stressed more engaged norms of citizenship. Despite these changes, the importance of citizenship norms is quite stable over time. None of the differences in Figure 2.1 are substantively large.[31]

I frankly would have expected some shift away from duty-based citizenship and toward engaged citizenship over a ten-year time period, if all else were held constant. For instance, the American National Election Study regularly asks whether it matters if one votes, which is widely interpreted as a measure of the civic duty to vote. This has slowly trailed downward over time, paralleling the decline in turnout. More generally, respect for authority has also decreased over the past several decades, eroding the foundation of duty-based norms of citizenship.[32] The entrance of the Millennial Generation into the electorate in 2014 should have also shifted citizenship norms. Perhaps the countervailing pressures of the Great Recession have held change in check. In the end, citizenship norms have changed only marginally over this decade.

WHAT KIND OF CITIZENSHIP?

If we return to President Bush's call for citizenship at the start of the chapter, how should it be interpreted based on our findings? Rather than a single model of citizenship, Americans define citizenship in two different ways. Duty-based citizenship evokes images of a civic republican model of the good citizen, with some variations. It stresses the duties and responsibilities of citizenship, with a limited participatory role. This is a constrained model of citizenship, which reinforces the existing political order and existing authority patterns. It is consistent with what is generally described as an elitist model of democracy, which implies a limited role for the citizen. This is also close to the description of the subject-participant political culture that Almond and Verba described, which combined a strong identification with the nation-state and a propensity to obey the laws, with a limited amount of political activity.[33]

In contrast, engaged citizenship has a more expansive view of the citizen's role. The engaged citizen stresses participation, and this includes direct-action and elite-challenging activities that go beyond voting in the next election. Participation is not just an expression of allegiance and duty but an attempt to influence policy outcomes. Significantly, engaged citizenship also includes a concern for the opinion of others, potentially an expression of support for a more deliberative style of political activity. In addition, these norms include a concern for others. Thus, engaged citizenship contains elements that are part of liberal and social traditions of citizenship.

These two aspects of citizenship have a long tradition in American politics and political thought. More than six decades ago, for instance, Charles Merriam and Robert Merriam described citizenship in terms of dual principles that are very close to the empirical patterns we have described:

> Certainly citizenship is something more than merely adding up a set of specific rights and duties or jobs to do, such as voting, paying taxes and obeying the laws. There is something beyond all that—something beyond the call of legal duties. We might expect of a good citizen, a distinctive if vaguely defined attitude—something akin to the idea of responsibility. Good citizenship properly embraces an acceptance of individual responsibility, moral as well as political, for the condition of the government and the general welfare of the community.[34]

Recognizing this duality of citizenship provides a way to understand and explain recent trends in American politics. I have suggested that the social transformation of society—rising educational levels, spreading cognitive mobilization, distinct generational experiences—are shifting the norms of citizenship among the contemporary public. Adherence to citizen duty is gradually eroding as attachments to norms of engaged citizenship increase. Other research shows that this pattern is occurring in other affluent democracies.[35]

I suspect that President Bush (and many others) was thinking of duty-based citizenship when he called for the renewal of American citizenship. This form of citizenship would encourage Americans to vote, obey the law, and respect their government. He would be surprised, and possibly concerned, to find that a new form of engaged citizenship has been increasing over the long term. This was probably not what he had in mind.

My reading of the literature suggests that many political analysts and politicians have focused only on the decline of duty-based norms and the consequences because these changes represent a shift in past patterns of behavior and thus are more apparent. This stimulates the criticisms of the American public as described in Chapter 1. In contrast, the consequences—both positive and negative—of greater attention to engaged citizenship are often overlooked or are reported in research that is not linked to discussions about citizenship. Integrating both perspectives should produce a more accurate—and more positive—image of democracy in contemporary America.

APPENDIX

To measure the structure of citizenship norms, I turned to a statistical technique called principal components analysis. The goal is to see if the large number of specific questions reflects a more limited, more fundamental set of political orientations. In other words, are the specific questions examples of general citizenship orientations?

This method first calculates the relationship between opinions on each of the possible pairs of questions and then looks for patterns among these correlations. The larger the correlations, the more the two items tap a common underlying "component." The method also determines how many underlying components are necessary to adequately represent the interrelationship among the items. In both 2004 and 2014, two components presented the most parsimonious and realistic representation of the patterns of citizenship.[36]

Table 2.A presents the empirical results from 2004 reported in the previous edition of this book on the left side and the results of merging the two surveys on the right side. Combing both surveys yields indices that can be compared across waves in the analyses that follow. Each of the values in the table is the relationship between the individual survey question and the underlying components. Both surveys yield a two-component pattern, with most questions correlating with only one component or the other. For example, the "Active in associations" item has a strong .75 relationship with the first component in the merged 2004/2014 results but only a .09 relationship with the second component. From these

TABLE 2.A	**Dimensions of Democratic Citizenship**			

	2004		2004 and 2014 (Merged)	
Variable	Engaged Citizenship	Duty-based Citizenship	Engaged Citizenship	Duty-based Citizen
Active in associations	.54	.39	.54	.09
Keep watch on government	.40	.51	.40	.17
Understand others	.59	.28	.59	.01
Political consumerism	.59	.22	.59	-.03
Help worse-off in world	.77	-.02	.46	.12
Help worse-off in America	.77	.02	—	—
Vote in elections	.17	.65	.49	.32
Obey the law	.10	.51	.06	.81
Never evade taxes	-.01	.65	.12	.80
Serve in the military	.07	.54	—	—
Eigenvalue	2.37	1.95	2.31	1.45
Percent variance	23.7	19.5	29.9	18.7

Source: 2004 and merged 2004/2014 General Social Surveys.

Note: Table entries are results from rotated principal components analyses.

relationships I name each component. Thus the "Active in associations" question is primarily a link to an engaged conception of citizenship, along with the other items that are strongly related to this first factor. Conversely, "Obey the law" and "Never evade taxes" are very strongly related to duty-based citizenship but only marginally related to engaged citizenship. In 2004 "Vote in elections" was strongly related to duty-based citizenship, and this relationship was clearly weaker in 2014. This might be due to changes in American politics between the two surveys that altered public perceptions of voting; but it also might be a statistical artifact. When the full ISSP cross-national data are released, we can examine whether this pattern occurs in other democracies.

These dimensions are most clearly seen in the separate analyses of the 2004 survey, especially when the "serving in the military" item is included.[37] The pattern is less distinct in 2014, in part because the large majority of items reflect an engaged notion of citizenship and only two duty-based examples remain because the military service question was not asked. In addition, with relatively more engaged citizenship items, the two items on helping those in need clustered more distinctly as a third dimension. This led to excluding one of these "Help worse-off" items to better balance the two dimensions of citizenship, as seen in Table 2.A.

This grouping of items and their interpretation as engaged or duty-based citizenship provide the empirical base for studying the norms of citizenship throughout the rest of this book. The dimensional analysis in Table 2.A was used to create component scores that are the indices of citizenship norms. These scores are constructed so they are statistically unrelated and have a standardized distribution; the average citizen gets a 0.0 score with a normal distribution around this value.

FORMING CITIZENSHIP NORMS

L et's begin this chapter with a small thought experiment. Several years ago, then Senator Richard G. Lugar, a Republican from Indiana, had a private meeting with the actress and activist Angelina Jolie in his Senate office to discuss the United Nations' Millennium Development Goals. Now, both these individuals are "good citizens" to most people. Senator Lugar had served in the U.S. Navy (1957–1960) and entered politics soon after returning home. He was first elected to the Senate in 1976 and was re-elected four times, serving as chairman of the Foreign Relations Committee and as former chairman of the Agriculture, Nutrition, and Forestry Committee. Ms. Jolie, besides her celebrity as an actress (and as wife of Brad Pitt and daughter of actor Jon Voight), has promoted humanitarian causes throughout the world and is noted for her work with refugees. She currently serves as goodwill ambassador for the Office of the United Nations' High Commissioner for Refugees (UNHCR).[1]

The senator and the actress/activist had met a couple of times before when Jolie was in Washington. They obviously shared an interest in foreign affairs and the plight of people in the developing world. Several years later Lugar cohosted a fundraiser for Jolie's charity, Global Action for Children. And yet one might imagine that if they discussed the meaning of "good citizenship," they would emphasize very different points. We might assume that Lugar places more emphasis on social order, and perhaps stresses the need for more people to vote and support their government. For instance, his U.S. Senate biography began with the statement: "Dick Lugar is an unwavering advocate of U.S. leadership in the world, strong national security, free-trade and economic growth." However, Jolie was there to discuss programs to benefit children and the needy in the developing world; thus we might expect her to stress solidarity and autonomy norms. And one hardly expects that social order is high on her priority list.

What causes these differences? There are many social contrasts between these two individuals that might explain their presumably different points of view: their early life experiences and family backgrounds. Lugar was born in 1932 and grew up on a family farm, and his Wikipedia biography begins with his early Boy Scout accomplishments. Jolie was born in 1975, and her upbringing in Hollywood was much different. Their careers and peer networks, their genders, and their partisan orientations also contrast.

One can't generalize from these two individuals, no matter how intriguing it might be to entertain such speculations. However, the Lugar-Jolie encounters illustrate a significant point: Although most Americans believe that all the elements of citizenship discussed in Chapter 2 are important, people differ in their emphasis on specific elements. Citizenship norms are not randomly distributed across the American public but instead reflect the social and political forces shaping these norms. For instance, to what extent do norms differ by generation, social status, race, or partisanship?

Even more important, the social distribution of citizenship norms indicates the source of these norms and how they may have changed over time. Chapter 2 described the distribution of these norms over the past decade. If we can project contemporary patterns over a longer time span, this yields more evidence of how America is changing. For example, to the extent that norms become fixed during early life, then generational patterns suggest how norms have changed over time. Similarly, if there are strong educational differences in citizenship norms, then the expansion of education during the late twentieth century should have contributed to norm shift (see Chapter 1). This chapter examines how citizenship norms vary across a basic set of social characteristics—generation, education, social status, gender, ethnicity, religion, and partisanship—and the implications of these patterns of citizenship.

A GENERATIONAL GAP?

We can assume, first off, that the tremendous changes in the content and context of American politics since the mid-twentieth century may have reshaped citizenship norms. We can't go back to the 1950s to ask Americans for their opinions on the citizenship questions. However, the legacy of these changing historical experiences should appear in generational differences in norms. Older Americans—those of the pre-1945 generations—were raised in a different era, with different expectations and practices of citizenship. This is the "Greatest Generation" that journalist Tom Brokaw wrote about, and who reflect the civic values that Robert Putnam and other contemporary authors have praised.[2] Brokaw articulately summarized the experiences of this generation and the impact of these events on their political norms:

> These men and women came of age in the Great Depression, when economic despair hovered over the land like a plague. They had watched their parents lose their businesses, their farms, their jobs, and their hopes. They had learned to accept a future that played out one day at a time. Then, just as there was a glimmer of economic recovery, war exploded across Europe and Asia. . . . When the war was over, the men and women who had been involved, in uniform and in civilian capacities, joined in joyous and short-lived celebrations, then immediately began the task of re-building their lives and the work they wanted. They were mature beyond their years, tempered by what they had been through, disciplined by their military training and sacrifices. . . . They stayed true to their values of personal responsibility, duty, honor, and faith.[3]

Indeed, previous research suggests that feelings of citizen duty are more common among older Americans and older Europeans.[4]

In contrast, most contemporary writings on the citizenship of young Americans are much less flattering. The postwar Baby Boom generation was on the cusp of the old order, and some were the driving force for the social changes of the 1960s and 1970s. Since then, however, there is a nearly universal agreement among pundits that the younger generation is what is wrong with American politics. To be sure, criticizing the young has a long tradition, but it has taken on a new intensity in the current discourse on citizenship. Compare the above description of the Greatest Generation with the following description of young Americans (by a young journalist):

> The Doofus Generation. That's what *The Washington Post* calls those of us in our twenties, who came of political age during the 1970s and 1980s. In the eyes of many observers, we are indifferent and ignorant—unworthy successors to the baby-boom generation that in the 1960s set the modern standard for political activism by the young. To an extent, they are right.[5]

This is not an isolated example, and other journalists and political analysts express these same harsh views.[6] A recent blue-ribbon study of civic life in the United States spelled out what older Americans think about the values of the young: "Each year, the grim reaper steals away one of the most civic slices of America—the last members of the 'Greatest Generation.' This is a cold generational calculus that we cannot reverse until younger Americans become as engaged as their grandparents."[7] What a cold-hearted description of American youth. But is it accurate?

I believe that these critical views of contemporary youth miss a larger reality. Older people typically castigate the young for not being like themselves—this has been true since the time of Aristotle—and they attribute negative political developments to the eroding values and poor behavior of the young. Older people are often experts at complaining. The fact that the young may not think of citizenship in the same duty-based norms as their elders is taken as evidence that the young lack good citizenship norms.

However, if feelings of *citizen duty* are eroding among the young, this may well be counterbalanced by new norms of *engaged citizenship*. Such a norm shift is consistent with evidence of the changing values priorities of youth. Ronald Inglehart's research argues that young people in the United States and most other affluent democracies more strongly favor self-expressive and participatory values and are more politically engaged just in different ways.[8] Similarly, other work points to the strong values of social justice, equality, and tolerance among younger Americans.[9] These norms of engaged citizenship may have benefits for democracy that are missed by focusing on the decline in duty-based norms.

I began the analyses by constructing indices of duty-based and engaged citizenship based on the findings of Chapter 2.[10] Figure 3.1 shows the level of both citizenship norms across generations.[11] The value of zero on each citizenship index represents the average for the entire American public; positive values in the figure mean that a generation scores above the average.

The generational shift in duty-based norms is quite clear. Older Americans who came of age (reached age eighteen) by the end of World War II and the postwar Boomer generation score highest on citizen duty. These sentiments then steadily weaken among the 1960s and later generations. In the first edition of this book there were too few Millennials in the 2004 survey to identify the values of this generation; and there has been much

FIGURE 3.1   **Generations and Citizenship**

▶ *Citizen duty decreases among younger generations, and engaged citizenship increases among the young.*

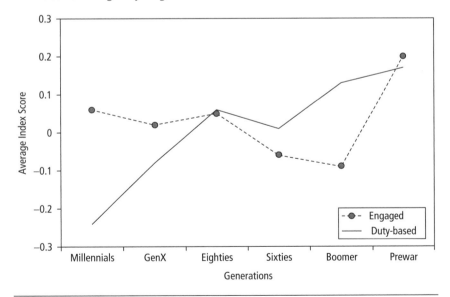

Source: 2004 and 2014 General Social Surveys combined.

Note: Figure entries are the average scores on the indices of duty-based and engaged citizenship.

speculation about this generation as they were coming of age. On the one hand, their education and life experiences broadly reflect the advances of American society described in Chapter 1. On the other hand, they were exiting school and entering the workforce in the midst of the Great Recession, and this might have produced a regression in values. By 2014 Millennials constituted over a tenth of respondents—and they are markedly lower on citizen duty than any other generation. If Millennials are the future, it is a future of significantly less citizen duty. This is the generational pattern that analysts typically discuss, leading to negative comments on the declining citizenship that the Millennials are accentuating.

The figure also shows that the erosion of duty-based norms among the young is partially offset by increased support for engaged citizenship, which stresses alternative forms of political participation, concern for the less privileged, and attention to the views of others. The anomaly is the oldest, prewar generation that scores high on engaged citizenship; I suspect this is because of the small size of this group and the effects of changing measurement because the pattern in the original 2004 survey placed them very low on engaged citizenship.[12] Otherwise, engaged citizenship moderately increases between the Boomer generation and Millennials. These norms are clearly beneficial to a vibrant democracy, although few analysts write about the lack of such values among older Americans.

The major challenge to this interpretation of Figure 3.1 is that these relationships do not reflect generational change but illustrate differences in the life-cycle position (age) of individuals. We can examine this idea by comparing generations on citizen duty because this is where contrasts across generations/age groups are more distinct. Experts often maintain that attention to duty and similar values increase as people age and assume more family and career responsibilities. Youth is a time to explore, test boundaries, and develop an identity; middle age is a time to pay taxes, work for the next promotion, and worry about your carefree children. With a single opinion survey we can't disentangle generational and life-cycle effects, but now there are two identical surveys separated by a decade. The Gen X respondents in the 2004 survey ranged from age twenty-two to thirty-one; by 2014 they were in their thirties and approaching the Big 4-0. And the same for other generations. Comparing the same generations over time can partially test whether generational or life-cycle forces are at play.

Figure 3.2 describes the levels of citizen duty across generations in both the 2004 and 2014 General Social Surveys. For three of the four generations with reliable samples in both surveys, support for citizen-duty was higher in 2014.[13] This shift also might reflect the changing climate of opinion because of the Great Recession, when many people became more insecure about their previous social condition. In either case, the average 2004–2014 shift was modest, and extrapolating this result across groups cannot account for the much larger differences across generations in both surveys. So while life-cycle forces (and possibly negative social conditions) are at work, norms of citizen duty appear to be changing more as a function of generational differences among Americans.[14]

FIGURE 3.2   **Comparing Generations over Time**

▶ *Citizen duty is lower among younger generations but increases slightly for three generations between 2004 and 2014.*

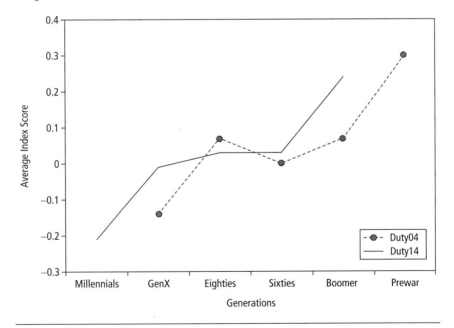

Source: 2004 and 2014 General Social Surveys.

Note: Figure entries are the average scores on the indices of duty-based and engaged citizenship.

These figures display a simple truth that we repeat throughout this study. Assertions about the decline in citizenship norms among younger Americans are incorrect. Rather, generations are changing in the types of citizenship norms they stress. Americans raised before and immediately after World War II generally define citizenship in terms of duties and obligations. Indeed, one might argue that these are the norms of a "loyal subject" (though not necessarily a good democratic participant).[15] In contrast, the young stress alternative norms that encourage a more rights conscious public, a socially engaged public, and a more deliberative image of citizenship. Both norms have positive (and negative) implications for the practice of citizenship and the workings of the democratic process—implications that we examine in the later chapters of this book.

THE RISING TIDE OF SOCIAL STATUS

Chapter 1 described the tremendous socio-economic transformation of America since the mid-twentieth century. The expansion of educational levels, improvements in living conditions, increases in leisure time, and the restructuring of employment added to the politically relevant skills and resources of the average American. In addition, the shifting social context has exposed people to new experiences and new norms of social action. These forces should affect norms of democratic citizenship.

Many studies emphasize the power of education and other social status traits to shape images of citizenship.[16] Norman Nie, Jane Junn, and Kenneth Stehlik-Barry, for example, showed that educational levels are strongly related to democratic participation and democratic enlightenment, although working in different ways.[17] Research consistently finds that the better educated are more likely to vote, more knowledgeable about politics, more accepting of the rule of law, and more politically tolerant. Thus, better-educated, higher-income, and higher-status Americans may be more likely to subscribe to duty-based citizenship norms. The formal and informal civics training of the educational system presumably stresses these norms, and people from higher status groups typically are more supportive of the norms of the existing system. These patterns are also consistent with the educational relationships for citizen norms in *The Civic Culture* study.[18]

Yet, once we realize that there is an alternative citizenship norm—engaged citizenship—the consequence of education becomes more ambiguous. If the skills and values produced by education are important in creating norms that one should obey the law, they should be even more important in stimulating participation in direct forms of engagement. Similarly, Nie, Junn, and Stehlik-Barry suggested that the cognitive skills linked to education should encourage engaged citizenship.[19] Recent political culture research documents a similar shift from allegiant patterns of citizenship to more assertive citizen orientations—led by the young and better educated—in most affluent democracies.[20] In short, if education and higher social status are valuable in developing the norms of a good subject, they may be even more relevant to developing the norms of an engaged citizen.

Figure 3.3 presents the relationship between education and the two indices of citizenship norms. The combined GSS surveys show that duty-based citizenship is actually lower among the better educated, but the difference is quite modest.[21] Individuals with graduate degrees are about a tenth of a point lower in citizen duty than those with less than a high school diploma. Conversely, education is strongly related to support for engaged citizenship. Separate analyses of the 2004 and 2014 surveys yields very similar results. This is additional evidence that social modernization is shifting the norms of the public to more assertive norms of engaged citizenship.

The logic of educational patterns should extend to other social status measures. For instance, the respondent's occupational prestige is positively related to engaged norms but not to duty-based citizenship. Family income displays a positive relationship to citizen duty but is unrelated related to support for engaged citizenship. These relationships are very modest in both waves of the GSS.

Taken together, this evidence suggests that social modernization—rising educational levels and improving living standards—beginning in the latter half of the twentieth century probably contributed to a shift in citizenship norms. Societal change encouraged a more engaged form of citizenship that goes beyond the deferential, subject-like role of duty-based citizenship. Participating in politics beyond voting and deliberating with others is more demanding than voting based only on a sense of duty. As more Americans possess these skills and resources, their norms of citizenship also change.

FIGURE 3.3	Education and Citizenship

▶ *Education substantially increases engaged citizenship and slightly diminishes duty-based citizenship.*

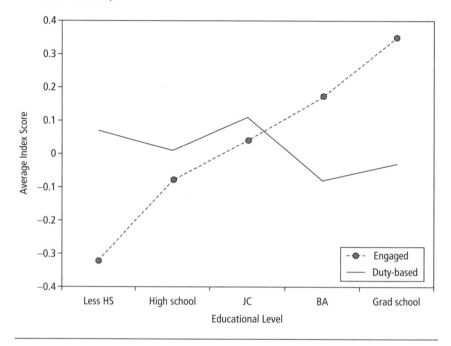

Source: 2004 and 2014 General Social Surveys combined.

Note: Figure entries are the average scores on the indices of duty-based and engaged citizenship.

GENDER AND ETHNICITY PATTERNS

My Facebook friends, perhaps because many are academics, regularly post articles on the gender gaps in American society and politics. Often the comments are variants of the familiar assertion that men are from Mars, and women are from Venus. Our question is whether this gender gap carries over to citizenship norms. For instance, if two people are standing on the street corner with a flashing "don't walk" sign but no cars in sight, is the man or the woman more likely to jaywalk? Who is more likely to be politically engaged or believe that one should question government actions?

Research on gender found that women traditionally were more conservative in their views and more concerned with a stable social environment when compared with men.[22] In part, this reflected the condition of most women as homemakers, where concern for family, security, and the duties of motherhood were paramount. However, one of the major social transformations in the past several decades involves the role of women in society: moving from positions of homemakers to active participants in the labor force. The entry of women into the workforce may have diminished gender differences in duty-based norms—because gender differences in life experiences have narrowed. However, in an analysis of the 2004 cross-national ISSP data, Bolzendahl and Coffe found that women place more importance on several aspects of citizen duty.[23]

The other half of the equation is the relationship between gender and the norms of engaged citizenship. We might expect that women are more socially conscious than men, and thus may express more concern for the welfare of others and the opinions of others—two elements of this mode of citizenship. Thus, as women have entered the workforce, participation in employment and exposure to these norms may have stimulated a more empowered self-image that encourages engaged citizenship. The cross-national research of Bolzendahl and Coffe showed that women are more likely to support norms of helping others, but differences in participation norms are insignificant.[24]

The gender differences in the two broad indices of citizenship norms are consistent across both the 2004 and 2014 surveys. Women are somewhat more likely to score highly on duty-based norms, which means following the rules, while men score below the average. Perhaps this is not surprising. The gender gap in duty-based norms persists even when controlling for marital status or employment status.[25] Gender differences in engaged citizenship are quite modest in both years. Although overall gender differences are modest, the tremendous transformation in the social status of women over the past fifty years still implies significant aggregate effects. The entry of women into the labor force has probably eroded support for duty-based norms and increased support for engaged citizenship.

Race and ethnicity present another case where the relationship to citizenship norms is potentially complex. If education or social status drives citizenship norms, then we might expect minority groups to display lower support for both citizenship dimensions since minorities have lower social status positions. However, the specific racial component of citizenship may function in a different manner. For instance, given the history of racial policies (explicit and implicit) in America, African Americans and other minorities may be more restrained in their sense of citizen duty. In addition, the emphasis on empowerment and engagement that accompanied the civil rights movement and other rights campaigns may stimulate norms of engaged citizenship. Coffe and Bolzendahl found more commitment to a rights-based definition of citizenship among minorities when they examined the 2004 survey.[26]

Figure 3.4 presents the citizenship norms of white Americans, African Americans, and a combined category of other racial groups for both surveys combined. White Americans score near the overall average on both dimensions and both years; the "other" category scores significantly above average in both years.[27] Perhaps the most interesting result, however, comes from comparing the norms of African Americans over time. African Americans scored slightly below average on engaged citizenship in 2004 (−.02) but substantially above average in 2014 (+.13). In contrast, black Americans scored below average on citizen duty in 2004, and this decreased further by 2014. Many factors may account for these shifts; the empowerment of Obama's election may have reinforced the participatory tendencies of this community, while their continued struggles for equality have eroded their attachment to citizen duty. The overall changes are still minor, however, and the cross-time patterns suggest that historical experiences and racial identifies do influence citizenship norms.

CITIZENSHIP AND RELIGION

Historically the discussion of American citizenship was often embedded in religious values and the imagery of religious fundamentalists (of various denominations) who played a prominent role in American history. Americans saw themselves as creating a new nation, a nation that differed from all others. More generally, religion instills norms of behavior that may carry over to the political domain because they define expectations about power relationships and appropriate social behaviors.[28]

FIGURE 3.4   **Race and Citizenship**

▶ *Racial differences in citizenship norms vary only modestly, with "other" racial/ethnic group displaying the highest support for both norms.*

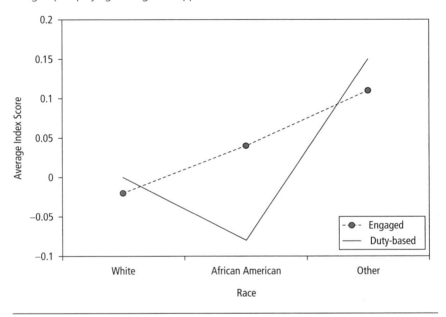

Source: 2004 and 2014 General Social Surveys combined.

Note: Figure entries are the average scores on the indices of duty-based and engaged citizenship.

Is there still a connection between religion and citizenship? For instance, it is typically argued that Catholicism increases acceptance of authority because of the structure of the Roman Catholic Church and its teachings. This might translate into duty-based norms of citizenship. The variations among Protestant denominations make it more difficult to offer clear predictions. Calvinists (Presbyterians, among others) might be more duty oriented; Reformation Protestants (Lutherans, Episcopalians, etc.) might lean toward engaged citizenship; Baptists probably divide by race.

In opinion surveys the number of respondents in discrete denominations is too small to examine these patterns in detail. Therefore, we compare Protestants, Catholics, Jews, and other religions and those with no religious affiliation. The largest contrast exists for feelings of citizen duty. Protestants and Catholics score above average for duty-based citizenship, while those with no religion score substantially below average. Thus religiosity seems most relevant in shaping a sense of duty. In contrast, norms of engaged citizenship are relatively similar across denominations. There are only a modest number of Jewish respondents, even combining both surveys. Yet their norms are distinct; they score substantially below average on citizen duty (−.20) and substantially above average on engaged citizens (+.20). Religious traditions do appear to influence citizenship norms, and differences in citizen duty actually increased between 2004 and 2014.[29]

The contrast between religious and nonreligious Americans can be seen more clearly using a question that asked about the strength of religious feelings.[30] Figure 3.5 shows that stronger feelings of religious attachments very clearly increase duty-based citizenship. The range from those with no religion to the strongly religious spans almost half a scale point on the citizen duty index.[31] Engaged citizenship shows a more complex pattern: Those high in religiosity are the only group that scores significantly above average on this dimension, presumably because their religious commitment stimulates a concern with others. However, the second highest score comes from those without a religious attachment, perhaps because of a humanist concern for the same set of values.

Like the other findings, the distribution of citizenship norms by religion suggests that these norms at least partially evolve from social experiences and identities. Duty-based citizenship norms tend to overlap with strong feelings of religiosity. This implies that the gradual secularization of American society during the late twentieth century also may have contributed to the erosion of duty-based norms and the increased attention to engaged citizenship.

PARTISAN DIFFERENCES IN CITIZENSHIP

For better, or perhaps for worse, America seems to be a nation divided by partisanship. The rhetoric of politicians and the varied selection of news on Fox TV and MSNBC suggest that there are at least two visions of what America represents. The adherence to good citizenship norms should span all the political parties in a well-functioning democracy. Support for

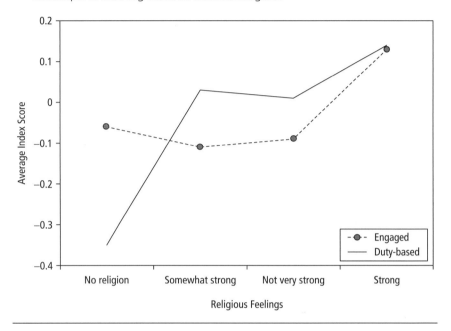

FIGURE 3.5 **Religiosity and Citizenship**

▶ *Religious feelings substantially increase citizen duty, but engaged citizenship is most important among the most and least religious.*

Source: 2004 and 2014 General Social Surveys combined.

Note: Figure entries are the average scores on the indices of duty-based and engaged citizenship.

democracy and the principles of good government and good citizenship should not be the domain of only one party. But contemporary discussions of citizenship suggest that adherents of different parties may vary in their definitions of good citizenship. That is, democracy functions best when Republicans and Democrats both believe it is important to obey the law and to keep a watchful eye on government, but one party may place more emphasis on the former and the other on the latter.

Philosophers' debates about the nature of citizenship also suggest that there is an ideological or partisan component to specific norms. Liberal, neoliberal, communitarian, and social-democratic images of

citizenship are often linked to specific partisan or ideological orientations.[32] Especially in the current political environment, the Republican Party seems to emphasize the duty-based elements of citizenship.
Ironically, the party that is most likely to favor smaller government
and greater individual autonomy is also more likely to stress the need
for greater respect for the authority of the state and its agents (especially during a Republican administration). Conversely, President
Obama's lofty rhetoric often stresses the social dimension of citizenship: the protection of those in need and the rights of individuals to
challenge the state. It is not that Republicans (or Democrats) favor one
aspect of citizenship to the exclusion of the other—they share both sets
of norms but with a different emphasis.

These contrasts seem apparent in the current party alignments, but
they may reflect more enduring images of citizenship rooted in party
history and ideology. For instance, Merriam's description of the Republican administrations of the late 1800s and early 1900s sounds surprisingly
similar to descriptions of the current Republican Party:

> Thus, the political mores of the leading group was divided against
> itself. On the one hand, it preached patriotism, devotion to the state
> in international affairs, and in internal affairs respect for law and
> order as often as it became necessary to call upon the government
> for protection of persons and property in industrial disputes; but on
> the other hand, the broader social interests of the state, the majesty
> of the public purpose, the supremacy of the common interests
> against the special, could not be too vigorously emphasized.[33]

Figure 3.6 shows that the partisan ties of Americans are clearly connected to norms of duty-based and engaged citizenship. Republican
Party identifiers score substantially above average (+.14) on citizen duty
and at the average (+.01) on engaged citizenship; if we isolate strong
Republican identifiers, they are even more distinct on both dimensions.
Conversely, Democratic Party identifiers score at the average on citizen
duty (0.0), but higher than average on engaged citizenship (+.12).
Independents are low on both dimensions, probably reflecting some apathy toward politics among many independents. Although the figure does

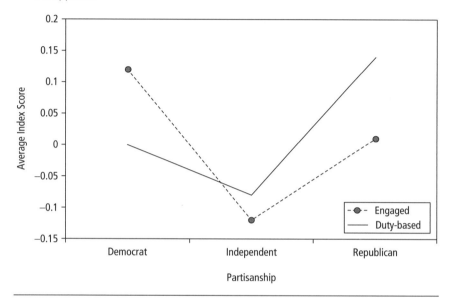

FIGURE 3.6   Partisan Differences in Citizenship Norms

▶ *Democrats emphasize engaged citizenship over citizen duty, and Republicans are the opposite*

Source: 2004 and 2014 General Social Surveys combined.

Note: Figure entries are the average scores on the indices of duty-based and engaged citizenship.

not present this evidence, people who voted for Ralph Nader in 2000 were among the lowest on citizen duty of any social group (−.46), while scoring far above average on engaged citizenship (+.27).

These partisan differences in citizenship norms can explain what might be described as a "dialogue of the deaf" on this topic. Both Democratic and Republican politicians, and a host of academics, argue that we need to strengthen citizenship through civic education programs, public service programs, and other political reforms.[34] Even if there are bipartisan calls for improving citizenship and expanding civics education in the schools, these views are inevitably linked to different definitions of what values of citizenship are lacking. Liberal and conservative politicians are both strong believers in good citizenship and advocates for more democracy—but they have very different ideas about how the values of Americans should be changed and what civic education should stress. These different citizenship emphases are reflected among party identifiers in the public at large.

BRINGING THE PIECES TOGETHER

Now that we've identified some of the basic social and political correlates of citizenship norms, let's integrate these separate discussions. As a first step, I mapped the norms of key social groups identified above so that we can compare their positions on both citizenship dimensions and how these have changed over time.

Figure 3.7 plots a group's average score on duty-based citizenship on the horizontal axis, and its position on engaged citizenship along on the vertical axis. A line connects a group's position in 2004 (a diamond) to its position in 2014 (a circle). For the sake of readability, I do not plot all groups; for instance, only the oldest prewar generation and youngest Millennial generation are shown here. Still, this figure provides a good mapping of the overall shifts in these norms.

The sharpest contrast is between alternative models of citizenship. The lower right quadrant identifies groups that are high in citizen duty but below average in engaged citizenship: The clearest examples are older Americans (the pre–World War II generation), Republican Party identifiers, and people with less than a high school education. Conversely, the upper left quadrant displays groups that are high in engaged citizenship but below average in duty-based norms. African Americans, Democratic Party identifiers, people with a graduate degree, and young people are the clearest examples of this pattern. This diagonal axis thus represents a political cleavage within the American public, between those who think of citizenship first in terms of duties and those who think of citizenship in terms of rights and engagement. It is no wonder that Democrats and Republicans (or young people and senior citizens) talk past one another when they discuss the abstract goal of good citizenship. They have different conceptions of citizenship.

The positions of some groups have noticeably changed over the 2004–2014 timespan. For example, African Americans placed greater stress on

FIGURE 3.7   Social Groups on Two Dimensions of Citizenship

▶ *Social groups generally changed their citizenship norms only modestly from 2004 to 2014.*

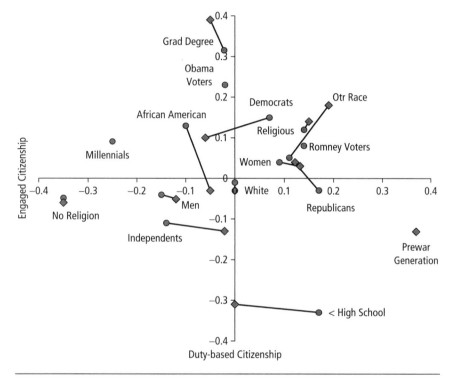

Source: 2004 and 2014 General Social Surveys.

Note: Figure entries are the average scores for each group on the indices of duty-based and engaged citizenship. The 2004 survey is denoted by a diamond at the end of a line, and the 2014 survey is a circle at the other end of the line.

engaged citizenship in 2014, while the "other" minority category places relatively less. But nearly all social groups remain located in the same general region in this space.

What complicates the separate comparisons of social groups is that many of these characteristics overlap. Sometimes the effects may be reinforcing, and sometimes they may encourage different patterns of citizenship.

For instance, are the contrasts across age groups a result of their distinct socialization experiences, or are they because the generations differ substantially in their educational level and other life conditions? Race, class, and education are also closely intertwined within the American public.

To calculate the unique effects of each social trait, I included them in a statistical model that estimates the effect of each trait while holding constant the effects of all the other items in the model.[35] For instance, what is the influence of age group if we statistically adjust the results so that differences in education, partisanship, and other factors are removed? This provides a purer measure of each characteristic's influence on citizenship norms separate from all the others. These results are presented in Figure 3.8.

The upper model in the figure presents the predictors of citizen duty combining the 2004 and 2014 surveys to identify basic relationships. The factors influencing citizen duty generally mirror the previous analyses. Older Americans, women, non-black minorities, and those with strong religious feelings are the most strongly correlated with citizen duty. Education has a weak effect in lessening duty-based citizenship. The first coefficient in the figure indicates that there is little change in duty-based citizenship between 2004 and 2014 once we control for the social characteristics of survey respondents.

The lower panel in Figure 3.8 displays the traits influencing engaged citizenship. Education is the dominant influence on engaged citizenship, while having little impact on citizen duty. Several characteristics also have contrasting effects. A Republican Party identification weakens feelings of engaged citizenship, while it strengthens duty-based norms. And while high income stimulates duty-based norms, it diminishes support for engaged citizenship.

Thus, most of the patterns we examined for single social characteristics also persist when we look at all these traits combined. The contrasts in citizenship norms because of education and generation support the logic that social modernization is shifting popular views of citizenship. In part because of these findings, I will often focus on generation and education in later chapters as we examine the forces that are reshaping American politics.

FIGURE 3.8   Predictors of Citizenship Norms

Citizen Duty

▶ *Age, income, gender, and religious attachments significantly increase citizen duty, but duty is lower among the better educated and African Americans.*

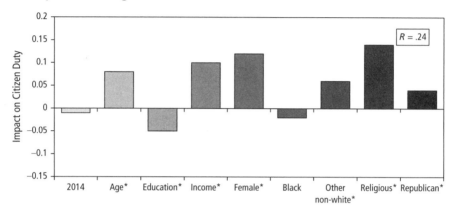

Engaged Citizenship

▶ *Education is the single most important factor encouraging engaged citizenship, but a religious attachment and Republican Party identification lower engaged citizenship.*

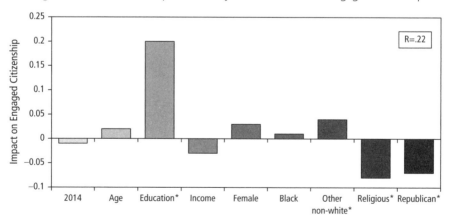

Source: 2004 and 2014 General Social Surveys.

Note: Table entries are standardized coefficients from a multiple regression analysis; each bar represents whether the predictor has a positive or negative effect on citizenship norms. Statistically significant effects ($p < .05$) are noted by an asterisk.

THE SOCIAL ROOTS OF CITIZENSHIP

The definition of "good citizenship" varies across subgroups of the American public. Older Americans are much more likely to stress duty-based norms, while younger generations tend to emphasize engaged citizenship. Republicans and Democrats display a similar contrast, as do religious and nonreligious Americans. The generalizations from the meeting of Senator Lugar and Angelina Jolie at the start of this chapter may be hypothetical, but they reflect many of the social patterns in citizenship norms demonstrated here.

Moreover, the social bases of citizenship norms follow patterns consistent with the themes of social change presented in Chapter 1. The social transformation of America appears linked to a shift in the meaning of citizenship. The age contrasts are especially significant. Some of the age differences might reflect life-cycle effects, in which the emphasis on authority and order increases as people age. But there appears to be a strong generational element to these patterns, derived from early political socialization and the changing context of American politics over the past half-century or more. If this interpretation is correct, it suggests that the slow, steady shift in citizenship norms will continue. As demographic change decreases the numbers of older Americans who subscribe to duty-based norms of citizenship, these trends also add new Millennials who are less motivated by a sense of duty and more motivated by norms of engaged citizenship. Moreover, these changes seem consistent with broader and deeper patterns that are transforming citizen values in America and other affluent democracies.[36] There is little evidence to suggest that younger generations can be persuaded to begin thinking like their grandparents. If this demography is our destiny, then we should begin a more serious discussion of how the shifting norms of citizenship will reshape democratic politics.

Another pattern occurs for education and citizen norms. Better-educated Americans emphasize engaged citizenship with effects that dominate other potential correlates. Republicans and those with strong religious feelings also give less weight to engaged citizenship. This suggests that rising educational levels have reinforced both set of norms, but the impact on engaged citizenship is proportionally greater. So even in this instance, social change increased the relative attention to engaged citizenship.

It is also important to note that most of these basic patterns are consistent across the decade spanned by the two GSS surveys, even though this was a period of dramatic economic change because of the Great Recession and the intensified political debate that followed. If citizenship norms are deeply embedded in a nation's political culture they should be relatively enduring over time. And I suspect that some of the altered relationships we do observe are due to slight changes in how the GSS measured citizenship norms.[37]

The larger lesson is the need to fully understand the nature of citizenship norms. Political commentators have often stressed the erosion of duty-based citizenship, praising those social groups that adhere to these norms and criticizing groups that are less duty oriented. Calls for renewing American citizenship are often equated with this dimension of citizenship. The social patterns in this chapter underscore the point that groups who are lower in citizen duty typically do not lack citizenship norms; they just emphasize different norms of engaged citizenship.

The remainder of this book examines the effects of both sets of citizenship norms. Both have positive implications for the functioning of the political process and the behavior of the American public—and both also carry limitations. Rather than lamenting the loss of duty-based citizenship, we should first understand the consequences of the changing emphases of citizenship.

BOWLING ALONE OR PROTESTING WITH A GROUP

A participatory public has been a defining feature of American politics and historically a strength of the U.S. political system. Alexis de Tocqueville, for example, was impressed by the participatory tendencies of Americans when he toured the nation in the 1830s:

> The political activity that pervades the United States must be seen to be understood. No sooner do you set foot upon American ground than you are stunned by a kind of tumult; . . . here the people of one quarter of a town are meeting to decide upon the building of a church; there the election of a representative is going on; a little farther, the delegates of a district are hastening to the town in order to consult upon some local improvements; in another place, the laborers of a village quit their plows to deliberate upon a project of a road or a public school. . . . To take a hand in the regulation of society and to discuss it is [the] biggest concern and, so to speak, the only pleasure an American knows.[1]

Thomas Jefferson also emphasized the importance of participation to the democratic process. Scholars maintain that political participation "is at the heart of democratic theory and at the heart of the democratic political formula in the United States."[2] Without public involvement in the process, democracy lacks both its legitimacy and its guiding force.

Studies of political participation in the 1960s and 1970s stressed the public's high activity levels. The political culture encouraged people to participate: Americans were active in voluntary associations, engaged in political discussion, and involved political affairs.[3] Tocqueville's description of America apparently still applied in the mid-twentieth century.

And yet a considerable body of contemporary research argues that fewer people are participating. Although education levels, socioeconomic status, access to political information, and the other resources of democratic citizenship have increased substantially over the past several decades (as described in Chapter 1), this has apparently not stimulated participation. Fewer Americans seem engaged in elections, and other evidence points to a drop in campaign activity.[4] In his influential book that stimulated the title for this chapter, *Bowling Alone,* Robert Putnam concluded: "declining electoral participation is merely the most visible symptom of a broader disengagement from community life. Like a fever, electoral abstention is even more important as a sign of deeper trouble in the body politic than as a malady itself. It is not just from the voting booth that Americans are increasingly AWOL."[5] John Hibbing and Elisabeth Theiss-Morse went a step further and claimed, "The last thing people want is to be more involved in political decision making: They do not want to make political decisions themselves; they do not want to provide much input to those who are assigned to make these decisions; and they would rather not know all the details of the decision-making process."[6]

Moreover, most analysts view the young as a primary source of this decline. A host of experts extol the civic values and engagement of the older, "Greatest Generation" with great hyperbole. At the same time, the young are described as the "narcissistic generation" or the "invisible generation," even by sympathetic journalists who are members of Generation X or the Millennials. Political analysts and politicians seemingly agree that young Americans are dropping out of politics, producing the erosion of political activity.[7]

Is the situation really so dire? In the years since the first edition of this book was published, there has been a growing recognition that young people are participating, albeit in new ways, and these new forms of action are increasing in overall terms.[8] Ronald Inglehart, for example, offered a much more optimistic image of contemporary citizen engagement: "One frequently hears references to growing apathy on the part of the public . . . These allegations of apathy are misleading: mass publics *are* deserting the old-line, oligarchical political organizations that mobilized them in the modernization era—but they are becoming more active in a wide range of elite-challenging forms of political action."[9] Political consumerism, contentious activity, deliberative action, and online participation have all increased since the halcyon days of the early 1960s. From this perspective, America is witnessing a change in the nature of citizenship and political participation that is leading to a renaissance of democratic participation—rather than a general decline in participation.

We suggest that the norms of citizenship may provide the key to understanding the changes in Americans' participation patterns. Duty-based norms of citizenship can stimulate certain forms of political engagement, especially turnout in elections. The decline of these norms thus may contribute to the erosion of electoral participation. In contrast, engaged citizens have ambivalent feelings toward elections and prefer more direct forms of political action, such as working with public interest groups, boycotts, or contentious actions. Let's first examine how political participation patterns are changing over time. Then, we can find out how the modes of citizenship are linked to participation patterns.

THE REPERTOIRE OF POLITICAL ACTION

Instead of starting with the common assumption that participation is synonymous with voting in elections, let's begin with a citizen-centered view of participation. How do people think of their participation options? Suppose a regulation was being considered by your city that you considered very unjust or harmful; what do you think you could do? This question has been asked of the American public several times, and the results are informative.[10] Few people, maybe a sixth, say they would use their vote or work through the political parties to influence policy.

Instead people mention a varied menu of participation opportunities. Around half say they would work with an informal group to address this issue. A growing percentage said they would directly contact city politicians or other political actors. There has also been a marked increase in the share of the public who say they would protest or circulate a petition on this issue.

In other words, there are expanding options for how people can influence their government. Moreover, the perceived growth in the participation repertoire has come primarily in forms of direct action—such as contacting and protest—that typify a style of participation that is much different from the institutionalized and infrequent means of electoral participation of prior years. If we had more recent survey evidence, or especially a survey of young Americans, we would find new forms of online activism that didn't exist a generation ago. Political blogs, social networking, and online political contributions further expand the options for political participation.

Americans thus see new avenues of political action available to them—but do they use these opportunities? Surprisingly, comprehensive long-term data on the participation patterns of Americans are relatively rare.[11] For example, the American National Election Study has a rich battery of items on campaign activity that extends back to the 1950s, but the study does not regularly monitor nonelectoral participation. The Political Action/World Values Surveys regularly ask about protest activities but not about more conventional acts. Even when surveys include a large battery of participation items, the wording of questions changes across surveys in ways that limit time comparisons.[12] Consequently, we use several different survey series to track activity patterns over time.

It's important to start the analyses as early as possible in order to describe patterns before the early 1970s, when some researchers maintain that participation began to erode. With a long time span, we can better see the long-term consequences of social change in the American public, effectively weeding out shifts in participation that result from the ebb and flow of specific events or specific election campaigns.

In summary, the boundaries of political action are much broader today than just electoral politics.[13] To truly understand the political activity of Americans, we need to expand our comparisons beyond voting and campaign activity, which are often the focus of those who criticize the public's level of participation. This chapter thus considers the range of choices available to Americans when they want to express their opinions, lobby politicians, or influence public policy.

VOTING AND ELECTIONS

Voting in elections is one of the most basic political acts for a good citizen. However, one of the verities of electoral research is that turnout has decreased over time, in both the United States and other established democracies.[14] And given the centrality of elections to the democratic process, it is a natural place to begin our comparisons.

Electoral statistics clearly demonstrate that the percent of the voting-age public (VAP) that shows up on Election Day has been decreasing. However, a growing proportion of the American public is not eligible to vote, either because they are not citizens or because criminal convictions have limited their voting rights. Consequently, it is also important to measure turnout based on the voting-eligible public (VEP) that adjusts for these factors.[15]

Figure 4.1 presents both the VAP and VEP trends in presidential elections over time. Turnout was significantly higher in the 1960s and trended irregularly downward until the late 1990s.[16] This is the evidence of declining citizen involvement that is most widely cited. Initiatives to simplify registration requirements (such as voter registration while getting a driver's license) and mail voting did not fundamentally alter the downward slide in turnout. However, participation in presidential elections has increased overall since 2000. Recent turnout peaked in 2008 with Obama's historic election, and it ebbed slightly in 2012. Turnout is also down in most other affluent democracies.[17]

Turnout in other elections has followed this same downward spiral. Without the stimulus of a presidential campaign, turnout is regularly 20 percent (or more) lower in off-year congressional elections and falling along with presidential elections. State and local turnout is even more embarrassing for American democracy. For example, in the 2013 election for mayor of Los Angeles, only 12.4 percent of registered voters actually

FIGURE 4.1   **Levels of Voting Turnout over Time**

▶ *Turnout in presidential and congressional elections is lower than during the 1960s.*

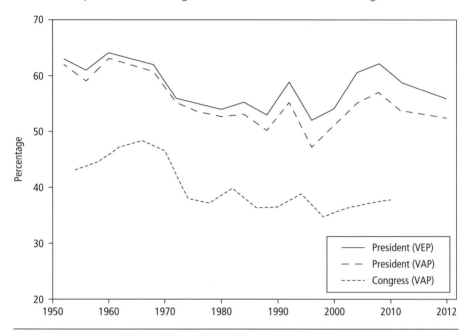

Source: U.S. Election Project at George Mason University (http://elections.gmu.edu/).

Note: Voting-age public (VAP) includes all adults in the nation; voting-eligible public (VEP) excludes noncitizens, felons, and others without the right to vote.

cast a ballot. And at least another 20 percent of the eligible citizens hadn't registered to vote, which would further decrease turnout.

Such election statistics are readily available across every political unit in America and are widely discussed after each election. This is the primary evidence that analysts cite for the decline in Americans' engagement in politics. Each election with lower turnout than the last generates anxious calls for reform in the media, as happened after the 2013 Los Angeles election. The decline in turnout is problematic for the vitality of democracy, especially for those who do not vote. But this is not the only way that people can participate.

CAMPAIGN ACTIVITY

Participation in campaigns extends electoral participation beyond voting. Fewer people are routinely active in campaigns because campaign work requires more initiative, more time, and arguably more political sophistication. It is much easier to mark an X on the ballot than to staff a campaign headquarters, show up for an election meeting, or even give money to a campaign. However, with greater costs to the activist comes greater influence. Campaign activities are important to parties and candidates, and candidates generally are more sensitive to, and aware of, the policy interests of their activists. Several analysts argue that campaign activity has also followed a downward spiral.[18]

The most extensive trends for campaign activity come from the time series of the American National Election Study (ANES) (Table 4.1).[19] The ANES asks about working for a party, going to a meeting, giving money, displaying campaign material, and persuading others how to vote. Between 1952 and 2012, there are ebbs and flows in campaign involvement related to specific campaigns. Campaign activity hit a low point in the late 1990s, which appears to reinforce the evidence of public disengagement for those writing about this period. But campaign activity has increased beginning with the 2000 election. The Obama campaign in 2008 built on an already increasing level of activity. Displaying a campaign button or a bumper sticker was more popular in the 1950s, but today personal discussion about the campaign is actually more common. Giving money to campaigns has also increased in recent elections, presumably stimulated by the potential for easy online contributions for small donors.[20]

The major change, however, has been the advent of online campaign participation. The Internet provides a new way for people to connect to others, to gather and share information, and to attempt to influence the electoral process.[21] While Web sites were unheard of in the 1992 campaign, they are now a standard feature of electoral politics. The electoral potential of the Internet became a reality with Barack Obama's 2008 campaign. The campaign developed a revolutionary model of a political social network ("MyBo") that allowed supporters to connect with like-minded people in their community. Fundraising rose to new heights

Trends in American Campaign Activity

▲ Campaign activity has fluctuated over time without a clear consistent trend, and participation has increased since its low point in 1996.

Activity	1952	1956	1960	1964	1968	1972	1976	1980	1984	1988	1992	1996	2000	2004	2008	2012
Work for a party or candidate	3	3	6	5	6	5	4	4	4	3	3	2	3	3	4	3
Go to a meeting	7	7	8	8	9	9	6	8	8	7	8	5	5	8	9	6
Give money	4	10	12	11	9	10	16	8	8	9	7	7	6	10	13	10
Wear a button or have a bumper sticker	—	16	21	17	15	14	8	7	9	9	11	10	10	21	18	13
Persuade others how to vote	28	28	34	31	33	32	37	36	32	29	38	27	34	48	45	40
Participate in two or more activities	—	16	21	17	16	17	16	12	12	12	14	11	11	30	20	14

Source: American National Election Study, 1952–2012.

through a sophisticated online solicitation/donation system. The Internet became a tool for political discussion, and not just the one-way dissemination of information. The political significance of online activity has steadily grown since 2008 in both the United States and other democracies.[22]

A Pew study found that online activity rose to new levels in the 2012 election. Many voters shared their voting preference via a social networking site (SNS) like Twitter, and others watched an online video about the campaign (see Figure 4.3). In contemporary elections more people probably forward election related emails or post a candidate/party button on Facebook than place placards on their lawns. The numbers of online activists are modest, and the uses are still growing, but the Internet is adding to the tools of campaign activism, especially among the young who are more active in most online forms of action.

Thus, the ANES suggests a relatively flat level of campaign activity over this sixty-year period. And if one factors in new forms of online campaign activity, participation has certainly increased. Even if fewer people vote, election campaigns still engage a significant share of the American public.

CONTACTING GOVERNMENT

Another form of political action is personally contacting a politician, government official, or media person about a political issue. This is a fairly demanding form of action, requiring a person to identify a political target and formulate a statement of his or her policy preferences. Table 4.A in the appendix shows that in 1967 a fifth of the public had contacted a member of the local government or a member of the state/national government. By 1987 both questions show that a third of the public had contacted politicians at both levels. Although data on this exact question are not available since 1987, the 2004 and 2014 GSS report that about a fifth of Americans contacted a politician or civil servant in the previous twelve months (and another fifth had done this "in the more distant past").[23] It thus appears that more and more people use this method of participation, which allows them to select the issue, the timing and means of communication, and the content of the message to policy makers. A century ago, active citizens marched en masse to the polls with their ballots held high over the heads and voted as their ward captain or union leader told them. Today, they sit in the comfort of their home and write politicians and the media about the issues of the community and the nation, often by email.

COLLECTIVE GROUP ACTIVITY

Another method of political action is working with others to address political or social issues—collective action. Collective action can take many forms. It often involves group efforts to deal with social or community problems, ranging from issues of schools or roads to protecting the local environment. From the PTA to local neighborhood committees, this is democracy in action. The existence of such autonomous group action defines the character of a civil society that theorists from Jefferson and Tocqueville to the present have considered a foundation of the democratic process. Today, participation in citizen groups can include involvement in public interest groups with broad policy concerns, such as environmental interest groups, women's groups, consumer protection, health care, or minority rights.

Group-based participation has long been cited as a distinctive aspect of the American political culture, but it is difficult to measure without representative survey data. Verba and Nie asked if individuals had *ever* worked with others in their community to solve some local problem. In 1967, 30 percent were active (see Table 4.A in appendix). By 1987, participation in community groups had increased to 34 percent. The Pew Center asked similar question in 2012, and 37 percent reported working with a community group on a social or political matter during the previous twelve months.[24] This activity is perhaps the closest to the Tocquevillian image of grassroots democracy in America, so it is very significant that informal collective action has become more common among Americans.

PROTEST AND CONTENTIOUS ACTIONS

One thinks of the 1960s as the protest era for modern American politics. This was the age of Aquarius, protests for civil rights, against the Vietnam

War, and for the social conscience of the nation. In a real sense, this experience transformed participation in America to include protest, demonstrations, and other contentious actions. But has this era, and the propensity to protest, passed into history?

Protest not only expands the repertoire of political participation, but it differs markedly from electoral politics in its style of action. Protest can focus on specific issues or policy goals—from protecting whales to protesting the policies of a local government—and can convey a high level of political information with real political force. Electoral activity seldom focuses on a single issue because parties represent a package of policies. Sustained and effective protest is a demanding activity that requires initiative, political skills, and cooperation with others. Thus, the advocates of protest argue that citizens can increase their political influence by adopting a strategy of direct action.

The early participation studies in the 1950s and early 1960s did not even ask about contentious activities. This partially reflected the low level of protest in the 1950s and early 1960s as well as the unconventional nature of these activities. Consequently, the most authoritative source of protest trends comes from Political Action/World Values Survey (WVS) that began in 1975. These surveys asked about participation in several types of contentious action (Figure 4.2).[25]

Overall protest levels grew across the 1980s and early 1990s and then peaked in the 1999 WVS survey before falling back slightly in the two surveys taken during the past decade. In the mid-1970s about a tenth of Americans said they had participated in a lawful demonstration; now the rate has increased to about a sixth of the public. Participation in petition signing, boycotts, and unofficial strikes have significantly increased over time. Other surveys suggest much higher levels of boycotting if it is described as political consumerism, that is, buying or not buying a product for ethnical, moral, or political reasons.[26] Moreover, if we could extend our time series back to the quieter times of the 1950s and early 1960s, the growth of protest activity would undoubtedly be more dramatic.

The WVS series may exaggerate participation levels because it asks if the respondent *had ever participated* in these activities instead of asking about participation over a specific time span. A fifty-year-old has had

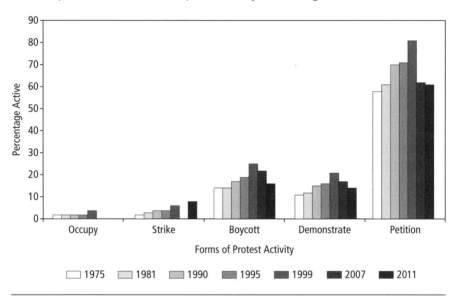

FIGURE 4.2   Protest Activity

▶ *Participation in various forms of protest activity is increasing.*

Forms of Protest Activity

☐ 1975   ☐ 1981   ☐ 1990   ■ 1995   ■ 1999   ■ 2007   ■ 2011

Sources: 1975 Political Action Study; 1981, 1990, 1995, 1999, 2007, and 2011 World Values Survey.

Note: Figure entries are the percentage who say they have done the activity. The occupy question was not asked in 2007 or 2011; the strike question was not asked in 2007.

more opportunities to participate than a twenty-year-old, and the former may be reporting activities from their youth. The Verba and Nie survey asked a different question in their 1987 survey, and 6 percent said they had participated in a demonstration, protest, or boycott in the past two years. The 2004 and 2014 GSS surveys asked people whether they had taken part in a demonstration, and 5 percent said they had done this during the previous twelve months (see Table 4.A in appendix).[27] An additional 15 percent said they had participated in a demonstration "in the more distant past." Another GSS question asked separately about boycotting, and 24 percent had done this activity in the past year in both surveys (and another 14–15 percent "in the more distant past"). Similarly, signing and circulating petitions online is now commonplace, as are virtual protests against the policies of the government or social institutions. About a third of GSS respondents in both surveys reported they had signed a petition in the last year, with an equal number doing this in the more distant past. The question wording and time span of a survey question affect the specific results, but undoubtedly contentious political activity has become much more common than during the relatively tranquil days of the 1950s and early 1960s. Protest has become so common that it is now the extension of conventional political action by other means.

ONLINE PARTICIPATION

Let's return to the point that the Internet is creating a forum for political activism that did not previously exist. The Internet provides a new way for people to connect to others, to gather and share information, and to attempt to influence the political process.[28] For instance, congressional reports state that emails are now the most common form of communications from constituents, and they are growing most rapidly.[29] The 2008 and 2012 Obama campaigns used the Internet to connect to prospective voters, share information, and mobilize voting. Fundraising in presidential elections rose to new heights through the campaign's sophisticated online solicitation/donation system.[30] The Internet became a tool for political discussion, and not just the one-way dissemination of information. The frequency of online activity has steadily grown since 2008 in both the United States and other democracies.[31] Moreover, the Web is the medium of the young—and is often unknown to their parents and grandparents.

The Pew Center surveyed Americans in mid-2012, before the party conventions, and asked about their political activities.[32] The intriguing part of this survey is that it separately asked about traditional offline forms of political participation and parallel activity online (Figure 4.3). For example, 25 percent of Americans had signed a petition (offline or both offline and online) in the previous twelve months, but an additional 8 percent had only signed an online petition. Similarly, 24 percent had contacted a politician by phone, mail, or email, but an additional 6 percent had only contacted by email. Some of this online-only activity is

FIGURE 4.3 **Offline and Online Political Participation**

▶ *The Internet creates new opportunities to expand citizen participation.*

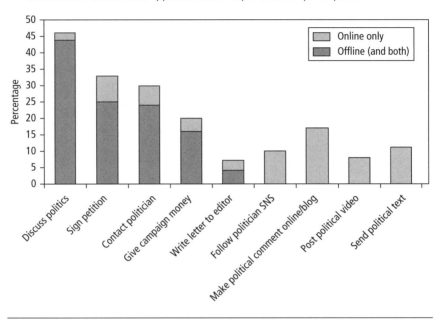

Source: 2012 Pew Civic Engagement Survey.

Note: The figure presents those who are active offline (includes those who do both offline and online) and those who are only online activists. The Pew questions asked about participation in the last twelve months.

because it is easier, so it substitutes for actions that were done only offline in the past. But undoubtedly this new medium opens the door to participation by individuals who might not otherwise be active, such as young people.

The same study found that two-fifths participated in some political activity as part of a social networking site.[33] Seventeen percent posted a political comment to an SNS or a blog, about a tenth posted a political video or sent a political text message. The numbers are modest, and the uses are still growing, but the Internet is adding to the tools of political activism, especially among the young who are more active in most online forms of action.

In summary, voting is but one form of political action. There are many doors into the political arena. Previous research has shown that people are drawn to different forms of action depending on their skills and their motivations. The voting decline literature misses this larger reality because it focuses only on elections and campaigns. When we expand our vision to the full repertoire of political action, people are actually participating more—not less. Some of these forms are expressive; others are more instrumental. But they share the common goal of giving people more voice in the course of society and government.

OLD REPERTOIRES AND NEW REPERTOIRES

Why has turnout in elections decreased while other forms of action have increased? There is no single answer because several factors shape the decision on whether to participate and then how to participate. However, something in this network of factors has changed.

Political activity makes time and cognitive demands upon the citizen. To be fully informed about the candidates and issues of an election is a challenging task, even if the act of voting is relatively simple. The demands increase substantially for other political activities, especially individualized, direct forms of action. For instance, to write a letter to a member of Congress or to speak at a city council meeting typically requires a deeper knowledge of politics, more personal initiative, and a significant time commitment.

Participation research thus stresses the importance of social status as a predictor of political activity. Better education, higher-status occupations, and higher incomes provide the resources of time and money that facilitate political action. In addition, these social traits normally indicate a set of cognitive abilities and organizational skills that facilitate activity. Thus, research commonly describes social status as the "standard model" to explain political participation.[34] This reality still holds true today; nearly all studies of participation display a positive correlation between social status and various forms of action.

Consequently, the rise in social status and other political resources discussed in Chapter 1 should stimulate political engagement. In large part, this has occurred—especially for individualized and direct forms of action, such as protests and direct contacting. But this has not happened for voting and participation in electoral campaigns. Fewer people are casting a ballot, and the drop-off in voting is proportionately greater among the young.[35] Arguments that complexity is pushing voters away from voting are inconsistent with the fact that more people are participating in activities that require more initiative, skills, and resources than voting.

Americans appear to be changing the ways they choose to participate. Voting is a form of action for those with limited skills, resources, and motivations—the simplicity of voting explains why more people vote than any other single political activity. As political skills and resources expand, people realize the limits of voting as a means of political influence, and many expand their participation to individualized, direct, and more policy-focused methods. In addition, we will shortly argue that changes in citizenship norms encourage participation in activities that are citizen initiated, more flexible, directly linked to government, and more policy oriented. In short, changing skills and norms encourage people to change their patterns of political action.

Age is another standard correlate of political participation. As a baseline model, we should expect increasing political involvement with age, as people assume more family and career responsibilities and become integrated into their political communities. This is generally known as the "life-cycle model" of participation.[36]

In addition, participation patterns may shift across generations. Several scholars have argued that the young are dropping out of politics. For instance, William Damon states: "Young people across the world have been disengaging from civic and political activities to a degree unimaginable a mere generation ago. The lack of interest is greatest in mature democracies, but it is evident even in many emerging or troubled ones. Today there are no leaders, no causes, no legacy of past trials or accomplishments that inspire much more than apathy or cynicism from the young."[37] Lots of experts echo these sentiments.

Are the young really this bad? Volunteerism and other forms of direct action seem especially common among younger Americans.[38] A generational shift toward other, nonelectoral forms of participation is so strong that it may reverse the normal life-cycle pattern. For example, Cliff Zukin and his colleagues examined the full repertoire of political action among the young, and they rejected the general claim of youth disengagement: "First and foremost, simple claims that today's youth . . . are apathetic and disengaged from civic life are simply wrong."[39]

Therefore, both social modernization and generational change may be reshaping the participation patterns of Americans. To display the interaction of both factors, one can define several "generational units" in terms of educational level and age. I divided the 2004–2014 General Social Surveys into better and lesser educated and into the six generations presented in earlier chapters.[40] Then, I compared these generational units for four types of political action that highlight the contrast between electoral participation and direct action: voting, being a member of a party, demonstrating, and boycotting.

Figure 4.4 presents the patterns of voting and party activity for these generational units. For example, the top panel in the figure displays the percentage of each generational unit who said they voted in the previous election; this percentage defines the center point for each of the circles in the figure. The width of each circle is proportionate to the relative size of each generational unit in the combined 2004–2014 GSS surveys. For instance, the oldest prewar cohort is now a small share of the public (with small circles), and the lesser educated outnumber the better educated; this pattern is reversed for the youngest cohort.[41] The bubble graph displays both the relative participation levels of different generational units and differences in the size of these units.

Voter turnout is significantly lower among the young for both educational levels. However, rising educational levels mean that the better educated (who participate more) constitute a growing percentage of younger cohorts. The increase in educational levels among the young has not reversed the general decline in turnout, but it moderates this downward trend.[42] Another way to think of this effect is that the greater relative size of the lesser educated among the older voters pulls down their average participation, and the greater size of the better educated among the youngest cohorts pulls up their overall participation rates.

Even this age relationship needs two caveats. First, participation tends to increase as people move through the life cycle. Second, since 1996 turnout among the young is increasing more rapidly relative to older Americans. Estimates from the Center for Information and Research on Civic Learning and Engagement (CIRCLE) found that turnout among 18- to 30-year-olds increased by 15 percent from 1996 to 2008, while turnout increased by 9.5 for the nation overall. Part of the explanation is the mobilization of youth by campaigns such as MTV's Rock the Vote and the efforts of various public interest groups. In addition, Barack Obama's candidacy in 2008 stimulated youth participation in the campaign's efforts to expand the electorate.[43] So if politicians speak to the issues of young people and civil society groups mobilize the young as the AARP does for seniors, then more young people will come to the polls on Election Day.

Party membership and activity show this same basic pattern across generational units in the lower half of the figure. The young are less engaged with political parties compared with the prewar generation and postwar Boomer generation. And within each generation the better educated are more involved. In overall terms, the movement away from party involvement across generations is greatest among the better educated, as they shift their focus to other forms of political action. Thus electoral politics fits this general pattern of decreasing engagement among younger generations.

While electoral activity is lower among youth, they may be more involved in other forms of contentious or direct participation. Two natural examples from the GSS are participating in a demonstration or buying/boycotting a product for political, ethical, or environmental research. Figure 4.5 shows examples of the new participation tools of the young—and they follow a much different pattern. The top panel displays the percentage of each generational unit that has participated in a demonstration in the past year. While over 10 percent of Millennials had demonstrated, barely 2 percent of older Americans had. And while education generally increases participation within a generation, these effects are quite modest. Younger generations may decrease their level of protest activity as they move through their lives, but early contentious action may morph to other forms of participation.

FIGURE 4.4	Voting and Party Work by Generation

▶ *Voting is more common among older age groups and the better educated within each age group.*

Voted in Previous Election

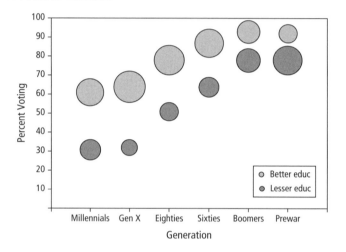

Member of Party Organization

▶ *Party membership is higher among older citizens and the better educated.*

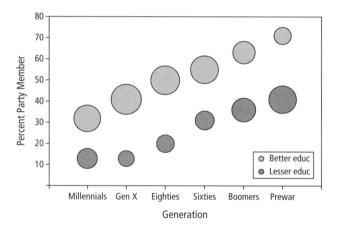

Source: 2004 and 2014 General Social Surveys.

Note: The width of the circles approximates the percent of the educational groups in each generation. The center of each circle is the percentage that has done the activity.

FIGURE 4.5 **Boycotts and Demonstrations by Generation**

▶ *Demonstrating is higher among the young and among the better educated in each generation.*

Attended a Demonstration

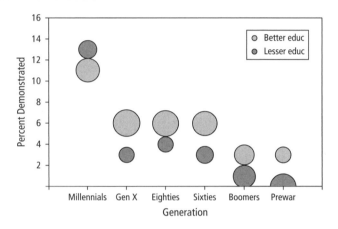

Boycotted a Product

▶ *Boycotting is more common among the young and the better educated in each generation.*

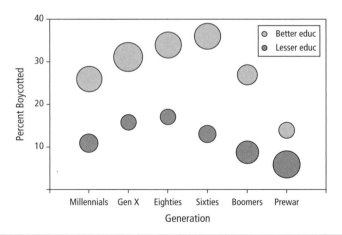

Source: 2004 and 2014 General Social Surveys.

Note: The width of the circles represents the percent of the educational groups in each generation. The center of each circle is the percentage that has done the activity.

The lower panel in Figure 4.5 displays the percentage of each generational unit that boycotted a product for political or ethical reasons in the past year. This activity is also more common among the young and among the better educated, so these two effects reinforce each other. For instance, only 6 percent of the oldest, less-educated cohort has engaged in these activities, compared with 26 percent among the better-educated Millennials. (In this instance, participation is highest among middle-aged Americans.) I would expect that as the disposable income of Millennials increases, so will their political consumption.

In summary, one cannot simply presume that young Americans are not politically active because they vote less than their elders. Activity can take many forms, and the young are more involved in contentious actions and online activity. In other areas age differences might be negligible or also contrast with voting. We need to examine the correlates of the full repertoire of political action—and the factors affecting participation—before we can accurately determine how politically engaged Americans are.

CITIZENSHIP NORMS AND PARTICIPATION

In addition to the social characteristics of education and generation, the norms of citizenship can lead people to different styles of participation.[44] Duty-based norms should reinforce traditional forms of political activity, such as voting and party activity, especially since citizen duty includes as one of its elements the duty to vote. Raymond Wolfinger and Steven Rosenstone, for example, stressed the role of duty in describing why people vote: "the most important benefit of voting [is] a feeling that one has done one's duty to society . . . and to oneself."[45] Andre Blais saw images of duty-based voting in even stronger terms: "To use a religious analogy, not voting can be construed as a venial sin: it is a wrong, one that weak human beings should be urged not to commit but may be forgiven for if they indulge in it."[46]

In contrast, engaged citizenship taps participatory norms that are broader than electoral politics. The engaged citizen is more likely to want more direct influence on government and its policies and to be skeptical of parties as political gatekeepers. This should stimulate participation in direct action methods such as boycotts, "buycotts," demonstrations, and other forms of contentious action.

Prior analyses of the 2004 GSS found robust relationships between citizenship norms and various forms of participation.[47] I want to build on these analyses by combining both the 2004 and 2014 studies to identify the impact of citizenship norms on participation, while controlling for the possible effects of other variables such as age, education, and cognitive skills (a vocabulary test asked in the GSS) (Table 4.2).[48] The activities in the table are organized with those where duty-based citizenship has the strongest positive effect on the left, and the strongest negative effect for the activities on the right.

From our perspective, the most interesting pattern is the differential effect of our two types of citizenship norms. Duty-based citizenship has a positive influence on electoral participation—voting and party membership— but there is a null relationship or negative relationship with all other forms of participation. This is consistent with Bolzendahl and Coffe's evidence on the negative effects of duty norms on participation in 2004.[49] Citizen duty encourages allegiance to the state but may actually undermine an elite-challenging view of participation.

In contrast, engaged citizenship is positively related to each of the political activities in the table. In part, this may reflect the inclusion of participation norms as one of the three areas in this index. However, even a revised index including only autonomy and social citizenship items (Chapter 2) shows significant positive relationships with each of these political activities.[50] So it is not just participatory norms; engaged citizenship represents a cluster of beliefs that encourage people to participate in politics and the decisions affecting their lives, often with a skepticism of government and a concern for those in need.

Since so much attention has focused on the low voting turnout of youth, it is worth focusing on the age relationship. Indeed, voting is much higher among older Americans (β = .25), the largest coefficient for any political activity. Only three other activities have age differences above .10, and these are all conventional forms of action. In three instances—boycotts, demonstrations, and Internet activism—younger people are slightly more active than their elders (albeit with statistically

TABLE 4.2 Predicting Participation

▶ The table describes the impact of citizenship norms and other predictors in explaining participation in each activity; citizen duty increases activities on the left of the table and decreases activities on the right.

Predictor	Vote	Be a Party Member	Sign Petition	Donate Money	Contact Politician	Attend Meeting	Boycott	Contact Media	Use Internet Forum	Attend Demonstration
Citizen duty	.06	.02*	.00*	–.01*	–.05	–.07	–.08	–.09	–.11	–.12
Engaged citizenship	.12	.15	.10	.16	.18	.18	.17	.08	.09	.14
Age	.25	.13	.07	.02*	.16	.11	–.03*	.06	–.04*	–.04*
Education	.20	.20	.11	.17	.16	.19	.16	.10	.08	.10
Cognitive level	.12	.12	.28	.16	.19	.10	.26	.11	.09	.10
Year of survey	–.01*	–.07	.01*	–.05	–.07	–.04*	.00*	–.05	—	.05
Multiple R	.42	.36	.38	.35	.43	.37	.43	.24	.22	.27

Source: 2004 and 2014 General Social Surveys.

Note: Table entries are standardized regression coefficients (ß); each coefficient represents whether the predictor has a positive or negative effect on each political activity independent of the other predictors. Participation items are coded (1) did not act and (2) did act; coefficients that are not statistically significant ($p < .05$) are noted by an asterisk.

insignificant coefficients). The conclusion is that age matters a lot for voting and party activity, which is where analysts focus their attention, but it matters much less for others forms of action. And even the youngest citizens today are likely to increase their participation in various ways as they move through the life cycle.

Participation in contentious action presents a distinct pattern. For the two items on the right side of Table 4.2—boycotts and attending a demonstration—the young are more active than older Americans. Furthermore, engaged citizenship stimulates these actions, while traditional norms of citizen duty have a substantial negative impact. Participation in an Internet forum displays the same pattern.

Finally, the four participation examples in the middle of the table represent forms of political action driven by a mix of forces. Contributing money, attending rallies, and contacting politicians are related to engaged citizenship but have weak negative relationships with citizen duty. These individualized forms of participation appear driven by multiple motivations, which implies that norm change within the American electorate does not have clear implications for participation in these activities.

Some other factors consistently influence different activities. Education and cognitive skills are strongly related to all forms of participation. These traits represent skills and resources that enable a person to better manage the complex world of politics and make their views known. Norms are important to participation, but so too are the resources to act on these norms.

In summary, the contrast in the normative basis of participation in electoral politics versus contentious politics highlights how different images of citizenship, combined with rising skill levels of the better-educated public, are altering the patterns of political action in America. Given the causal forces behind these participation patterns, this shift may be a continuing feature of democratic politics.

ENGAGED DEMOCRATS

I first presented this evidence on participation trends to a group of government officials at a lunch talk in Washington, D.C. I began by sharing the academic argument that Americans are disengaging from the political process, which may undermine the bases of American democracy.

To the audience of government officials and administrators, I asked how many of them worried that too few Americans were contacting their offices for advice or in attempts to influence government policy—how many worried that citizens were too passive. No one raised a hand. As you might imagine, just asking this question generated laughter about the unrealistic claim. Few members of Congress, for instance, complain that they receive less input from their constituents than in the past; few administrators yearn for a lobbyist to break the dullness of their daily routine. Instead, they see individual citizens, lobby organizations, and public interest groups as part of an expanding network of activism that had developed in Washington over the previous generation. As stated in the introduction: the good news is . . . the bad news is wrong. America remains a participatory society.

Election turnout has declined, but this is not typical of all political activity. The repertoire of action has actually expanded, and people are now more engaged in more forms of political participation. Participation in election campaigns is still common. People are working with informal groups in their community to address local problems—and this has grown over time. More people today make the effort to directly contact their elected representative or other government officials. The repertoire of political action now includes a variety of protest activities. When one adds political consumerism and Internet activism, the forms of action are even more diverse.

There are three major lessons from our findings. First, turnout rates in elections provide a poor indicator of overall political involvement. It is the most easily available statistic for local, state, and national politics, and it extends back in time, but there is more to democracy than elections. Other nonelectoral forms of individualized or direct political action have increased over time. Ironically, Putnam's 2000 Social Capital Survey replicated four questions from the Verba-Nie participation series: general interest, attending a rally, working with a community group, and protest. None of these four questions displays a statistically significant decrease from the Verba-Nie participation levels of 1967 and 1987. Rather than disengagement, the repertoire of political action has broadened.

Changes in political participation are analogous to changes in the contemporary media environment. Compared with a generation ago,

Americans are consuming much more information about politics, society, and other topics. People are also consuming information from a greater diversity of media sources, some of which did not exist a generation ago. If one only tracked the viewership of the news programs on the major television networks, however, the statistics would show a downward trend in viewership over time. The declining viewership for ABC, CBS, and NBC is not because people are watching less television (they are actually watching more) but because they have more alternatives today. This is the same with participation: People are more active in more varied forms of action.

Certainly we should not dismiss the decrease in voting turnout. Elections are important because they select political elites, provide a source of democratic legitimacy, and engage the mass public in the democratic process. If large proportions of young (and older) Americans do not vote, this lessens their representation in the political process (and may change election outcomes). It is not healthy for democracy for half or more of the public to voluntarily abstain from electing government officials. This is especially problematic when the elected government does not represent all the people and makes decisions that a full majority of Americans do not support. For instance, given the differential turnout rates by age, it is not surprising that the government devotes increasing resources to programs benefiting seniors while providing proportionately less support for the young. However, the goal of participation reforms should not be only to encourage young people to act like their grandparents (and vote out of a sense of duty) but also to show them how engaged citizenship should lead to voting as well as new forms of participation.

Second, changes in citizenship norms and the social composition of the American public are shifting the nature of political action. Turning out to vote requires little initiative since this activity is institutionalized and often mobilized by social or political groups. The clearest examples are the "get out the vote" drives that are a common part of American elections. At the midpoint of the twentieth century, when most Americans had only limited formal education, modest living standards, and limited access to political information beyond the local newspapers, voting and campaigns were the primary focus of political action—and norms of duty-based citizenship encouraged individuals to participate.

As the political skills and resources of the public have increased, this alters the calculus of participation. More people today can engage in more demanding forms of political action, such as individualized activity and direct action. Writing letters to a government official, for example, is less likely when three-fifths of the public has less than a high school education (the electorate of 1952) than when three-fifths have some college education (the electorate of 2012).

In addition, changing norms reinforce a new style of political action. Engaged citizenship stimulates people to be active, especially in methods that give them more direct say and influence. Engaged citizens will still vote because of the importance of elections to the democratic process. However, their participation repertoire includes more direct and individualized forms of action. The engaged citizen is more active on referendums than elections and more active in direct action than campaign work; volunteering is preferred to party activity.[51]

Third, the changing mix of participation activities has implications for the nature and quality of citizen influence. Verba and Nie, for example, describe voting as a high-pressure activity because government officials are being chosen; but there is limited specific policy information or influence because elections involve a diverse range of issues.[52] The public's influence may increase when elections extend to a wide range of political offices and include referendums. Still, it is difficult to treat elections as mandates on specific policies because they assess relative support for broad programs and not specific policies. Even a sophisticated, policy-oriented electorate cannot be certain that its policy interests are represented in an election or that the government will follow these policies once elected into office. Consequently, many people vote because of a sense of civic duty, because of involvement in a campaign, or as an expression of partisan support rather than as a major means to influence policy. Indeed, the importance of citizen duty as a predictor of voting turnout and party work illustrates how these citizenship norms motivate turnout.

In contrast, direct action methods allow citizens to focus on their own issue interests, select the means of influencing policy makers, and choose the timing of influence. The issue might be as broad as nuclear disarmament or as narrow as the policies of the local school district—citizens, not elites, decide. Control over the framework of participation means that people can convey more information and exert more political pressure than they can merely through election campaigns. Political institutions are also adapting to accept and encourage these new forms of citizen access.[53] In short, the control of political activism is shifting to the public and thereby increasing the quantity and quality of democratic influence.

APPENDIX

Comparable statistics on participation rates over time are quite rare, almost an endangered species. Because the data are limited and the time points are few, I summarize overall trends in the appendix. The body of the chapter focuses on the separate studies that examine specific forms of participation.

The first comprehensive assessment of participation was Sidney Verba and Norman Nie's classic, *Participation in America*.[54] In 1967 they asked people about their involvement in a range of political activities. The study identified four distinct modes of political action that people use: voting, campaign activity, communal activity (working with an informal group in the community), and contacting officials. Subsequent research has built upon this framework.

In 1987 Sidney Verba, Kay Schlozman, and Henry Brady repeated the 1967 participation battery.[55] In the meantime, I used a subset of the items asked in the 2004 and 2014 GSS series to update these trends with similar examples. All four surveys use in-person interviews with high-quality sampling and they were conducted by the same research organization, which ensures the same surveying standards.[56]

Table 4.A describes participation patterns over time. As a starting point, the 1967 survey asked about general interest in politics. Two-thirds of the public said they were very or somewhat interested in politics.[57] Indeed, in the midst of the Vietnam War and the civil rights controversies of the 1960s, this should have been a time of broad political interest. Twenty years later, however, rather than a decline in interest, interest held steady in 1987 and remained at this higher level when the question was repeated in 2004 (the question was dropped in 2014).[58] Meanwhile, the Gallup Poll and Pew Center found a slight increase in political interest between 1952 and 2000.[59]

TABLE 4.A	Trends in Political Participation, 1967–2014

▶ *Participation in elections and voting has decreased, but most other activities have increased or held fairly constant.*

Question	1967	1987	2004	2014
Are you interested in politics and national affairs?	66	66	70	56
Voting				
Report voting in the last presidential election	66	58	68	70
Official vote statistics in last presidential election (voting eligible public)	62	55	61	59
What about local elections—do you always vote in those?	47	35	—	—
Campaign Activity				
Do you ever try to show people why they should vote for one of the parties or candidates?	28	32	—	—
Have you done (other) work for one of the parties or candidates?	26	27	—	—
In the past three or four years, have you attended any political meetings or rallies?	19	19	13	8
In the past three or four years, have you contributed money to a political party or candidate or to any other political cause?	13	23	31	24
Contacting				
Have you ever personally gone to see, or spoken to, or written to some member of local government or some other person of influence in the community about some needs or problems?	21	34	—	—
Contact state/national government	20	31	22	18
Community Action				
Have you ever worked with others in this community to try to solve some community problems?	30	34	—	(37)
Protesting				
Have you participated in any demonstrations, protests, boycotts, or marches in past two years?	—	6	5	5

Sources: 1967 *Participation in America* Study; 1987 NORC General Social Survey participation module; 2004 and 2014 General Social Survey. Community action is from the 2012 Pew Civic Engagement Survey.

Note: The 2004–2014 participation questions asked about activity in the last twelve months.

The questions on voter turnout show the typical over-reporting of whether respondents voted, even though official electoral statistics show a clear decline in turnout. About two-thirds of Americans still claim they voted in the previous presidential election.

It is important to note that the Verba et al. questions for other activities were open-ended about the time frame ("have you ever"), while the GSS surveys ask about participation in the last twelve months. This inevitably decreases levels of expressed participation in the 2004–2014 surveys.

Two measures of campaign activity are tracked over time. Attendance at political meetings shows a decline, while financial contributions show an increase over this roughly five-decade time span. These two patterns are consistent with the ANES findings in the chapter. Electoral campaigns that focus on media presentations have diminished the centrality of meetings and rallies in campaigns, while the financial needs of campaigns have steadily grown over time.

Contacting shows little change over time, but this is a question with significant wording differences between the 1967–1987 time points and the 2004–2014 surveys. And the 2004–2014 surveys asked about participation only in the last twelve months. Protest activity was first asked in 1987. Despite frequent claims of protest ebbing and flowing over time, these three surveys show a fairly stable pattern, although the GSS surveys only asked for activity in the previous twelve months. As other examples of contentious activity, the GSS shows much higher levels of petition signing in both surveys (35 and 32 percent, respectively) and boycotting products for political or ethical reasons (24 percent in both surveys).

In summary, my rough calculations—trying to adjust for changes in question wording and splicing together the separate survey series in this chapter—suggest that overall political activity has increased by roughly a third from the 1960s until today. Turnout in elections is down, but the most reliable survey evidence suggests that virtually every other form of activity is stable or increasing over time. In addition, new forms of activity, such as political consumerism and Internet activism, have been added to the participation repertoire.

Moreover, preliminary results from the GSS 2010–2014 panel survey that exactly replicated the 1967 to 1987 trends in wording and methodology became available during the production of this book, and these data reinforce this conclusion. Campaign persuasion, political contributions, and protest activity are significantly higher than in the earlier surveys, while political interest, local contacting, and community action are stable since 1967.[60] In simple terms, overall political participation is increasing if we consider the full range of citizen activity.

5

FREE SPEECH FOR EVERYONE?

On a recent Saturday morning we were having breakfast outdoors in Newport Beach. The group of senior citizens at the next table was intensely discussing their views that President Obama was the worst president in U.S. history; they were especially critical of his policies toward immigrants. The irony was that Obama's most vociferous critic had a distinct foreign accent. She seemed to favor immigration for herself but not for "them." Then literally a few days later, a colleague in the economics department was so irate at a conservative talk show host that he threatened violence if they should meet. It sometimes appears that political debate is deteriorating in America to the point that reasonable people only tolerate the opinions of those with whom they agree—and talk show hosts often are the worst examples of intolerance.

Many pundits claim that political tolerance is decreasing and America is becoming a more divided nation. There are vague images of a more tranquil America of the past. But let's do a reality check. Turn the clock back sixty years from the 2014 General Social Survey to consider the levels of political tolerance in America in 1954. This is an auspicious year to select because it was marked by Sen. Joseph McCarthy's notorious Army–McCarthy hearings. Following the lead of the earlier House Un-American Activities Committee, McCarthy brought a series of military, political, and social figures before his Senate subcommittee investigating Communist Party influence in America.[1] Intertwined with the Red Scare was the Lavender Scare, as Congress targeted homosexuals as potential security risks.[2] By the end of 1954, approximately 2,200 individuals had been removed from the federal workforce as security risks because of their political views or sexuality. The Senate eventually censured McCarthy for his outrageous behavior, but only after he threatened and intimidated a long series of witnesses, compiled millions of words of testimony, and broadcasted the hearings on live television. McCarthy was not an isolated case. In mid-1954, the Supreme Court upheld the constitutionality of the Internal Security Act, thus making membership in the Communist Party sufficient grounds for the deportation of aliens. Nineteen states had legislation banning communists from public service or politics.[3] Thousands had been removed or encouraged to leave positions in state and local governments, and loyalty oaths were prerequisites for employment in many workplaces.[4] Earlier in that year the U.S. Information Agency, which ran America House libraries around the world, banned Henry David Thoreau's *Walden* because of its socialist orientation. In 1954 a system of "voluntary" censorship existed in the movie industry, and a growing number of screenwriters were being added to the blacklist because of their supposed communist ties.[5] To link religion to patriotism, President Dwight D. Eisenhower signed legislation to add "under God" to the Pledge of Allegiance. The Supreme Court handed down the landmark *Brown v. Board of Education* ruling on racial desegregation of schools in 1954, but this was only necessary because seventeen states mandated segregated education. Anti-Semitism remained common in America, and nearly all of the Ivy League universities discriminated against Jewish students, minorities, and women in their admissions.[6] I could continue—1954 was a very busy year for intolerance.

Moreover, the first surveys of Americans' political tolerance were conducted in 1954, and they painted a clear image of public prejudice. James Gibson noted that nearly 5,000 people were surveyed in Stouffer's seminal study of tolerance, and barely 100 were willing to give communists the right to free speech, assembly, or employment as a school teacher.[7] Socialists and atheists fared only slightly better. Racial prejudice was still widespread—and one can easily imagine what the average American would say about gay rights in 1954. Despite the rhetoric of American politics and the promises of the Constitution and Bill of Rights, America in the 1950s was not a society of broad political and social tolerance.

The extent of political tolerance is vitally important to the functioning of democracy. The Bill of Rights begins by enumerating the freedom of religion, speech, press, assembly, and petitioning the government to underscore the importance of these rights. A study of tolerance in the mid-1970s began by noting that "The founding fathers of this country prescribed tolerance in the marketplace of freely flowing ideas as the key to the democratic process and the necessary condition for orderly change and innovation in a democratic society."[8] A more recent book states that "support for the freedom of expression of unpopular views represents an understanding of the meaning of an open and democratic polity. To a substantial extent, tolerance is the cornerstone of a democratically enlightened citizenry."[9]

Thus, political tolerance is a key feature in judging the vitality of American democracy. And in contrast to the alarmist claims of some pundits, opinion surveys over the past half century generally describe spreading tolerance among the public.[10] Furthermore, the processes of social modernization described in Chapter 1—such as rising educational levels, generational change, and the empowerment of minorities—is often linked to the growth of political tolerance. Therefore, this chapter examines how changes in citizenship norms may have contributed to increasing political tolerance among Americans.

Let's begin by reviewing the prior public opinion research on political tolerance in America and the changes in political tolerance over time. Then we'll examine the relationship between citizenship norms and political tolerance.

HOW TO MEASURE POLITICAL TOLERANCE

Analyses of political tolerance have a long—and controversial—history in public opinion research. The first study by Samuel Stouffer examined tolerance for socialists, atheists, and communists by asking people's willingness to allow each group to give a public speech in the community, to teach in a college, to have books on their views included in the public library, and other activities.[11] Stouffer concluded that tolerance of these specific groups was limited, despite widespread public support for abstract democratic principles of free speech and minority rights. Stouffer's research occurred in a context where the increasing tensions of the Cold War overlapped with a society that had not accepted principles such as racial and gender equality. However, Stouffer believed that tolerance would gradually increase among Americans because of rising education levels and generational change.

Further research in the 1970s and early 1980s seemingly justified Stouffer's optimistic projection of tolerance trends. Replicating Stouffer's core measures of tolerance for atheists, communists, and socialists, James Davis found that tolerant responses had increased significantly by 1972.[12] Similar patterns occurred for tolerance of other nonconformist activities, such as protesting the Vietnam War, showing pornographic movies, or teaching sex education in the schools. The study concluded that "this is a critical shift [in American public opinion] since the existence of a tolerant majority greatly enhances the prospect that expansion of support for civil liberties will be accelerated."[13]

Other researchers soon challenged the evidence of increasing tolerance on methodological grounds.[14] They argued that Americans had not become more tolerant; rather, the perceived threat attached to the anti-system groups of the 1950s—communists, socialists, and atheists—had waned by the 1970s, and so people expressed more tolerance of these less-threatening groups. The researchers argued for a "content-controlled" method of measuring tolerance: One should first identify the specific groups a person dislikes and then measure tolerance for these groups. Consequently, when surveys asked about the contentious groups in the 1970s—such as antiwar protesters—this yielded a less positive view of political tolerance. In addition, the Stouffer items were criticized for only focusing on extreme leftist groups, so that a person's ideological position could bias the results.

The debate over the measurement of political tolerance has continued to the present. One step forward was the expansion of the tolerance battery to include extreme groups on both the left and right, which lessens the ideological bias of a tolerance scale. However, research also found that tolerance is generalized and is normally applied to extremist groups on both the left and right,[15] which undermines the argument of

the content-controlled approach. Other studies showed that the correlates of tolerance were quite similar for both the balanced Stouffer
items and the content-controlled measures, again suggesting that both
methods tapped a common reality.[16]

Tracking levels of tolerance over time is admittedly difficult, because
the groups that test the tolerance of a nation will change. For instance,
until September 11, 2001, few survey researchers in the United States
thought that Muslim fundamentalists were a major test of political tolerance.[17] And questions about tolerance of communists now seem quaint
antiques as the memory of the Soviet Union fades into history. By including a mix of groups and using alternative methodologies, however, I
believe we can monitor the broad contours of political tolerance in
America—and see how these feelings are linked to norms of citizenship.

THE UNCONVENTIONAL EVIDENCE: RISING POLITICAL TOLERANCE

As just noted, measuring tolerance is not a simple task. Since 1976 the
General Social Survey has asked questions to measure tolerance toward five
social groups: communists, atheists (antireligion), homosexuals, militarists,
and racists. The GSS methodology tries to avoid the content of tolerance
problem by including groups on the left and right. In retrospect, this is
difficult to do over a long time because the political context changes so
much over three decades. When the battery began in 1976, one could not
foresee the collapse of communism in 1989–1991. The political efforts of
the gay/lesbian movement have also changed the public impressions of
this group over time. The survey series spans the period from the end
of American involvement in Vietnam to the conflicts in Afghanistan and
Iraq and the continuing war on terrorism at home and abroad. These varied
experiences might affect attitudes toward militarism. We thus might expect
that Americans have a highly variable image of different potential extremist
groups over time, so that tolerance waxes and wanes.

For each group, the GSS asked if members of the group:

- Should be allowed to speak in the respondent's community
- Should be allowed to teach in a college or university
- Should be allowed to have their books in a local library

Table 5.1 displays the percentage giving tolerant responses on each of the three activities for each of the five groups. Five time points show the general patterns: 1976, which begins the survey series; 1988, before the tumultuous political upheavals in Eastern Europe of 1989–1991; 1994, early in the Clinton administration; 2004, in the midst of the Bush administration; and 2014, the most recent survey.

Americans' tolerance toward all five groups has gradually broadened over the past several decades. Averaging together the three activities, tolerance of leftist groups has steadily increased: communists (+20 percent), atheists (+22 percent), and homosexuals (+28). Similarly, there is increased

TABLE 5.1	Tolerant Responses for Five Target Groups

▶ *Americans have become more tolerant toward all five groups over the past four decades.*

Target Group	Action	1976	1988	1994	2004	2014	Change
Communist	Allow to speak	53	62	68	70	70	+17
	Allow to teach	40	50	57	66	66	+26
	Allow book in library	55	61	68	71	73	+18
Atheist	Allow to speak	62	71	73	77	79	+17
	Allow to teach	39	47	54	66	67	+28
	Allow book in library	58	65	71	73	78	+20
Homosexual	Allow to speak	62	73	81	84	89	+27
	Allow to teach	52	60	72	80	89	+37
	Allow book in library	56	63	70	74	81	+20
Militarist	Allow to speak	53	58	64	67	71	+18
	Allow to teach	35	39	47	54	60	+25
	Allow book in library	55	59	65	69	71	+16
Racist	Allow to speak	60	63	62	62	61	+1
	Allow to teach	41	43	44	47	48	+7
	Allow book in library	60	64	68	66	64	+4
Average		**52**	**59**	**64**	**68**	**71**	

Source: 1976, 1988, 1994, 2004, and 2014 General Social Surveys.

Note: Table entries are the percent giving a tolerant response on each question.

tolerance of militarists (+20 percent) and racists (+4 percent). Allowing a representative of these groups to teach at a university was originally the least tolerated activity for each group, but tolerance for this increases the most over time—and all three activities show increases.

Most striking is the consistent shift toward tolerance across groups. We might assume that the demise of communism altered images of communists, for example, but much of the change occurred by 1988, before the Berlin Wall collapsed. The increased tolerance of communists since 1988 seems like a continuance of the earlier trend. We might expect that the U.S. involvement in Iraq and Afghanistan might have shifted opinions toward militarists in the past decade, but the most recent surveys seem a continuation of a general trend. These trends could also reflect different patterns within subgroups of the population: liberals becoming more tolerant of liberal groups and conservatives growing more tolerant of conservative groups—with both remaining intolerant of their opposites. This is not the case, however—the trends in tolerance are broadly comparable for self-identified liberals, centrists, and conservatives.[18] Indeed, this evidence speaks to a slow, broad increase in political tolerance over this thirty-eight-year span.

The shift in tolerance is even more apparent in Figure 5.1. This figure charts the average number of tolerant responses by year, with a maximum of fifteen different items asked in each year (three activities for five groups). Again, the steady increase in tolerance over time is striking; it is a relatively continuous trend rather than abrupt shifts in reaction to political events or changes in political context. In the mid-1970s, the average American gave less than eight tolerant responses out of fifteen. The high point in tolerance is 2014 with 10.5 tolerant responses, which is up slightly since the 2004 survey. These tolerance trends would be even more dramatic if we could extend these series back to the 1960s or 1950s.

Other research describes the growth of political tolerance in other areas. There is growing racial tolerance and support for gender equality over time.[19] Robert Putnam tracked increasing support for racial integration, civil liberties, and gender equality among the American public. He concluded that "behind each of these statistical trends stands a category of Americans increasingly liberated from stigma and oppression."[20]

FIGURE 5.1 Rising Political Tolerance

▶ *Americans' tolerance of the activities of challenging political groups has increased over time.*

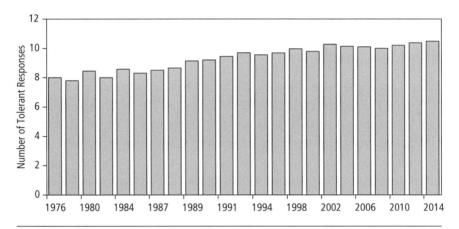

Source: 1976–2014 General Social Surveys.

Note: The figure presents the average number of tolerant responses across the fifteen items in Table 5.1.

On most dimensions, Americans are more tolerant today than at mid-twentieth century.

Certainly intolerant aspects of the American political culture still exist, so we should be cautious about an overly optimistic reading of these trends. There are still too many examples of intolerance toward others because of their political beliefs, religion, or lifestyle choices. Some people are still unwilling to grant the rights assured by the Constitution to those with whom they disagree. Racial, ethnic, religious, and political divisions remain part of the American experience. New tensions, such as those with some Muslim fundamentalists in America and Europe, test the boundaries of tolerance.[21] In addition, expressions of tolerance are distinct from actual behavior. News reports often share examples of people doing unreasonable things to their fellow citizens—and too many people watch this happen and remain silent.

Still, while the media and the political pundits would have us think that the situation is getting worse, the evidence from public opinion surveys argues just the opposite. People were once openly hostile to those they disagreed with, ready to withhold freedom of speech, freedom to publish, or the ability to teach. Today, such expressions of intolerance are much less common. Americans have moved closer to the Jeffersonian ideal that the democratic response to extreme political beliefs is to engage in discussion and debate.

WHO IS TOLERANT AND WHO IS NOT

Researchers generally agree on the main factors related to feelings of tolerance; they disagree on the interpretation of these influences. Education is strongly and consistently related to tolerance for extremist groups at either end of the political spectrum. Some scholars argue that education increases cognitive sophistication, and this stimulates tolerance.[22] Others maintain that education leads to critical and moral reasoning and thus support for tolerance.[23] This educational effect is likely reinforced by the apparently increasing attention to tolerance and diversity in the educational system. Consequently, the absolute increases in educational levels over the past several decades should have systematically increased tolerance levels.

Alternatively, educational differences in tolerance may represent the social stratification of Americans. Upper-status individuals have more social resources and privileges, which may make them less sensitive to extremist threats or diminish their concern about alternative groups. Thus, education might identify this social ranking rather than having independent effects. Such a stratifying effect would diminish the impact of rising educational levels on tolerance because the top strata would simply be identified by a higher education level (the bachelor's degree of the 1960s is equivalent to the master's degree of today). Stratification by education can be a constant effect over time, just measured by different cutting points (the same with income). I evaluate this idea in the following analyses.

Another standard predictor of tolerance is age or, more precisely, generation. Typically, younger generations are more tolerant than older generations.[24] Generation is a surrogate for the different socialization experiences of individuals. While there is much that is positive about American society in the 1950s, the period was not noted for its tolerant political environment. It is still shocking to remember that older Americans raised before the mid-1960s grew up in a nation that tolerated and institutionalized racism and consciously restricted the role of women. McCarthyism was an extreme example of political intolerance under the guise of national security, but anticommunism was official doctrine.

In contrast, the efforts of the civil rights movement and women's movement transformed public opinion in these two instances, and they exemplified a general process of increasing political tolerance and greater consciousness of basic human rights.[25] Successive generations have been raised in environments that were progressively more tolerant in both their social norms and legal protections. Presumably, different socialization experiences left their imprint on the values of each generation.

However, some analysts question the existence of a generational trend in tolerance. Robert Putnam, for instance, argued that Generation Xers were no more tolerant than the early Boomers, and he felt the cohort born around 1940 to 1945 (pre–Baby Boom) represented the high point of tolerance.[26] In addition, some generational differences may result from rising educational levels rather than generational experiences per se. For Putnam, the biggest generational gains in tolerance were already behind us, and the erosion of social capital held negative implications for political tolerance. (It should be noted, however, that we now have more than a decade of additional survey data, and the tolerance trend continues.)

Thus, growing tolerance may partially depend on a process of generational change and the public's increasing educational levels. To illustrate the effects of generation, Figure 5.2 tracks the generational scores on the overall tolerance index in both 2004 and 2014. One can see a clear pattern of lower tolerance among the older generations. The prewar generation in 2004 gave only 7.6 tolerant responses compared to 10.0 among Millennials in 2014. Moreover, the other generations change very slightly between 2004 and 2014, implying that tolerance levels within generations are relatively stable.

If we were to plot the relationship between education and tolerance it would closely resemble the generational figure. Those with less than a high school degree gave tolerant responses to slight more than 7 of the 15 items in the GSS. Those with a graduate degree expressed tolerance

| FIGURE 5.2 | Tolerance by Generations |

▶ *Overall political tolerance is higher among younger generations and is markedly lower among the prewar generation.*

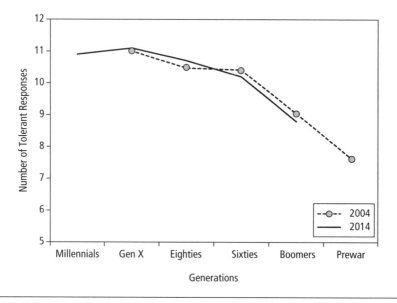

Source: 2004 and 2014 General Social Surveys.

Note: Figure entries are the number of tolerant responses by each generation to the five groups in Table 5.1.

on more than 12 items. These patterns are virtually identical in 2004 and 2014, and this applies to both liberal and conservative groups. Consequently, demographic change is a major contributor to growing tolerance levels in America. As older and less-educated generations leave the electorate, to be replaced by younger and better-educated citizens, then overall political tolerance will generally increase.

CITIZENSHIP AND TOLERANCE

Education and generation help to map the social distribution of tolerance, but political tolerance should also be embedded in definitions of citizenship. Democratic citizens should be socialized into tolerant beliefs, but this may vary across different beliefs about what good citizenship means.

On the one hand, respect for the majority, social order, and the rule of law are essential elements of the democratic contract. But too strong an emphasis on these values may discourage dissent and promote intolerance of unconventional political and social views. For those who value duty and social order, tolerance of political dissidents may sometimes be seen as threatening this order and consequently undesirable. Thus, although Tocqueville admired Americans' emphasis on participation and equality, he also believed that the majoritarian elements of the American political culture created pressures for conformity and limited tolerance of minority beliefs.[27] Empirical research similarly shows that the values underlying social order orientations are negatively related to tolerance attitudes.[28] Thus, those who follow a duty-based definition of citizenship may be less tolerant of unconventional or antisystem political groups.

Meanwhile, norms of engaged citizenship may encourage political tolerance. A concern for social rights and the protection of the disadvantaged is embedded in this conception of citizenship, and these orientations should promote tolerance. The ability to sympathize with others and the acceptance of unconventionality in interpersonal relations is linked to political tolerance.[29] Libertarian/postmaterial values are similarly linked to engaged citizenship as well as political tolerance.[30] Tolerance thus requires a more expansive definition of citizenship, and so engaged citizenship may contribute to the spread of tolerance.

Figure 5.3 shows the relationship between citizenship norms and tolerance in the 2014 GSS citizenship module.[31] Attachment to engaged citizenship slightly increases political tolerance; there is roughly a half-point difference in tolerance as a function of these norms ($r = .03$). However, high levels of citizen duty have a much stronger effect on decreasing political tolerance by two whole scale points ($r = -.18$). Combining these two effects, the shift in citizenship norms between duty-based and engaged citizenship provides a strong stimulant for increasing political tolerance in America over the past several decades.

Age, education, and citizenship are all interrelated, and thus it is difficult to know if the influence of citizenship is separate from the effects of education, generation, or other factors. We can address this point by statistically estimating the independent effects of citizenship norms, age, education, and other potential factors. For instance, a measure of cognitive

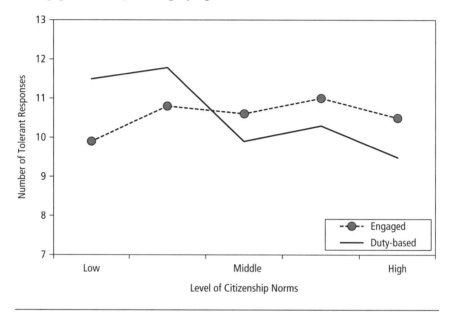

FIGURE 5.3   **Citizenship Norms and Tolerance**

▶ *Those high in citizen duty have lower overall political tolerance, while those high in engaged citizenship have slightly higher tolerance levels.*

Source: 2014 General Social Survey.

Note: The figure plots the number of tolerant responses on the five groups in Table 5.1 by both measures of citizenship norms.

skills (based on a vocabulary test) can separate cognitive skills from formal education—and both can be isolated from generational patterns. Including party identification provides a way to see if political identities are linked to tolerance levels overall (although it is inevitably linked to which groups are tolerated and not).

Table 5.2 presents these statistical analyses predicting a summary index of overall tolerance, plus each of the specific groups included in the 2014 GSS. The coefficients in the table indicate the relative importance of each predictor, while statistically controlling for the effects of the other predictors (also see the statistical primer in the appendix). Education and cognitive abilities are strongly related to tolerance in each of the models, which reaffirms the importance of both social learning and cognition in promoting

TABLE 5.2	Predicting Tolerance

▶ *Citizen duty and age generally lower tolerance levels even when we control for other factors; education and cognitive ability systematically increase tolerance for all groups.*

Predictor	Tolerance Index	Communist	Atheist	Homosexual	Militarist	Racist	Anti-US Muslim
Citizen duty	−.11*	−.07*	−.10*	.00	−.12*	−.07	−.17*
Engaged citizenship	−.02	.01	.04	.01	−.04	−.04	.07*
Age	−.15*	−.13*	−.15*	−.16*	−.17*	.00	−.03
Education	.23*	.23*	.17*	.16*	.17*	.14*	.19*
Cognitive ability	.27*	.21*	.27*	.23*	.20*	.14*	.25
Party identification (R)	.03	.01	.02	−.03	.03	.07	.03
Multiple *R*	.46	.40	.42	.36	.38	.26	.44

Source: 2014 General Social Survey.

Note: Table entries are standardized regression coefficients with pairwise deletion of missing data. Coefficients significant at $p < .05$ are denoted by an asterisk.

political tolerance. This implies that rising education levels have contributed to increases in tolerance, even beyond the public's cognitive skills. Older Americans generally express less tolerance. These patterns persist even when we control for education, cognitive skills, and partisanship. Somewhat surprisingly, a person's party identification is not significantly linked to their tolerance level once we control for these other factors.

Citizenship norms shape feelings of political tolerance even when other factors are controlled. Those who emphasize a duty-based image of citizenship are less tolerant toward nearly all of these groups regardless of the political issue. In our previous analysis of the 2004 GSS, engaged citizens were substantially more tolerant of challenging groups.[32] Now, engaged citizenship displays insignificant relationships, except for tolerance of Muslim clerics who hold anti-U.S. positions. The sum of these findings suggest that social modernization should continue to increase tolerance (all else being equal) as education levels and cognitive skills increase and as the citizenship norms of the public shift from duty-based to engaged citizenship.

The norms of citizenship also shape other aspects of tolerance and inclusion in America. For instance, the 2004 General Social Survey included a short battery on attitudes toward immigrants. Engaged citizens are more favorable toward immigrants, with relationships even stronger than for the Stouffer tolerance questions.[33] Engaged citizens are more likely to feel that immigration improves American society, that the government does not spend too much on immigrants, and that citizenship should be extended to immigrants. The effect of citizenship norms is often substantial; for instance, among those lowest in engaged citizenship, 79 percent said the government spent too much on immigrants versus only 32 percent among those highest in engaged citizenship. Conversely, duty-based norms of citizenship encourage the opposite policy positions. Thus, how one defines what it means to be a citizen shapes how he or she applies the rights of citizenship to others.

Citizenship and Tolerance: A Second Look

The sources of political division today look far different from those that preoccupied Stouffer and researchers in the 1950s and even different from a generation ago. The collapse of the Soviet empire and the end of the Cold War made communism an example of another era. Problems such as racial intolerance and gender discrimination remain, although in dramatically different forms than a half-century ago. Homosexuals have moved from the dark shadows of society toward broader social acceptance. And in a post–September 11 world, the threats of religious fundamentalism and international terrorism loom large.

Tolerance measures should reflect these changing realities. To explore these points we turn to an earlier survey (the 2005 CDACS survey) that used a content-controlled measure of political tolerance.[34] The survey first asked people to identify their least-liked group from a list provided by the interviewer. The choice of the least-liked groups differed across the two indices of citizenship. Those high in citizen duty mentioned groups that span the political spectrum: the Ku Klux Klan (34 percent), radical Muslims (19 percent), people who are against churches and religions (12 percent), and American Nazis (9 percent). Those high in engaged citizenship listed their least-liked groups as the Ku Klux Klan (52 percent), American Nazis (11 percent), radical Muslims

(8 percent), and those against churches and religions (7 percent). Several of the groups in the Stouffer battery no longer seem to concern many Americans: 6 percent mentioned militarists, 4 percent said communists, and only 3 percent listed gay rights activists.

After identifying the least-liked group, the CDACS survey asked whether this group should be allowed to make a speech in the community, be banned from running for public office, or be allowed to hold rallies in the community. This content-controlled measure should be a more rigorous test of political tolerance because individuals are first asked which group they dislike the most—and then tolerance is judged for this group. It is easy to imagine being tolerant of groups that one is ambivalent toward; the real test of tolerance comes when one's values conflict with an opponent.

Figure 5.4 presents the relationship between citizenship norms and this content-controlled measure of tolerance. Those high in engaged citizenship express higher levels of tolerance. Conversely, as commitment to citizen duty increases, political tolerance decreases. These two comparisons are in reference to different groups, but they are the groups that are most disliked by each person. Thus, this analysis yields similar conclusions: The norms of citizenship shape how we apply the rights of citizenship to others, even those we dislike the most.

Citizenship and Tolerance: A Third Look

In the post–September 11 world there is a lively and important debate on how America can balance its commitment to freedom and civil liberties while protecting its citizens. The continuing public deliberations on the terms of the Patriot Act and its renewal illustrate these issues. The treatment of prisoners at Guantánamo Bay, the CIA secret prisons, and debates over government surveillance programs raise the specter of the United States ignoring its democratic legal commitments to gain vital national security information. Similarly, some of the legislators involved in the drafting of the Patriot Act and related government policies argued that we are living in a new age where past rules of privacy and civil rights no longer fit reality. These debates intensified in 2013 when Edward Snowden released information on the National Security Agency's data collection efforts in the United States and abroad and the potential

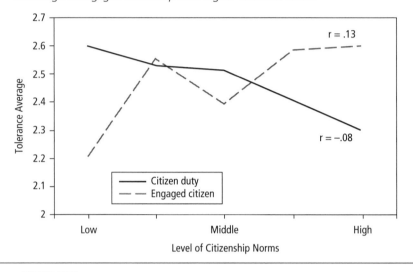

FIGURE 5.4   **Citizenship and Tolerance of Least-Liked Group**

▶ *Those high in citizen duty have lower tolerance toward the least-liked group, but those high in engaged citizenship have higher tolerance levels.*

Source: 2005 CDACS Survey.

Note: The figure plots the average score toward the least-liked political group by both citizenship dimensions; 1 = *low tolerance* and 5 = *high tolerance.*

violation of individuals' privacy rights. These are the new examples of tolerance and civil liberties in contemporary America.

To tap these concerns, the 2005 CDACS survey asked Americans about their support for civil liberties when the political system was challenged. One set of questions focused on domestic dissent, such as the government investigating protestors, requiring that high school teachers support government policies, and expanding the government's investigative powers.[35] Other items focused explicitly on terrorist threats: making it illegal to belong to a group that supports terrorism and making it legal for the government to detain noncitizens indefinitely if they are suspected of belonging to a terrorist organization.

Loyal and patriotic Americans can honestly debate these issues and disagree on the answers, but it is clear that citizenship norms at least partially shape how people feel toward these issues. The first set of items in Figure 5.5 deal with civil liberty issues generally involving dissent (or at least separate from a terrorist connection). The strength of the correlation is represented by the length of the bars in the figure and the direction

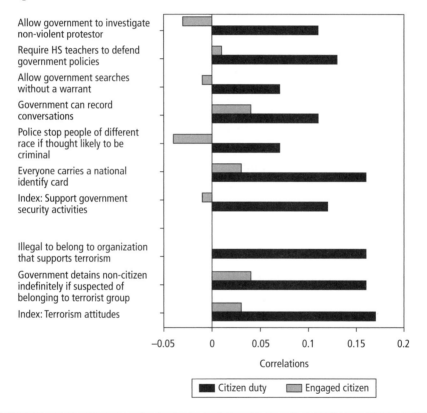

FIGURE 5.5   Citizenship and Civil Liberties

▶ *Those high in citizen duty show more support for strong government action to promote security, while those high in engaged citizenship are less supportive of government action and more concerned with civil liberties.*

Source: 2005 CDACS Survey.

Note: Figure entries are correlation coefficients (Pearson's *r*) that measure whether citizenship norms have a positive or negative effect on these civil liberties questions.

of the relationship. For each of these items, feelings of citizen duty encourage people to support a policy restricting civil liberties. In contrast, engaged citizenship has essentially no relationship or even a negative relationship with these same policy choices. The lower part of the table presents two items that explicitly involve a potential terrorist threat. Citizen duty has an even stronger effect, prompting people to support policies that would restrict potential terrorists, even if these policies raise basic civil liberty questions. Again, engaged citizenship is essentially unrelated to these policy choices.

For instance, only 28 percent of those low in citizen duty strongly approve of a law that would make it illegal to belong to or contribute money to a group that supports international terrorism, but this percentage rises to more than 50 percent among those high in citizen duty. On first blush, we might say that such a law is needed in today's uncertain and insecure world. But life is more complex, and in reality one might belong to a group without knowing about all of its activities. Americans also disagree on what is a terrorist act and what is a defensible use of violence. This is not to argue that people should be free to support terrorism, only that this is a complex issue, subject to different interpretations, and so caution is warranted before accepting a blanket statement.

One can legitimately debate each of these policy options. It is easy to understand that in the present world many Americans feel that stronger actions must be taken to limit crime and the terrorist threat. At the same time, some people are sensitive to the potential loss of civil liberties engendered by these actions. Certain analysts might decry the limited support for strict measures to ensure public order among those low in citizen duty; but others might insist that duty-based citizenship too easily sacrifices liberty for security. The point is that citizenship norms shape these political positions and thus partially define the two sides of this debate.

IMPLICATIONS OF CITIZENSHIP AND TOLERANCE

I encourage you to watch the movie *Pleasantville* as you are reading this book. *Pleasantville* stars Tobey McGuire and Reese Witherspoon as teenagers in the 1990s. Through movie magic, they are transported back to Pleasantville in the 1950s. The town is familiar to anyone who has watched *Leave It to Beaver, The Andy Griffith Show,* or any of those idealistic portrayals of American life back in the day. The two teenagers soon realize that all is not as pleasant as portrayed on television (and in some academic writing). Life appears perfect, but there is little diversity in the town, women lack rights, nothing is challenged, and life is defined by narrow boundaries—and everyone is a shade of gray. When the two teenagers encourage someone to explore a new idea or experience, the Pleasantville resident shifts from grey to full living color. These color shifts generate opposition from the townsfolk including new restrictive laws, book burnings, and a crowd stoning a café that hosts those who have developed color. Gray residents even post signs that say "NO COLOREDS" (ironically, no African Americans live in Pleasantville). Eventually, the town broadens its horizons and the gray residents appear in color, and the teenagers return home to the 1990s.

The point was that the idealistic images of the past often overlook the narrow social and political norms of the era. Intolerance was largely unchallenged in mid-century America. After their visit to Pleasantville, the teenagers returned to the 1990s with a new appreciation. Intolerant acts still happen in America, but less often than in previous decades. Yet this evidence of increasing political tolerance runs counter to much of the contemporary punditry about the current political culture. While politicians and public figures decry the intolerance and polarization of Americans, the evidence from public opinion surveys describes a slow, steady increase in tolerance toward a range of contentious groups over the past several decades.

Given the recent history of American politics, it would be surprising if feelings of tolerance had not changed.[36] The civil rights movement dramatically altered the landscape of American politics, and a wealth of survey data document the fundamental transformation of public opinion on racial discrimination. The women's movement similarly transformed attitudes toward gender equality, and it helped to reinforce the rights revolution in America. Some may look back to the 1950s as a golden age of American politics, but this was not so for persons of color, women, other minorities, and those concerned about social equality.

Furthermore, these political changes are linked to shifting norms of citizenship, from duty-based norms that are less accepting of difference to norms of engaged citizenship that encourage tolerance. This places the core support for political tolerance among young, better-educated Americans—with the least support among older and less-educated citizens. Thus, the expansion of citizen rights and tolerance for others during the second half of the twentieth century is one of the major historic achievements of American democracy—and changing citizenship norms contributed to these processes.

Why, then, have these trends been missed by politicians and pundits who insist that Americans are becoming less tolerant of others? In part, the explanation may simply be that as a nation becomes more tolerant, it is less accepting of remaining intolerance. The "political correctness" emphasis that is so common on university campuses and liberal parts of society arises because, although most Americans believe we should be tolerant of others, some take this goal to an unreasonable degree. However, the political correctness in the 1950s would have worked in the opposite direction, to discourage differences. In much the same way, the rights revolution creates a new set of forces that heighten claims that one's rights have been violated—sentiments that people would not have expressed several decades ago. In short, as tolerance becomes more common, this increases pressure on remaining examples of intolerance.

This positive image of the political culture conflicts with a mindset that social analysts should be critics. Treatises on the crisis of American democracy or the imminent collapse of American society draw more attention than a book announcing that *the sky is not falling*. That is why few of the recent books on the crisis of the American spirit note the spread of political tolerance. Even Putnam, when summarizing the evidence of increasing political tolerance, discounts the significance of these trends, and the positive evidence is even presented in a chapter titled "The Dark Side of Social Capital."[37] Any description of the "Greatest Generation" as politically intolerant does not fit the image of this cohort as the font of social capital.

At the same time, some critical reflection is warranted if it builds on the facts. Although expressions of tolerance have grown over the past several decades, we know that there is a gap between statements and behavior. The change in public sentiments has not been fully matched by the reality of public actions or public policy. The reality of life is improving, but it is lagging behind the even larger shift in public opinion. In short, more must yet be done to make America a tolerant society.

In addition, although we might embrace tolerance as an ideal, we should recognize the need to balance social needs and individual freedom. America and other Western democracies are now struggling to balance tolerance of diversity and multiculturalism with real worries about tolerance of political and religious extremists who themselves do not tolerate others. Some challenges to the status quo are presenting ideas we might dislike, yet which should be tolerated. Other contemporary challenges present real threats that test democracy's ability to balance social needs against individual rights. The difficulty is to identify the nature of the challenge and the appropriate response. The evidence of the rising political tolerance and broadening views of citizenship by Americans suggests, to me, that the nation is now better suited to address these questions than in earlier periods of American history, when intolerance was openly tolerated.

6

IS GOVERNMENT THE
PROBLEM OR THE SOLUTION?

S everal years ago, I gave a talk about public opinion at the Leisure
World retirement community (now Laguna Woods) that is a few
miles away from my university. The audience was attentive and informed;
they asked lively questions and challenged my ideas—perhaps even more
than in a typical university class. In informal discussions after the talk, I
met residents who had fought in World War II, and some had worked on
postwar reconstruction in Japan or Germany. They followed politics and
voted. The turnout of registered voters in the community was 78.5 percent
in 2012 (the national turnout for eighteen- to twenty-four-year-olds was
under 60 percent of registered voters). As I left the community center, I
noticed the range of other lectures, social groups, and other activities
scheduled during this week. More than 200 informal groups are listed on
the community's homepage with a range of social, cultural, and political
themes. This, clearly, was a sample of the generation that Brokaw and
Putnam admired, and these seniors displayed many of the positive political
traits identified with this generation.

Much of the current discussion about citizenship focuses on such
examples of political engagement and the individual's expected role
within the political system, as discussed in the previous chapters. In addition, however, citizenship norms shape images of the role of government
and its public policies. For example, the residents of Leisure World hold
fairly conservative political views, as might be expected of a community

where the average age is seventy-eight years. Nearly three-quarters supported Mitt Romney in the 2012 election, while their grandchildren likely leaned toward Obama. In discussing politics after the lecture, these seniors favored lower taxes, and they remembered and preferred an earlier era when government was less active—of course, they made exceptions for Social Security, Medicare, and other programs benefitting seniors. Some people were interested in new issues such as environmental protection, but these were not priorities. The typical senior felt that the government was doing too much or doing it wrong.

When a politician calls for a return to traditional images of citizenship, this implicitly includes expectations about the appropriate role of government and even specific government policies. For instance, when George Bush called for a renewal of citizenship in his 2001 Inaugural Address, he presumably expected that this would include a more limited role of government. And when Barack Obama talks about the need for greater civic engagement, it is connected to a specific, but very different, policy agenda.

This chapter examines the potential impact of citizenship norms at three levels. First, how do citizenship norms shape an individual's view of the overall scope of government activity? Although the overall size of government grew during the past five decades, debate over its appropriate size continues. Second, what specific policy areas should receive more or less government spending? For instance, should government spend more on social programs, or focus its priorities on providing security and basic public services? Embedded in the two models of citizenship are different expectations about what policies should be the priority of government and which policies should receive less attention. Third, what is the relationship between citizenship norms and a range of domestic and foreign policy issues? All this evidence provides a better understanding of the range of political values linked to contemporary norms of citizenship.

WHAT SHOULD GOVERNMENT DO?

Because theories of citizenship typically focus on the individual's role in the political process, the implications of citizenship norms regarding the role of government are not always clear. However, we can extract some ideas from previous writings. For instance, several theoretical models of citizenship (for example, neoliberalism) imply that these norms should favor limited government. Neoliberalism holds that an expanding role of government means that "individualism is sacrificed to equality; privacy, to bureaucracy; and furthermore, security is bought at the price of stigma and the loss of that very dignity of citizenship it was designed to enhance."[1] Many neoliberals see more personal freedom emanating from a smaller government that requires less of its citizens (and provides less in return). Even when social rights are recognized, this perspective would limit the government's responsibilities by stressing the individual obligations of citizens.[2] To an extent, theory expects that these orientations are linked to duty-based citizenship, similar to those articulated by many Leisure World residents. In short, duty-based citizenship might prompt individuals to favor a smaller role for government.

This image of limited government is ingrained in an American political culture that emphasizes individual freedom and skepticism of a powerful government. The Republican Party has actively advocated these goals. In his first inaugural address in 1981, President Ronald Reagan stated:

> Our government has no power except that granted it by the people. It is time to check and reverse the growth of government which shows signs of having grown beyond the consent of the governed.
>
> It is my intention to curb the size and influence of the Federal establishment and to demand recognition of the distinction between the powers granted to the Federal Government and those reserved to the states or the people.[3]

This mantra guided Reagan's presidency as well as the succeeding Republican administrations of George H. W. Bush and George W. Bush. The Tea Party movement absorbed Reagan's imagery, even if they have moved beyond what Reagan actually advocated.

In contrast, the idea of social citizenship implies a more expansive view of the role of government. A top priority of engaged citizenship is social rights, and it primarily falls upon the government to secure these rights.[4] In much the same way, the traditional social-democratic perspective of citizenship stresses the potential economic and social hardships that face the disadvantaged and thus the need for government to redress these conditions. Engaged citizenship presumably represents a more proactive view of government as a means to address social needs. Part of this no doubt stems from the concern for others that prevails among engaged citizens (see Chapter 2). Many of the policies of the Obama administration—such as the expansion of health care, the emphasis on minority rights, and efforts to aid immigrant communities—might be interpreted within a framework of engaged citizenship.

Thus, duty-based citizenship and engaged citizenship may affect specific policy preferences. An emphasis on duty and individual responsibility could restrict support for social programs, redistributive policies, and the "big government" initiatives normally identified with the Democratic Party. In contrast, engaged citizenship could lead to almost diametrically opposed policy priorities: support for an activist government that provides for the needy, develops social service programs, and is a guarantor of basic civil rights.

The clearest contrast in the policy implications of citizenship norms may come in the foreign policy domain. Citizen duty should encourage support for defense spending and a commitment to national security. In contrast, engaged citizenship should encourage support for foreign aid and a more cooperative foreign policy style. Expressed in the vernacular of Washington, norms of citizen duty are most apparent in support for the Department of Defense, while norms of engaged citizenship may lean toward support for the Department of State. Or more colloquially, duty-based citizens are from Mars, and engaged citizens are from Venus.[5]

Admittedly, the theoretical literature on citizenship includes contradictions to the positions just described, with various political philosophers providing contrasting statements on the appropriate scope of government. Our questions on citizenship norms focus on the role of individuals and their responsibilities as a citizens, and the questions do not explicitly ask about specific public policies or the overall scope of government. However, by examining the relationship between citizenship norms and policy attitudes, we can illustrate how these norms are affecting the agenda for government action.

WE WANT GOVERNMENT TO BE A BIG SPENDER

One of the broadest policy attitudes involves support for the overall role of government—whether government should be large and active or small and limited in its goals. Public opinion surveys use various ways to measure opinions on the role of government. We consider whether Americans believe their government should increase or decrease public spending.[6] This focus is partially based on theoretical concerns because it broadly describes public expectations of their government. I also chose this focus because the General Social Survey includes questions tapping these preferences.

The GSS asked people whether the government should spend more or less in a variety of policy areas.[7] Figure 6.1 presents the overall trend in spending preferences over the past four decades, and the results are a

| **FIGURE 6.1** | **Increasing Support for Government Spending** |

▶ *Americans' average preferences for spending in eleven policy areas have increased over time.*

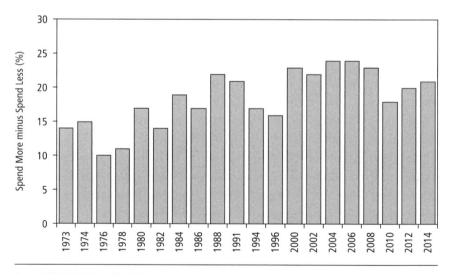

Source: 1973–2014 General Social Surveys.

Note: Figure entries are the percentages saying "too little" is being spent on the problem minus the percentage saying "too much" averaged across eleven separate policy areas (see Table 6.1).

surprising contrast to the conventional wisdom. Across eleven different policy domains (see Table 6.1), I counted the percentage who thought government should be spending more and subtracted the percentage who thought the government should spend less. In every year, those who want more government spending exceeded those who want less spending by a considerable margin. Over the past forty years, public support for greater spending generally trended upward. Ironically, conservative administrations (like that of George W. Bush) often stimulate the public to express more support for government spending, while liberal administrations (like that of Barack Obama) have the opposite effect. Stuart Soroka and Christopher Wlezien describe this as a thermostatic model of public opinion: When government gets too hot in one direction or too cold in another, then the public readjusts to have a policy balance they prefer.[8]

These patterns are not unique to the General Social Survey. Other opinion time series find that most people expect the government to do more in most policy areas, even while complaining that taxes are too high or government must be more efficient.[9] Moreover, even when spending is paired with the costs of these programs, such as in higher taxes, more people generally support an active government. Bennett and Bennett concluded that when faced with the alternatives of limited government and a larger role of government, Americans "have made a choice, and it is in favor of big government." Americans have grown comfortable living with the leviathan.[10]

Averaged within these overall statistics are preferences on specific policy goals. Table 6.1 displays the difference between the percentage of Americans who say there is too little spending in each policy area minus those who say there is too much spending for a few time points. These statistics describe a long-term consensus for increased government spending on crime prevention, education, health care, preventing drug addiction, environmental protection, and solving the problems of urban America. Only welfare, the space program, and foreign aid are consistently viewed as candidates for budget cuts.[11]

Americans' priorities for spending on specific programs do, however, respond to changes in the federal budget and the political environment in a manner consistent with the thermostatic model.[12] For instance,

TABLE 6.1 Budget Priorities of the American Public

▶ *This table tracks the changes in public spending priorities over time.*

Priority	1973	1976	1980	1984	1988	1991	1996	2000	2004	2008	2014
Halting rising crime rate	64	61	65	62	64	59	61	55	52	55	52
Protecting the nation's health	58	57	49	53	65	66	60	69	75	72	46
Dealing with drug addiction	64	55	56	57	64	50	48	53	45	47	47
Protecting the environment	57	47	35	54	60	63	50	55	58	60	49
Improving the educational system	42	42	44	59	60	62	65	67	69	65	66
Solving problems of big cities	41	26	21	31	36	35	45	40	29	36	31
Improving the condition of blacks	12	2	0	19	19	20	13	21	20	24	21
Supporting the military and defense	−28	−2	48	−21	−22	−13	−15	−2	9	−19	5
Supporting welfare	−33	−49	−45	−16	−19	−15	−43	−19	−17	−13	−29
Supporting space exploration program	−53	−51	−21	−27	−16	−26	−32	−29	−24	−22	−3
Providing foreign aid	−70	−75	−69	−65	−63	−68	−69	−52	−53	−47	−57
Average	14	10	17	19	22	21	16	23	24	23	21

Source: 1973–2014 General Social Surveys.

Note: Table entries are the percentages saying "too little" is being spent on the problem minus the percentage saying "too much"; missing data are excluded from the calculation of percentages.

there was relatively high level of support for defense spending in the early years of the Bush administration; after spending increased, opinions shifted to a preference for cuts by 2008. Another recent example is health care. Since about 1990 two-thirds or more of Americans favored more spending on the nation's health. After President Obama spent more with the Affordable Care Act, support for more health spending dropped by 26 percent.

These patterns may be surprising to those unfamiliar with these public opinion trends, since the political rhetoric of the Republican Party for the past three decades has called for less government spending, and this appeared to be a generally successful electoral strategy. In fact, the Republican appeal to voters has had a different focus—cutting taxes— while being less than forthcoming on how this will impact spending. The public's endorsement of increased spending on specific policy areas is typically paired with criticism of taxation levels as too high (and general cynicism about government). Similarly, U.S. senators with Tea Party credentials lobby against any tax increase but then favor spending that directly benefits their state. These contrasting orientations, I will argue, are embedded in the norms of citizenship.

Our Spending Priorities

How do the norms of citizenship shape policy preferences? Duty-based citizen norms seem more consistent with conservative and neoliberal images of the role of government, which would limit support for overall government spending and favor a narrow definition of the role of government. In contrast, engaged citizenship should prompt a more encompassing view of the scope of government. These norms should lead individuals to accept a larger government role across a range of policy areas, especially those that address social needs.

To link citizenship norms to support for more government spending overall, I simply counted the number of policy areas in 2004 where an individual favors more spending minus the number of policies where he/ she favored less spending.[13] Figure 6.2 plots these spending preferences by citizenship norms. As expected, duty-based citizens cite fewer areas where they support more government spending. Engaged citizens see almost twice as many policies where they want more spending. To

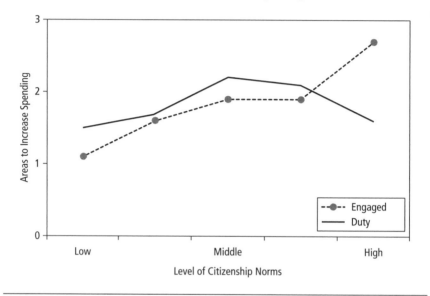

FIGURE 6.2   Citizenship and Government Spending

▶ *Engaged citizenship significantly increases support for government spending, while citizen duty is not systematically linked to overall spending.*

Source: 2014 General Social Survey.

Note: Figure entries are the average number of areas where respondents favored more spending minus the number of areas where they favored less spending.

address the social interests of engaged citizenship, these individuals feel that the government should be larger. This general pattern is quite similar to what appears in the initial analyses of citizenship and spending in the 2004 GSS survey.[14]

But overall spending attitudes can hide more than it shows, because citizenship norms differentially affect support for spending across specific policy areas. Duty-based norms may encourage a conservative preference to focus spending on defense spending, infrastructure, transportation, and similar programs. These are the policy preferences one most closely identifies with the residents in our Leisure World example. In contrast, engaged citizens—perhaps the grandchildren of the Leisure World residents—may favor more spending on government programs that protect the environment, provide social services, and protect the needy. The policy priorities of the Obama administration are presumably closer to the priorities of the young. Thus, the different definitions of citizenship should be translated into contrasting public policy priorities.

Figure 6.3 presents the relationship between citizenship norms and spending for each of the eleven policy areas (positive values mean a preference for more spending; negative values mean a high level on a citizenship norm favors lower spending). The table is arranged by the policy priorities of engaged citizens; their strongest positive correlations are at the top of the figure. The social dimension of engaged citizenship yields support for greater spending on support for blacks, drug rehabilitation, foreign aid, and aid to the poor. These are all examples of how the solidarity norms of engaged citizenship stimulate concern for the underprivileged. Each area displays a strong positive relationship with engaged citizenship (and a weak or negative relationship with duty-based norms).

In contrast, those who score high on citizen duty generally favor less spending on social programs and more spending on defense and law enforcement—the only areas where engaged citizenship is linked to cuts in spending. An illustrative contrast is protecting the environment: Engaged citizens favor more environmental spending, and duty-based citizens want to spend less. If you apply these results to debates on the direction of government, it is easy to see why these two views of what it means to be a good citizen translate into different priorities for government.

Combining Predictors

The citizenship patterns in policy priorities are striking, but they may reflect the influence of other attitudes. For instance, there is a strong partisan element in attitudes toward government spending, and this may underlie the patterns in Figure 6.3.[15] Democrats typically support greater government spending, especially on the social programs emphasized by engaged citizens. Republicans are more likely to hold the line on total government spending and focus spending on other priorities such as national security. Similarly, policy priorities may reflect different generational or educational experiences that are related to citizenship norms.

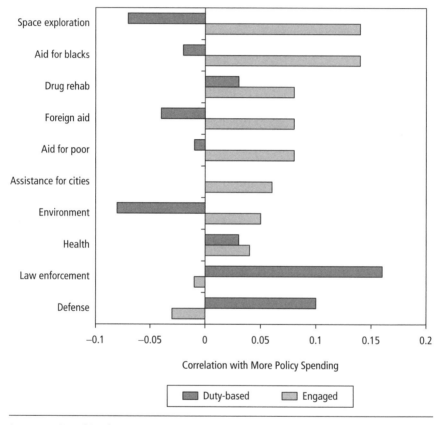

FIGURE 6.3   Citizenship and Spending Priorities

► *Engaged citizenship increases support for spending more on most policies, while citizen duty is linked to more spending on defense and law environment while spending less on most social programs.*

Correlation with More Policy Spending

Duty-based   Engaged

Source: 2014 General Social Survey.

Note: Figure entries are the correlations (tau-b) between citizenship norms and favoring more spending in each policy area. A positive correlation means the norm is related to a preference for more spending; a negative correlation means the norm is related to less spending.

To determine if citizenship norms are really important for spending attitudes independent of other characteristics, I did a statistical analysis to control for other factors such as partisanship, age, and education.

Table 6.2 displays the results from these analyses. The first column shows that support for overall government spending is positively related to engaged citizenship and, to a lesser extent, duty-based citizenship, even while statistically controlling for the substantial impact of partisanship and the other predictors.

The second column in the table examines support for spending on social programs such as education, assisting the poor, and health care.[16] Here, the impact of partisanship outweighs nearly all the other possible predictors of spending support. Neither citizenship variable has a significant effect. In contrast, the third column analyzes support for defense spending and law enforcement. Duty-based citizens favor more spending for these policies, despite the general negativity of duty-based citizens toward spending overall. Evidence from the 2004 GSS would add highway improvement, mass transit, and other infrastructure programs. Finally, a last cluster of policies deals with foreign aid, helping cities, and space exploration. For these policy areas partisanship has

TABLE 6.2   Predictors of Spending Preferences

▶ Engaged citizens and Democratic partisans strongly favor more spending overall, while older Americans want to spend less. The weight of citizenship norms varies across specific policy areas.

Predictor	Overall Spending	Social Spending	Defense/ Security	Aid to the Needy
Duty-based citizens	.07*	.06	.16*	−.03
Engaged citizens	.13*	.03	.01	.18*
Democrat partisan	.27*	.47*	−.20*	.02
Age	−.18*	−.17*	.16*	−.09*
Education	.03	−.05	.02	.11*
Gender	.04	.07*	−.02	−.06
Multiple R	.37	.48	.30	.25

Source: 2014 General Social Survey.

Note: Table entries are standardized coefficients from a multiple regression analysis; each entry represents whether the predictor has a positive or negative effect on citizenship norms. Statistically significant effects ($p < .05$) are noted by an asterisk.

little independent impact, and engaged citizenship stimulates support for government action. All four examples also speak to the issue of generational change. Older Americans clearly favor smaller government, wanting to spend less overall, on social spending, and on aid to the needy. Their only priorities are security and defense. This is another indication of how generational change can reshape the nation's policy priorities.

In summary, citizenship norms influence how Americans think about the scope of government in general and how they define the specific policy priorities of their government. Feelings of citizen duty lead to a more restrictive view of government overall and a more limited policy mandate reflecting more conservative traditions. In contrast, engaged citizenship encourages an activist image of government, especially on the social programs that reflect the values embedded in these norms of citizenship.

PUBLIC POLICY PREFERENCES

Spending priorities provide one aspect of the public's policy priorities, but often the goals of policy are more distinct than their funding levels. As this chapter was being drafted in 2014, the U.S. Congress was debating a range of issues where the amount of spending was secondary to the basic policy goal: reactions to Russian actions in the Ukraine, citizenship rules, privacy laws, the XL pipeline, Medicare reform, the recent flare-up in Palestinian-Israeli relations, and various policies to address international terrorism. Often the choice is not how much to spend but which policies to pursue.

The GSS had a limited number of specific policy questions. Therefore, I again turn to the earlier Georgetown CDACS survey that included questions on specific policy choices. To highlight the differences between citizen duty and engaged citizenship, Figure 6.4 organizes these policy items into three categories. The first category at the top of the figure includes those items where citizen duty strongly promotes approval of the policy (a positive correlation) and engaged citizenship generally stimulates disapproval (a negative correlation). This category includes four different policies that reflect a strong national security orientation: the United States was justified in the Iraq war, people should

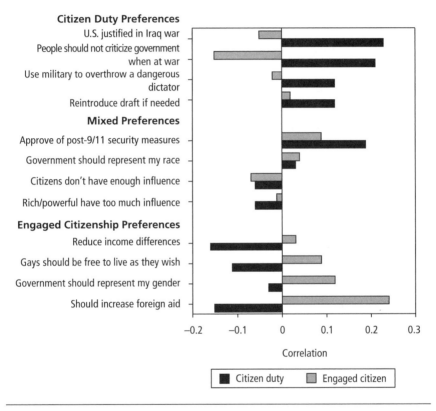

FIGURE 6.4   Citizenship and Policy Preferences

▶ *Citizen duty increases support for military action, while engaged citizenship increases support for social programs, multiculturalism, and foreign aid.*

Source: 2015 CDACS Survey.

Note: Figure entries are the correlations between each dimension of citizenship and favoring more spending in each policy area. A positive correlation means the norm is related to a preference for the policy; a negative correlation means the norm is related to opposition to the policy.

not criticize the government when at war, military force can be used to overthrow a dictator, and we should reintroduce the military draft. Think of U.S. Senator John McCain as typifying these orientations.

In contrast, the items at the bottom of the figure are policies favored by those high in engaged citizenship (a positive correlation) and generally opposed by those high in citizen duty (a negative correlation). This includes support for increased foreign aid, the representation of women in government, gay rights, and the reduction of income differences. Doesn't this sound like the mantra of the Obama administration, at least one wing of its supporters? (A third category in the middle of the figure includes issues where citizenship norms do not have strong effects.)

The policy contrasts as a function of citizenship norms could not be starker. While citizen duty promotes support for national security and allegiance, engaged citizens are advocates for a liberal cultural agenda and economic liberalism. Perhaps the rhetoric and actions of recent administrations in Washington have polarized citizenship norms around these contemporary issues and made images of citizenship more partisan in the current environment. One can imagine that many elements of public policy can appeal to both norms of citizenship or even be independent of such norms. The Bush administration developed its policies oriented by traditional norms of citizenship and government that encourage such images of national security, duty, and loyalty as their base. Its calls for a renewal of citizenship reflect a desire for Americans to develop values that will support such policies. Similarly, the Obama administration pursued a different policy agenda because Barack Obama and his top aides saw the role of government in terms of a different set of political norms. This is how citizenship norms shape the policy preferences of Americans.

ARE CITIZENSHIP NORMS ANOTHER TERM FOR PARTISANSHIP?

By now, something should be jogging your brain: It seems like the policy views of engaged citizens overlap with the Democratic Party, and the policy priorities of duty-based citizens overlap with the Republicans. This is accurate, but only partially so.

Citizenship norms are not just another term for partisanship. The evidence on spending preferences (Table 6.2) shows that these norms can affect policy views independent of a respondent's party loyalties. (And to some degree party loyalties might be influenced by one's definition of good citizenship.) Part of the complexity of contemporary American politics is that citizenship norms do not fully align with the political parties. There are libertarian elements of the Republican Party that share a great deal in common with some liberal Democrats. Paying taxes, following the law, and other duty-based elements of citizenship are not practiced only by Republicans—or else the IRS would fall way short on tax collections. Both parties contain a mixture of both citizenship types.

At the same time, it was clear in 2012 and even more so in 2008 that Obama had a special appeal among younger Americans.[17] Part of this appeal was that he spoke to the policy concerns of the young: environmental protection, concern about the needy at home and abroad, social equality, and the special needs of youth. This is what drew young people to his campaign in the Iowa caucuses in 2008, what drew the student canvassers in the early primary states, and what led to the social networking innovations of the Obama campaign. In 2012 Obama spoke to youth with the agenda of an engaged citizen, as much as Romney spoke to others about a duty-based agenda for America. These policy priorities overlap with the evidence of the policy preferences of engaged or duty-based citizens.

The 2014 GSS asked people for whom they voted in the 2012 presidential election, and Figure 6.5 describes the relationship between citizenship norms and vote choice. A full 69 percent of those who scored high on engaged citizenship said they voted for Obama, compared with only 51 percent among those high on duty-based citizenship. And while Obama's support rose with the level of engaged citizenship, it dropped even more sharply with higher levels of duty citizenship. As a reference point, the size of these voting differences is roughly comparable to the generational gap in Obama support, which has received widespread media attention. Citizenship norms matter just as much, or more.

Early voting preferences tend to establish party identities, and younger Americans have twice supported Obama's candidacy. Young people today are less likely than previous generations to identify with a political party; but among those who identify, Democrats now outnumber Republicans by a considerable margin.[18] Given their early voting records and their disproportionate support for norms of engaged citizenship, this Democratic leaning among the young may be a continuing feature of the electoral landscape—with predictable results if the young will only vote.

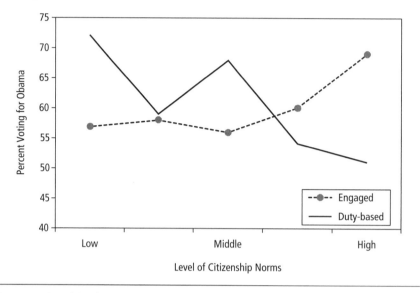

FIGURE 6.5   **Citizenship and Party Choice in 2012**

▶ *Obama gained more votes from engaged citizens in 2012, and fewer votes from duty-based citizens.*

Source: 2014 General Social Survey.

Note: Figure entries are the percentage saying they voted for Obama in 2012 for each level of citizenship norms.

CITIZENSHIP AND PUBLIC POLICY

Norms of citizenship guide what people think a "good citizen" should do. Thus, much of the discussion about America's need for stronger citizenship focuses on its impact on civic engagement, political engagement, and political tolerance—themes examined in previous chapters. This chapter shows how citizenship norms also affect expectations of what a "good government" should do.

Norms of citizen duty encourage a more limited view of government that is focused on providing minimal policy outputs, such as national security, domestic order, and basic infrastructure needs. In contrast, engaged citizenship stimulates a more expansive view of government and its role in society, including addressing the social concerns included in engaged citizenship. So engaged citizens favor more government spending overall, especially on social programs, minority aid, foreign aid, education, and the environment. These preferences can exist even independent of the partisan leanings of individuals, although one sees these orientations reflected in the policy positions of the Republicans and Democrats.

Ronald Inglehart has extensively described how this pattern of changing policy goals is a common feature in most affluent democracies.[19] He explains how new postmaterial values are generating support for new social and quality-of-life issues. In a sense, I am arguing that the American public is following a similar course of changing citizenship norms.

Despite the imagery that Americans expect less from government—fueled by the rhetoric of conservative pundits and politicians—the public's spending preferences actually have moved in the other direction since the 1970s. Americans today favor more government spending than they did four decades ago. Engaged citizenship is inevitably intertwined with a belief that government exists to address a range of societal needs. As the balance of citizen norms shifts within the American public, this increases expectations for a more active government, especially on social programs. The trends from 1973 until 2014 show that some of the greatest increases in support for more government spending occur for improving the educational system, protecting those in need, and improving the condition of minorities. Thus, the public is changing its policy priorities in ways that are not as apparent in everyday political discourse.

Perhaps policy conflicts have become so harsh in contemporary American politics because they arise from these different images of citizenship. In earlier periods, when most Americans' shared norms of citizen duty, policy debates drew upon a common value set. But now, some policies tap different norms and identities about what a good citizen and good government should do. In part, this may arise because citizenship norms are becoming more closely linked to partisan ties. It also presumably reflects a tension between contrasting citizenship norms that now exist within the American public.

For instance, the immigration debates can devolve to calls to either strengthen the border or advance immigrant rights as in the Dream Act, and norms of citizenship may shape these policy preferences. A range of other issues—such as carrying firearms, abortion and gay rights, and specific foreign policies—might evoke much different responses from duty-based citizens and engaged citizens. (Don't even mention proposals to legalize marijuana.) It is not that one policy alternative is completely wrong and the other is completely right, but they reflect a different set of priorities.

Thus, one could visit the Leisure World retirement community and discuss the norms of engaged citizenship—being active in associations, understanding others, buying products for political reasons, and being concerned with those less well-off—and these seniors would broadly accept these values as part of the American creed. However, if one then argued that these American norms should lead to policies supporting gay rights, more foreign aid, and gender equality, they might not agree because of their conceptions of a good citizen. These value differences are embedded in shifting norms of citizenship, and this may be why certain policies deeply divide sectors of American society.

IS A GOOD CITIZEN TRUSTFUL OR SKEPTICAL OF GOVERNMENT?

Try an experiment. Sit in a Starbucks and start a conversation with the people at the next table. Ask their views about how the government in Washington is doing its job. If they will talk to a stranger who asks them about politics, they usually share a list of complaints. Taxes are too high, services are too low; government is doing too much in one area, and not enough in another area. And often they cite a favorite example of where the government has done something foolish or even corrupt. I have done this experiment when George Bush and then Barack Obama occupied the White House, and only the examples differ, not the overall pattern of dissatisfaction.

Dissatisfaction is now commonplace in politics. The average American is dissatisfied with the performance of government—almost no matter whether he or she is a Democrat or a Republican. The contemporary political culture features "critical citizens" and "dissatisfied democrats" who expect more of their elected officials.[1] We are Monday morning quarterbacks, complaining about the miscues and the missed opportunities and thinking that a skilled government could (and should) do better.

This cynicism has become a normal part of politics, but during the 1950s and early 1960s, good citizenship meant support for the political system and a strong sense of national pride. In comparison to the other nations studied in *The Civic Culture*, Americans had "a high degree of pride in the political system. Americans' attachment to the political system also includes both generalized system affect as well as satisfaction with specific governmental performance."[2] At about the same time, the American National Election Study found that 73 percent of those surveyed felt the government could be trusted most of the time to do what is right, 71 percent believed politicians cared what people think, and 64 percent thought government was run for the benefit of all. Indeed, political scientists described such supportive and allegiant attitudes as fundamental elements of a democratic civic culture.[3]

Since the mid-1960s, however, these positive images of government gave way to doubts about politicians and skepticism of our democratic political institutions.[4] In 1979, President Jimmy Carter warned that declining public confidence "was a fundamental threat to American democracy." Political trust ebbed and flowed over the subsequent years but never returned to the allegiant and supportive orientations that *The Civic Culture* had described. Diminished support for government and political institutions has stimulated widespread debate about the vitality of democracy, since allegiance and trust were once considered essential to a democratic political culture.[5]

How have changing norms of citizenship affected these images of government? A strong link exists—but in more complex forms than often recognized. Your discussion partner at Starbucks is not just reacting to the actions of government but to citizenship norms that define what is expected of a good government—and a good citizen.

CHANGING IMAGES OF GOVERNMENT

Public doubts about the government normally begin with questions about the incumbents of public office. Americans might initially criticize Richard Nixon's actions during Watergate, Bill Clinton's marital indiscretions, George W. Bush's presentation of the facts leading up to the Iraqi war, or Obama's enactment of the Affordable Care Act. If dissatisfaction persists, then these feelings can generalize beyond the specific politicians of the day. Cynics may begin to distrust politicians as a group, thinking that those who attain public office are generally untrustworthy or are corrupted by the temptations of office. If these sentiments deepen, they may touch the institutions of government beyond the individual officeholders.[6]

These examples illustrate the point that political support includes several different orientations. I separately compare political support at three levels:

- **Political authorities** are the incumbents of political office, or in a broader sense, the current government and the pool of elites from which government leaders are drawn.
- **Regime** refers to the institutions and offices of government rather than the present officeholders. This level of support also involves public attitudes toward the procedures of government and political institutions, such as the principles of pluralist democracy.
- **Political community** implies a basic attachment to the nation and political system beyond the present institutions of government.

Attitudes may differ across these three levels, and each is examined in this chapter.

TRUSTING POLITICAL AUTHORITIES

You might be cynical about politicians and the government, and today you have lots of company. But you have nothing on William Hungate. Hungate, a Democrat from Missouri, served as a member of the U.S. Congress from 1964 to 1977. He served on the powerful Judiciary Committee and was one of the primary authors of the articles of impeachment against President Richard Nixon. He voluntarily left Congress in 1977, tired of the politics, the logrolling, and the shortcomings of government. In one of his last addresses to Congress he said his farewells: "May the future bring all the best to you, your family and friends—and may your mothers never find out where you work."

Cynicism about government has a long tradition in America and is deeply ingrained in political lore and humor.[7] Yet, in the 1950s and early 1960s, most Americans were positive toward their government. There was an enthusiasm in the American political spirit, and political analysts viewed such positivism as critical to a successful democracy.

However, public images of politicians and government have followed a downward spiral over the past several decades. The most extensive evidence comes from the American National Election Studies, which describe a deepening skepticism of politicians over time (Figure 7.1). Trust in political authorities started to decline in the late 1960s. Conflict over civil rights and Vietnam paralleled Americans' eroding public confidence in their leaders; in concert with Watergate and a seemingly endless stream of political scandals, support declined even further over the next decade.

Trust in government officials reached a low point in 1980 and then temporarily improved during Ronald Reagan's upbeat presidency. The practiced symbolism of Reagan's administration and the allegories of the "Great Communicator" stressed the positive aspects of American society

---

FIGURE 7.1   **Trust in Government**

▶ *Americans' trust in government dropped in the 1960s to 1970s and has remained low since then.*

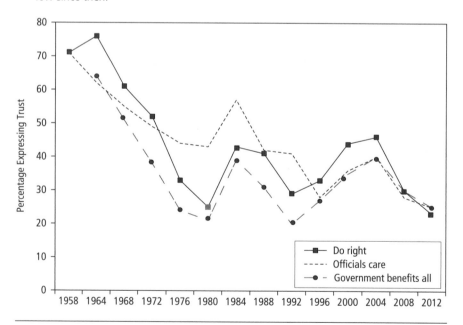

Source: 1958–2012 American National Election Studies (ANES).

Note: Table entries are the percentage giving a trustful response.

and politics. Opinions rebounded in 1984, but the decline continued in later years. By the end of the first Bush administration in 1992, trust levels hovered near historic lows.

Trust improved somewhat by the end of the Clinton administration, following a decade of unprecedented economic growth and the end of the Cold War, but levels of support remained far below those of the late 1950s and early 1960s. After the terrorist attacks on the World Trade Center and the Pentagon in September 2001, people were more trustful of politicians and more confident in political institutions. As these events receded in time, however, opinions slipped back to their pre–September 11 levels. By the 2004 presidential election, trust in government was roughly the same as in 2000. Cynicism declined further by the end of the Bush administration and further still during the Obama administration. The 2012 ANES found that only 23 percent of Americans trusted the government to do right, 25 percent felt that politicians cared what people think, and only 25 percent thought government was run for the benefit of all.

Nearly all other long-term public opinion series show the same downward trends in trust in government. For example, since 1966 the Harris poll asked, "The people running the country don't really care what happens to you." In 1966, only 29 percent shared this opinion; in 2013 a full 85 percent thought politicians didn't care. The Pew Center for People and the Press studied attitudes toward government in 2010 and concluded, "By almost every conceivable measure Americans are less positive and more critical of government these days."[8]

The Sources of Change

The trends of decreasing trust in authorities are now well known, described by a host of academic and popular books. In many analyses of American opinions, researchers point to unique and specific characteristics of American politics as explanations. The presidency supposedly suffers from the accumulation of scandals that range from Watergate and Iran-Contra to Bill/Monica and new scandals since. Other explanations focus on the institutional structure of American government and the need for reform. Congress suffers from its own set of scandals and various problems of the legislative process.[9] Politicians seem more concerned about pleasing special interests than the voters at large. Other analysts suggest that the media are to blame, and the growth of investigative and attack journalism have demoralized the American public—thus the media should be reformed.[10] Perhaps the most perverse view is that the United States suffers from too much democracy and that limiting the democratic process will improve public images of government.[11]

While scandals, government performance, and institutional deficits likely contributed to the decline in political support, broader forces of social change are also at work. Joseph Nye and his colleagues noted that these specific explanations are not generally consistent with the patterns of decreasing trust in government.[12] For example, the ebb and flow of trust does not seem to follow the performance of the economy; and when scandals pass and the public votes a new government into office, the skepticism continues. In addition, cross-national studies document a similar trend of decreasing political trust in most affluent democracies.[13] The breadth of this pattern, across a wide range of nations and different institutional structures, suggests that a common pattern of social change is affecting citizen images of government.

This book maintains that citizenship norms reflect these broader changes in political values produced by the modernization of American society (and other affluent democracies) over the past several decades. The decline of duty-based norms decreases respect for authority of all types, including respect for government officials and political institutions. Thus, the erosion of duty-based citizenship may contribute to declining trust in government authorities. Such a relationship would be another reason why some politicians seek a revival of traditional, duty-based norms to create a more supportive and allegiant public.

Engaged citizenship has a more uncertain impact on images of government. These citizens expect government to be active across a wide set of policies (see Chapter 6), so they may be more positive toward the politicians and government agencies that carry out these programs. However, engaged citizenship includes a desire for citizen autonomy and support for challenging political actions; this suggests that they may be more critical of government. For instance, a growing emphasis on post-material and self-expressive values, which overlap with norms of engaged citizenship, stimulates criticism of the established leaders and institutions of government.[14]

To test these ideas, let's relate citizenship norms to several measures of support for politicians and the government (Figure 7.2).[15] The patterns in the figure are less distinct than the original analyses of the 2004 data, but they mirror the same results. Duty-based citizenship generally has a stronger tendency to increase support of government; every relationship is positive and statistically significant. Engaged citizens are a bit more skeptical of government, especially of elections and general political corruption. Only half of the relationships for engaged citizens are statistically significant. In short, citizen duty taps the type of allegiant citizenship that earlier democratic theorists admired—citizens who have positive images of their government and the political authorities in office. Engaged citizens have mixed images of government and politicians. Those who score

| FIGURE 7.2 | Citizenship and Evaluations of Government |

▶ *Citizen duty promotes more support for government, while engaged citizens have mixed images of government.*

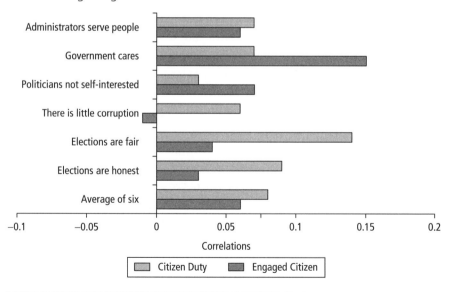

Source: 2004 and 2014 General Social Surveys combined.

Note: Figure entries are correlation coefficients (Pearson's *r*) that measure whether citizenship norms have a positive or negative effect on these evaluations of government.

high in engaged citizenship are slightly more trustful of government and politicians. However, their critical ethos appears in feelings that corruption is more common and in their doubts about the honesty and fairness of elections.

Another insightful set of questions asked about how the democratic process has been working in the past, today, and in the future.[16] The first finding is that Americans gave democracy "today" a 6.6 out of 10 in 2004, but they thought democracy ten years in the future would only rate a 6.1 (a real drop from their 6.8 rating of democracy ten years prior). In fact, by 2014 Americans gave the working of the democratic process only a 5.9— even lower than their earlier prediction. And their prediction for 2014 was a 5.4 score; the downward spiral is projected to continue.

When one looks at the relationship between citizenship norms and these three measures of democratic performance, an intriguing pattern appears. Both types of citizenship norms are linked to more positive evaluations of government. But this relationship is stronger for duty-based citizens looking backward to ten years ago; they look longingly toward the way democracy used to be. Engaged citizenship shows a slightly stronger relationship for democracy ten years from now; they look more positively toward the future. These are small differences, but when the contrasting effects of citizen duty and engaged citizenship are jointly considered, the cumulative effect is larger.

Americans are redefining what it means to be a good citizen, and this reshapes their images of government. If the person sitting next to you in Starbucks holds duty-based norms of citizenship, he or she will be more supportive of politicians and look back to an idyllic image of the past, when duty, social order, and allegiance were in greater supply. In contrast, if the next coffee drinker holds norms of engaged citizenship, he or she will be more skeptical of the current political authorities but also be more optimistic about the political process working better in the future— better than it did in the past.

TRUSTING POLITICAL INSTITUTIONS

Declining faith in politicians and government officials might not be too worrisome because democracy exists to "vote the rascals out" when we are dissatisfied with the government's performance. However, democratic theorists worried that if cynicism generalized to the institutions of democracy, the implications would be more problematic.

Thus when surveys began to document decreasing confidence in Congress, the executive branch, and even the Supreme Court, political scientists became concerned. The best evidence of this erosion of political trust comes from the General Social Survey, which has asked questions about institutional trust that continued a series the Harris poll began in 1966 (Figure 7.3). There was a dramatic drop in confidence in all three branches between 1966 and 1971. Then the GSS surveys describe an erratic downward trend in confidence in the executive branch and Congress. In 2014 both trends hit historic lows. Only 12 percent of Americans had great confidence in the executive branch and

FIGURE 7.3   Declining Confidence in Political Institutions

▶ *Americans have become less trustful of the key institutions of the democratic process.*

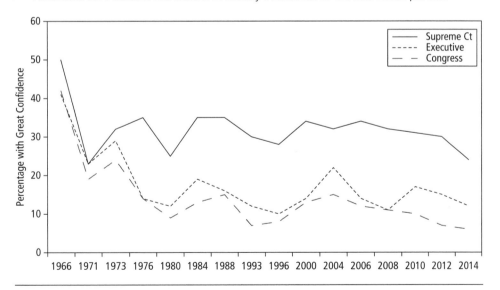

Sources: 1966 and 1971 from Harris Poll; 1973–2014 from General Social Surveys.

Note: Table entries are the percentages expressing a "great deal" of confidence in the people running each institution.

a mere 6 percent had confidence in Congress; a majority (55%) had hardly any confidence in Congress. Separate trends from the Harris Poll show confidence in the executive branch and Congress dropping to historic lows in recent years. These are the sentiments that fuel public criticism of Washington, and any actions the government takes are shrouded in suspicion.

Many factors might contribute to the declining confidence in political institutions: the performance of elites, media coverage of politicians' shortfalls, frustration with the policies enacted (or not enacted) by government. If people are frustrated over a long enough time period, they may generalize this to the institutions themselves. In addition, we expect that changing citizenship norms are another factor. Duty-based citizens are more likely to express an allegiance to the state and its institutions; this is the duty of a good citizen. Conversely, engaged citizens are likely to be ambivalent; trust must be earned rather than bestowed by tradition.

When we correlated citizenship norms with institutional trust, the results were quite similar to trust in politicians (Figure 7.2). People high in duty-based citizenship express more confidence in the executive branch, Congress, and the Supreme Court. An index summarizing all three questions has an $r = .12$ correlation with citizen duty. Conversely, engaged citizenship has an ambivalent relationship with institutional trust, and trust in Congress actually is lower among those who score high on engaged citizenship. The index of institutional trust thus yields an insignificant relationship ($r = .04$) with engaged citizenship.

Is the decline in political trust important? When these trends first became apparent, one of the cofounders of the ANES said this was the most significant trend in American public opinion that had no effect. Now as the level of trust drops to very low levels, it is becoming more apparent that this is changing citizens' behaviors. I used to be more sanguine about these trends, because democracy benefits when citizens question power. But the extensive period of very low trust can erode the foundation of democracy. Like many things, there is a "Goldilocks point"; too much or two little is not good, and government functions better if we find a balance. So far, meaningful reforms to address public concerns are still limited, and thus dissatisfaction endures.

One effect of declining trust is political participation. In place of the habitual party support of the past, more voters are now skeptical of parties, which means they are less likely to vote and more often change parties between elections. Political distrust also encourages protest, social movement activism, and other elite-challenging political activities. These new forms of activism often strain the democratic process, as demonstrators challenge established political elites and current government structures. There are benefits from an assertive citizenry, but these benefits come with additional costs.[17]

A skeptical public is likely to act differently.[18] In late 2014 and early 2015 there was an outbreak of measles in Southern California, and it spread because an increasing number of parents were not vaccinating their children. Often the most vocal antivaccine voices came from affluent, middle-class people who were skeptical of the advice from public health officials. Research suggests that people who think the government is unresponsive to their interests or wastes tax money are more likely to feel it is okay to fudge a bit on their taxes or bend the law in other ways. The skeptical citizen may be hesitant to serve on a jury or perform other public service activities. In short, political support is part of the social contract that enables democracies to act without coercion and with the voluntary compliance of the citizenry. Decreasing support can erode this part of the social contract.

DEMOCRATIC VALUES

On your next trip to Starbucks, if you began a political conversation about the value of democracy rather than performance of the current administration, I suspect the conversation will be much different.[19] Despite our negative evaluations of government, Americans broadly endorse the democratic ideal. Most people readily agree with Churchill that democracy is better than other forms of government, even if it has its limitations. Americans believe that democracy ensures life, liberty, and the pursuit of happiness that is central to our political traditions. Public endorsement for democratic values is essential in sustaining democracy. Moreover, social modernization—the expansion of education and other social trends—should have reinforced democratic values, much as we saw in the spread of political tolerance in Chapter 5.

Public support for democracy is a complicated attitude to measure, however. Democracy contains several distinct political principles. Political tolerance, as examined in Chapter 5, is one central element of democratic values, but there are others. The 2004 General Social Survey tapped a set of democratic principles that were derived from previous research on democracy:[20]

- **Democratic inclusion and equality**: the importance of government treating everyone equally and protecting the rights of minorities.
- **Citizen participation**: the importance of giving people a chance to participate and citizens engaging in acts of civil disobedience.
- **Effective participation**: the importance of politicians considering the views of citizens.
- **Social democracy**: the importance of ensuring people have an adequate standard of living.

This is not an exhaustive list but it includes many key themes discussed in the philosophical literature on democracy. As you might expect, Americans broadly accept the importance of most of these democratic principles. On a 7-point importance scale, all but the item on civil disobedience have a mean score above 6 (the items are listed in Figure 7.4).[21]

However, our question is whether the norms of citizenship are related to support for democratic principles. Are there different relationships for duty-based and engaged citizenship? Duty-based citizenship promotes support for the politicians and the government as we have just seen, but do these norms also stimulate support for democratic values? Democratic norms possess an egalitarian and autonomous element that might conflict with the hierarchic and orderly norms of citizen duty. In contrast, engaged citizenship should more openly embrace democratic values. The participatory norms, social concerns, and autonomy of engaged citizenship are broadly and directly compatible with democratic values as measured in this survey. Thus, engaged citizenship may have an even stronger impact on democratic values.

Figure 7.4 presents the correlations between the two citizenship dimensions and the six democratic values items. The democratic values index combines all six items.[22] In every case but one, both sets of

| FIGURE 7.4 | Citizenship and Democratic Values |

▶ *Both sets of citizenship norms generally increase support for democratic values, and these effects are strongest for engaged citizenship.*

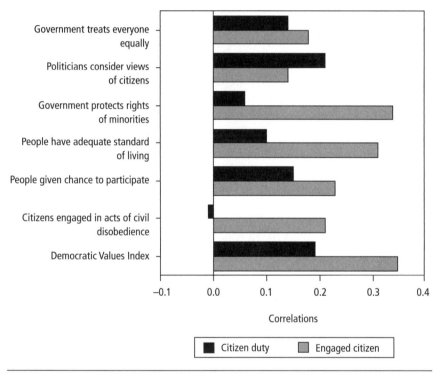

Source: 2004 General Social Survey.

Note: Figure entries are correlation coefficients (Pearson's *r*) that measure whether citizenship norms have a positive or negative effect on these democratic values.

citizenship norms strengthen democratic values. However, citizen duty has a notably weaker relationship with most democratic values and in fact has a negative relationship with the civil disobedience item. Engaged citizenship, in contrast, strongly correlates with all six items. Often this contrast is quite striking. For instance, engaged citizenship strongly encourages the protection of minority rights, but this is only slightly more common among those with high levels of duty-based citizenship. Similarly, engaged citizenship is clearly linked to defining democracy in terms of adequate living standards, but this is only weakly the case for duty-based citizenship.

Most Americans support democratic values when asked separately and in abstract terms. Who would disagree? Motherhood, apple pie, and democracy—this is the American way. A more robust way of measuring preferences is to ask people to choose between contrasting alternatives. The 2005 CDACS survey asked about the trade-off between majority rights and social order on the one side, and minority rights and preserving individual freedoms on the other. Both sets of options are reasonable and important goals of a democratic government, but they reflect values that can potentially come into conflict. Four items focused on these trade-offs:

➢ For democracy to work best, the will of the majority must be followed, **OR**, For democracy to work best, the rights of minorities must be protected.

➢ In times of war, American should have a strong leader who unites the country, **OR**, In times of war, it is as important as ever to be able to disagree about our country's political direction.

➢ In order to curb terrorism in this country, it will be necessary to give up some civil liberties, **OR**, We should preserve our freedoms above all, because otherwise the terrorists will win.

➢ People should respect the rules/policies set by the government, even if they disagree with them, **OR**, When they disagree with the government, people should act according to their own sense of what is right/wrong.[23]

These are difficult questions to answer because both alternatives have a strong basis in democratic theory, and many people presumably agree with both options. The challenge for democracy is to find the appropriate balance between both. Indeed, in the post–September 11 world these items reflect the debates over issues such as the renewal of the Patriot Act, the domestic spying programs run by the National Security Agency, and the government's role in protecting the nation from further terrorist acts. Politics often means that we must choose between two desired goals, and citizenship norms shape the trade-offs people are willing to make.

I've combined these four items into a single measure; at one end is greater support for minority rights and civil liberties, and at the other end is support for majority rights and social order. As we might expect, those high on citizen duty support the majoritarian/order alternative on these four items (Figure 7.5). This is a very large difference as a function of duty-based norms. In contrast, engaged citizenship promotes support for minority rights and civil liberties when faced with these trade-offs. The challenge of democracy is to balance both these sets of values; but when Americans are faced with these choices, citizenship norms shape the direction of their choices.

In summary, much as we saw for attitudes toward political tolerance and civil liberties in Chapter 5, duty-based citizenship produces a more

---

FIGURE 7.5   **Citizenship and Majority/Minority Rights**

▶ *Citizen duty increases support for majority rights over minority rights, and engaged citizen increases support for minority rights over the majority.*

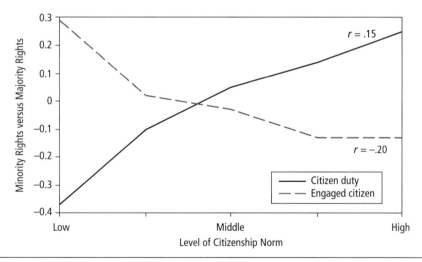

Source: 2005 CDACS Survey.

Note: Negative values indicate support for minority rights, and positive values indicate support for majority rights. See note 24 on the creation of this measure.

restrictive image of democracy based on conformity and acceptance of authority. The good citizen is a good subject. In contrast, engaged citizenship reinforces Americans' commitment to norms of autonomous action and inclusion. Engaged citizens stress minority rights and the social dimensions of democratic politics in keeping with their self-definitions of good citizenship. Engaged citizens may be less trustful of contemporary politicians and political institutions because they have higher expectations for the democratic process.[24]

FEELINGS OF NATIONAL PRIDE

A European friend was visiting the University of California, Irvine, right after the terrorist attacks of September 11, 2001. He was amazed by the outpouring of generosity by Americans who lived 3,000 miles away from New York. People contributed money to telethons, the businesses in Irvine had jars for contributions near their cash registers, and restaurants had a 9/11 night and donated the proceeds to New York. However, he was even more amazed by the patriotic outpouring of Americans. As many writers have noted, the sales of American flags skyrocketed in the weeks after the terrorist attacks. Even a few university staffers from the 1960s generation displayed the American flag on their office doors. The terrorist attacks brought Americans' deep feelings of patriotism to the surface.

Patriotism and strong feelings of national pride are a distinctive element of the American political culture—and were even before September 11.[25] However, these sentiments may not be immune to the dissatisfactions that have affected other aspects of political support. Expressions of patriotism seem less common today than they did a generation ago (with the exception of the period immediately after September 11). A growing emphasis on multiculturalism and the spreading ethnic diversity of America have led to debates on the breadth and depth of a common national identity.[26]

To what extent are feelings of national identity linked to definitions of citizenship? Allegiance to the nation seems inimitably tied to duty-based citizenship because both stress loyalty, commitment, and support for the political order. These orientations seem to form a single array of political beliefs. In contrast, the link between engaged citizenship and national pride is more ambiguous. In abstract terms, a strong sense of citizenship should encourage attachment to the nation. However, engaged citizenship represents a questioning view of government, and these sentiments may be even clearer when measuring national attachments.

The contrasting effect of citizenship norms is clearly seen for feelings of national pride (Figure 7.6). Only 66 percent of people who are lowest in citizen duty say they are very proud to be American, and this increases to almost 90 percent among those highest in citizen duty. In contrast, engaged citizenship has no relationship with feelings of national pride. While duty-based citizenship may lead one to raise the flag on the Fourth of July and endorse national ambitions, the engaged citizen has a more reserved feeling toward the nation.

FIGURE 7.6 **Citizenship and National Pride**

▶ *Citizen duty greatly increases national pride, while engaged citizenship shows no relationship.*

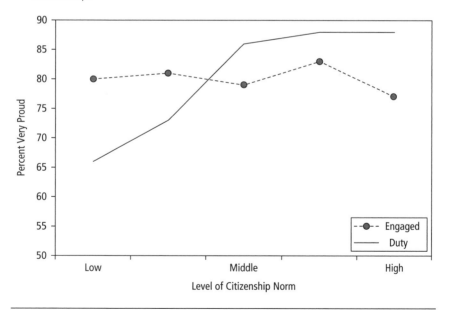

Source: 2004 and 2014 General Social Surveys combined.

Note: Figure entries are the percentage saying they are "very proud" to be an American.

Certainly engaged citizens can be proud of their nation, but we expect that the nationalist and potentially ethnocentrist elements of national pride conflict with the inclusive solidarity aspects of engaged citizenship (being concerned with others in need in the nation and the world). For instance, a set of questions in the 2004 survey taps pride in various elements of the American experience (Figure 7.7). While citizen duty positively stimulates pride in the armed forces and American history, engaged citizens see these same traits negatively. Conversely, engaged citizens are prouder of America's social programs, science, and the arts. Thus, these different groups of Americans think of the nation in terms of distinct parts of U.S. history and society. This is clearly illustrated in the last question in Figure 7.7. When asked if there are things in America today that make them ashamed, those high in citizen duty generally say no, while engaged citizens tend to say yes.

To one group of Americans, we are still the first new nation that reflects the positive potential of humankind; when they think of America, they think of the nation's positive experiences. Another group of Americans see the nation's performance as falling short of its ideals; they look at America and see things that should be improved. Both are expressions of national pride, but one accepts the status quo and the other sees a need for change.

AMERICA, RIGHT OR WRONG

It's a slogan we have all seen many times. During the turbulent 1960s it was prominently used in the debates over the Vietnam War; and it was reprised during the debates on the Iraq War. It is occasionally seen as a bumper sticker or on a sign posted in a store (often in rural America). In its full form, it highlights the findings of this chapter.

My country, right or wrong.

If right to defend it, if wrong to correct it.

This phrase, attributed to the late Senator Carl Schurz of Wisconsin, has unfortunately become politicized in the cultural divide about citizenship in America. Conservatives typically embrace the first line while

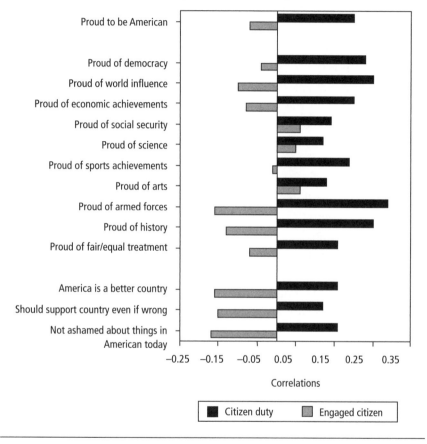

FIGURE 7.7   Citizenship and Different Aspects of National Pride

▶ *Citizen duty strongly encourages feelings of national pride, while engaged citizenship produces a mixed image of America's strengths and weaknesses.*

Source: 2004 General Social Survey.

Note: Figure entries are correlation coefficients (Pearson's *r*) that measure whether citizenship norms have a positive or negative effect on these questions on national pride.

glossing over the second line. Liberals often skip over the first line and accept the second. The strength of this credo is the combination of both elements, but politicians and political commentators often give them different emphases.

This chapter shows that norms of citizenship lead to different images of government. (The chapter appendix shows that the impact of the two citizenship dimensions on images of government and other support attitudes is consistent even when controlling for other factors.) People high in duty-based citizenship think of the United States as that shining city on the hill that President Reagan and other conservative political figures describe. They are more trustful of politicians, have more confidence in political institutions, and are more enthusiastic in their national pride. They have a positive relationship to their government and nation, even while wanting a smaller government. Support and allegiance have first priority, much as in the first line of Schurz's phrase. Thus, it is not surprising that expressions of trust and patriotism are stronger among those who accept duty-based norms of citizenship.

Engaged citizens, meanwhile, are less supportive of political elites and the government. They probably are also more skeptical of paying taxes, less willing to contribute to government, and less supportive of the institutions of representative democratic government. This creates the strains on democracy noted in recent scholarship.[27] The diminished political trust of engaged citizenship presents a challenge to government and the effective operation of the political system.

At the same time, engaged citizenship stimulates support for democratic values, especially an emphasis on equality and the protection of minority rights and expression. Consistent with their self-definition of citizenship, engaged citizens expect more of the government than social order and more of citizens than allegiance. Combined with the evidence of previous chapters, these individuals have a more proactive and socially responsible view of citizenship. To a degree, these are the dissatisfied democrats or assertive citizens who have higher expectations for their government.[28]

This is the paradox of the contemporary American political culture: People have become less trustful of government while simultaneously becoming more supportive of democratic ideals. And the citizenship norms that encourage one of these sentiments tend to be less important to the other.

A democratic society needs both sets of beliefs to function effectively and function democratically. Ideally, these different orientations would be mixed within individual citizens who could see both the need to respect politicians and the need to question politicians and who find the right balance between these two orientations: "My country right or wrong. If right to defend it, if wrong to correct it." In a democratic nirvana, this might be the case. However, for contemporary American politics, these two beliefs are concentrated in different groups of citizens. Some political analysts might lament the decline of duty-based citizenship; but if the consequence is a closer balance between these two democratic norms, the process and the nation may benefit. Indeed, only through the desire for democracy to better fulfill its ideals does the democratic experience progress, and the shift in citizenship norms contributes to this progress.

APPENDIX: MULTIVARIATE ANALYSIS

To ensure that the impact of citizenship norms discussed in this chapter does not simply reflect other sources of political support, I combined the citizenship variables with other potential predictors in a statistical analysis to distinguish between independent and shared influence.

In the first step, I created separate indices of political beliefs. I computed an additive scale of the trust in politicians items (Figure 7.2) and confidence in political institutions (Figure 7.3). I used the democratic index in Figure 7.4 and the question on national pride (Figure 7.6). Then, I conducted multiple regression analyses using the citizenship variables, age, education, cognitive level, party identification, gender, and year of survey. These multivariate analyses are similar to those presented and discussed more extensively in Chapters 4, 5, and 6.

Table 7.A shows that the two citizenship indices have contrasting effects. Citizen duty is positively related to satisfaction with the political process, democratic values, and national pride even while controlling for the other variables in the analysis. In contrast, engaged citizens only weakly related to trusting in politicians and political institutions or to national pride, but they are much more supportive of democratic values. In other words, the independent effects of these two citizenship dimensions persist while controlling for other characteristics. With the more distinct measures of citizenship norms in the previous edition of this book, these patterns are even stronger in 2004.

TABLE 7.A	Predicting Political Support

► *Citizen duty increases political trust, democratic values, and national pride. Engaged citizenship is virtually unrelated to political trust and national pride while even more strongly related to democratic values.*

Predictor	Trust in Politicians	Confidence in Institutions	Democratic Values	National Pride
Citizen duty	.17*	.13*	.20*	.11*
Engaged citizenship	.07*	.04	.35*	−.01
Age	.03	−.10*	.02	.15*
Education	.19*	.10*	−.05*	−.03
Cognitive level	.10	.08*	.15*	.00
Party identification (R)	−.05*	.05	−.13*	.14*
Gender (F)	.02	.03	−.05	.02
Year of survey	−.05*	−.20*	—	−.08*
Multiple R	0.41	0.29	0.46	0.41

Source: 2004 and 2014 General Social Surveys.

Note: Table entries are standardized regression coefficients. Coefficients significant at the $p < .05$ level are denoted by an asterisk.

Another significant feature of Table 7.A is the impact of cognitive variables. Both education and cognitive level (measured by a word skills test asked in the GSS) show positive relationships with political trust and weaker relationships with national pride, but cognitive level is positively related to democratic values.

IN TOCQUEVILLE'S FOOTSTEPS

Imagine Alexis de Tocqueville's amazement as he traveled through the United States in 1830–1832. He started in New York, then went to Buffalo and Detroit, where he had his first contact with Native Americans, and then traveled back to the East through Canada. The following year he headed west through Pennsylvania by horse, down the Ohio River on a steamboat (which nearly sank), and eventually reached the port of New Orleans after three months of travel.

In the midst of a rough and rugged new world, he saw a new democratic nation that differed dramatically from the autocratic political systems of Europe. *Democracy in America* was his tribute to the America public.[1] Tocqueville saw Americans' emphasis on participation, freedom, and equality as the foundation of this new democratic process. Americans were directly involved in governing and had created the modern world's first democracy. The special nature of the American polity is central to our ideas about nation and citizenship. From John Winthrop's description of colonial America as the "City upon a Hill" to Ronald Reagan's reiteration of this imagery (as a "Shining City upon a Hill," no less), Americans view the United States as the first new nation.

Tocqueville's description of the American political culture was based on comparing it with European political cultures. In other words, Tocqueville recognized what was distinct about Americans by comparing them with Europeans. There is a long history of such cross-national comparisons to gain insights into the American political culture (or the culture of any single nation).[2]

These past studies yield valuable evidence of the American political culture, but they often make conflicting claims. For instance, some observers stress Americans' antistatist and antigovernment traditions, while others argue that our sense of national pride and allegiance to government are exceptional.[3] Some repeat the Tocquevillian observation about the participatory tendencies of Americans, but others lament the erosion of the very civil society that Tocqueville praised.[4] There are assertions about the tolerance and pluralism of the political culture, while others point to America's history of slavery and racial discrimination. I could easily expand this list of contradictions.

Some of these contrasting images can coexist because the United States is a large and diverse nation, and different parts of the society can hold different political values. In addition, American society is changing. Some scholars discuss American traditions at the founding of the republic, in the twentieth century, or in contemporary times. In addition, these descriptive studies often lack systematic evidence. Even an insightful observer such as Tocqueville was limited by the evidence he could collect and by his inability to see beyond the observable behavior of the Americans he encountered to assess their inner values.

Many of these same debates about citizenship exist in Europe and other contemporary democracies.[5] Participation in election campaigns has decreased in most affluent democracies, and there are similar complaints about declining civic engagement. Analysts of European democracies cite the rise of individualism as a threat to the social compact of good citizenship. And just as in the United States, the youth are held to blame. Or as Liam Fay satirically wrote about generational differences in the 2015 Irish elections, "Distrust of the upcoming generation is a trademark of our species. Human society has been in a permanent state of decline and decadence since our ancestors first learned to spell the words, and the scruffy degenerates responsible for dragging us to hell in a handcart are invariable identified as feckless youth."[6]

I follow a Tocquevillian logic in this chapter—comparing American norms of citizenship with other democratic publics. Such comparisons should show what is distinctly American about the political values examined here. The great chronicler of American society and politics Seymour Martin Lipset offered an important insight when he stated that "those who know only one country, know no country."[7] In addition, cross-national comparisons can identify common processes of social and political change that transcend any nation's unique historical experiences.

Our journey of comparison is much easier than Tocqueville's—no horses or steamboats—because the surveys of American public opinion are part of a larger cross-national study of citizenship. The 2004 International Social Survey Program (ISSP) studied these themes with coordinated opinion surveys across dozens of nations, including the 2004 GSS. (The 2014 ISSP, which replicated these citizenship questions, will not be available until all the participating nations have completed their surveys, presumably sometime in 2016.) Thus, I compare the meaning of citizenship between Americans and other publics based on the 2004 ISSP and then examine how these norms shape other features of the political culture.

THE NORMS OF CITIZENSHIP

Do Americans think of citizenship differently than most Europeans? In recent years many observers have stressed the supposed differences across the Atlantic. Robert Kagan's popular book summarizes these sentiments: "It is time to stop pretending that Europeans and Americans share a common view of the world. . . . Americans are from Mars and Europeans are from Venus."[8] Kagan was writing primarily about international orientations, but his statement reflects a broader comparison of the social elements of citizenship that supposedly vary between Americans and Europeans. This harks back to the tradition of treating the United States as exceptional in its social and political values.[9]

So let's focus on the norms of citizenship and how they compare across contemporary democracies. Before comparing American and European opinions, we should ask what differences might be expected in citizenship norms. Comparisons may vary between specific pairs of nations: Americans may be stronger adherents of one trait than the British but weaker adherents of that trait than the French. But should we expect broad differences in citizenship norms between Americans and other democratic publics?

Citizen Duty. These norms are the foundation of citizenship in almost any nation (Chapter 2). Previous research yields an ambiguous image of Americans as distinctly high on norms of duty. On the one hand, analysts frequently cite the revolutionary origins of the United States as the basis of a populist and antistatist tradition, in which people question the government and their duty to obey.[10] The constitutional framers structured government to limit its actions. This antiestablishment tradition is also seen in current elections when even incumbents run as outsiders and rail against the government in Washington. On the other hand, it is unclear whether this antistatist tradition affects feelings of citizen duty. For instance, the World Values Survey finds that Americans are less likely than the French, Germans, or British to say that cheating on one's taxes or falsely claiming government benefits can be justified.[11] Americans' strong religious traditions may also stimulate feelings of duty in the political realm. Allegiance and patriotism are commonly cited elements of the American political culture. This is a paradox of the American political culture: The praise for autonomy and resistance to government appears as common as support for allegiance and duty. Perhaps the explanation, as presented in previous chapters, is that different individuals emphasize these two differing sets of norms.

Citizen duty also embraces the responsibility to vote. Americans might score low on this norm because we know that turnout in U.S. elections is quite low. Yet Chapter 3 found that Americans strongly endorse a norm that people should vote—even if they do not vote themselves. Low turnout partially reflects how elections are managed in America. Again, the evidence from prior research is ambiguous.

Engaged Citizenship. This combines several different parts: participation, autonomy, and solidarity (see Chapter 2). Election turnout aside, most analysts stress the participatory traditions in the United States. America is supposedly the nation of joiners and doers, spurred on the populist spirit of the American political culture. The political creed of activism is interlaced throughout U.S. history, as portrayed in Tocqueville's early description of American democracy. In addition, populist traditions should stimulate norms of autonomy. Good citizens will believe that they should be informed and politically independent. Previous cross-national surveys generally find that Americans are more politically active than other democratic publics, and I similarly expect stronger participatory and autonomy norms.[12]

Engaged citizenship also includes solidarity norms promoting a concern for others. Such sentiments are widely identified with European democracies and their large social welfare programs. These values flow from the Social Democratic and Christian Democratic traditions in Europe.[13] Typically, analysts describe the United States as a contrasting case. America is the land of rugged individualism, and critics cite underdeveloped social policies and income inequality as consequences of these American values. Thus, we might expect that Americans should give less importance to solidarity norms than European publics do.

These contrasting images of citizenship between Americans and Europeans would provide a rich basis for theoretical debate—which would never be resolved if it remained a debate between pundits and philosophers. In fact, Tocqueville himself saw these contradictions and said America was "a mixture of vices and virtues that is rather difficult to classify and that does not form a single picture." However, I can compare Americans' citizenship norms with other nations using a cross-national survey that asked the citizenship questions. The 2004 International Social Survey Program included these questions in coordinated surveys of nineteen established democracies including the United States.[14]

Figure 8.1 presents the average importance Americans attach to each of the ten citizenship norms and the average for the other eighteen established democracies. The duty-oriented items are to the left of the figure, and the engaged citizenship items are to the right. Americans broadly place more importance on citizenship, ranking almost all the items as more important than other democratic publics do. In a few instances the gap is substantial—serving in the military, keeping watch on government, social activism—and these items span both duty and engagement norms. There is one exception. Concern for the needy is significantly lower among Americans than among other publics. This may reflect the stronger traditions of social citizenship in many European democracies as well as their large welfare state programs.

The specific national patterns of citizenship are seen in Figure 8.2. To create this figure, I calculated scores on the two dimensions of citizenship

FIGURE 8.1   **Comparing the U.S. with Other Democracies**

▶ *Americans attach more importance to most citizenship items than do people in other affluent democracies.*

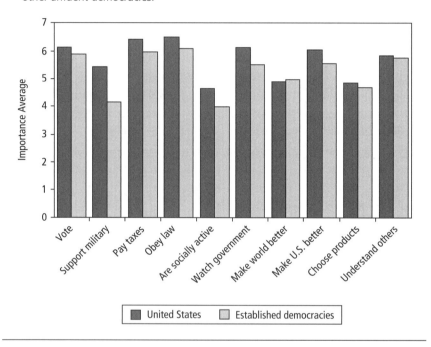

Legend: ■ United States   □ Established democracies

Source: 2004 International Social Survey Program. Eighteen nations are combined for the established democracies scores.

for people in all nineteen nations.[15] Then, I computed the average score for each nation on both indices. The horizontal dimension in the figure represents where the average person in a nation scores on the citizen duty index; the vertical dimension is the nation's score on engaged citizenship.

American citizenship norms are not unique, but they are distinctive. Americans are second highest in citizen duty. More than most other publics, Americans believe a good citizen pays taxes, serves in the army, obeys the laws, and votes. Several other nations that are high in citizen duty also share a British heritage—Canada, Australia, and Ireland, plus Britain itself. This suggests that cultural elements of citizen duty derive from this legacy, perhaps from a tradition of popular sovereignty and the expectation of citizen allegiance in response. Most Scandinavian nations

---

| FIGURE 8.2 | Citizen Duty and Engaged Citizenship by Nation |

▶ *Americans are very high in feelings of citizen duty and are above average in feelings of engaged citizenship.*

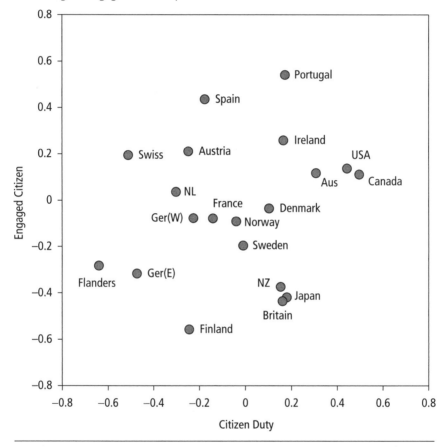

Source: 2004 International Social Survey Program.

Note: Figure entries are national positions based on mean scores on the citizen duty and engaged citizenship factor scores.

---

are located near the midpoint on citizen duty. In contrast to national stereotypes, the lowest nations include several that have a German background: East and West Germany, Austria, and Switzerland.

Americans also score above most nations in engaged citizenship, as shown on the vertical axis. Given the tradition of social citizenship in

Europe, the relatively high placement of the United States is surprising since the public in several welfare states (such as Britain, Germany, Sweden, and Norway) score at or below the overall average. As Figure 8.1 suggests, Americans' positive scores on engaged citizenship reflect participatory norms beyond voting and feelings of political autonomy. However, Americans are not dramatically different from Europeans on the two combined measures of social citizenship.

The high levels of citizenship norms among Americans—both citizen duty and engaged citizenship—are surprising. The book opened by citing the mounting claims that citizenship and democracy are at risk in the United States. Yet Americans display a stronger sense of citizen duty than most other established Western democracies. And despite claims of the individualism of the American political culture, the norms of engaged citizenship are also relatively strong in the United States. In short, if contemporary democracies are supposedly at risk because of their citizens, then the risk is lower in the United States because the American public holds stronger citizenship norms than most other established democracies.

Because the current cross-national data are from only a single time point, I can't track how citizenship norms have changed across all these nations. However, as noted in Chapter 3, generational comparisons can suggest how these norms have been changing and thus show the citizenship trajectories of nations over time. I presume that citizenship norms reflect core values that become fixed in political identities early in life and then generally persist over time, as seen in previous comparisons of American norms in 2004 and 2014. Thus, comparing the distribution of citizenship norms across generations suggests how norms have shifted across the decades.

Figure 8.3 displays the citizenship norms for five generations in the United States and for the other established democracies.[16] To simplify the comparison, I calculated the difference between scores on citizen duty minus scores on engaged citizenship. A positive value means a generation scores higher than average on citizen duty, and a negative value means a higher than average score on engaged citizenship. Two findings stand out. First, the pre-WWII generation emphasizes duty norms by a large margin, while Generation X gives almost equal attention to both norms. The shift is a bit larger in the United States because

FIGURE 8.3   **Generations and Citizenship Norms**

▶ *The difference in citizenship norms shifts toward engaged citizenship for younger generations, although each generation of Americans emphasizes duty more than other nations.*

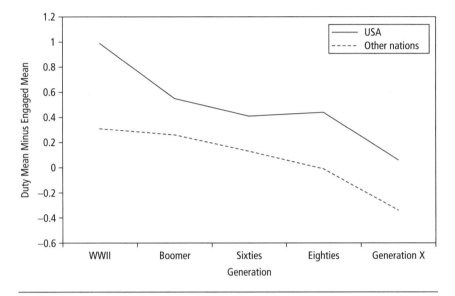

Source: 2004 International Social Survey Program.

Note: The figure entries are the national mean scores on citizen duty minus the mean scores on engaged citizenship for each generation.

the growth of engaged citizenship is greater among younger American generations relative to other democracies. This common pattern reinforces this book's thesis that social modernization is producing a norm shift through changing generational experiences, increased affluence and education, changing economic and social structures, and the other forces of modernization.

Second, for each generational grouping, Americans are significantly more duty oriented than other democratic publics. This was evident in Figures 8.1 and 8.2 as well and shows that the American culture still broadly encourages feeling of citizen duty compared with other nations.

If we combine both findings, this may explain why the process of generational change—and political change—is so apparent in the United States. The norms of "the Greatest Generation" of Americans heavily emphasize citizen duty and give much less importance to engaged citizenship. Younger Americans are sharply different; they give roughly equal weight to both sets of norms. Thus, generational change in the United States has markedly altered citizenship norms, and this is more easily noticed by political analysts and has more obvious effects on the style of politics. In Europe and most other established democracies, in contrast, the generation shift in citizenship norms is more modest. These publics have shifted toward engaged citizenship, but at a slower rate.

In summary, although generational change in citizenship norms is more modest outside the United States, the shift from citizen duty to engaged citizenship is broadly occurring across most affluent democracies. Consequently, norm shift is not a unique American experience but reflects the forces of social modernization touching all these nations.

COMPARING THE CONSEQUENCES OF CITIZENSHIP

Citizenship norms should shape peoples' attitudes and behaviors since these norms define what people feel is expected of them in political life. Having examined a host of effects for the American public, I now extend these analyses to other established democracies. While Americans may be distinct in the levels of citizenship norms or the specific social conditions that shapes these norms, the effects of citizenship norms should be similar across nations. For instance, if engaged citizenship generally encourages contentious political action in America, then we should also see this in other nations. So let's examine three traits that were central to our descriptions of the impact of citizenship norms in the United States: political participation, political tolerance, and democratic values.

Participation since Tocqueville

On his travels through America, Tocqueville was struck by the participatory tendencies of Americans, especially compared with Europeans. This has remained a common description of the American political culture until recently (see Chapter 4). A growing number of politicians, pundits, and political scientists have asserted that the American political spirit has fundamentally changed. For instance, a 2006 report by the National Conference on Citizenship warns that "without strong habits of social and political participation, the world's longest and most successful experiment in democracy is at risk of losing the very norms, networks, and institutions of civic life that have made us the most emulated and respected nation in history."[17] This notion that political participation is dropping to unprecedented levels has become the clarion call of those who see American democracy at risk.

The evidence in Chapter 4 showed that nonelectoral forms of participation are actually increasing among Americans, even while election turnout has decreased. Indeed, similar patterns are occurring in many other advanced industrial democracies.[18]

The 2004 ISSP survey allows us to compare Americans with other democratic citizens—much as Tocqueville did on the basis of his personal experiences.[19] Figure 8.4 displays the percentage of Americans who have engaged in eleven different political activities in comparison with citizens in other established democracies. Clearly, Americans fall behind most other nations in voting; only 63 percent of Americans say they voted in the last national elections, compared with 84 percent in the other democracies. Looking at participation beyond voting, however, Americans generally participate more than other democratic publics. For example, Americans are more active in signing petitions, donating funds to political groups, contacting politicians, attending meetings, and participating in Internet forums. This high level of American participation beyond elections is documented in other recent comparative studies.[20]

Another perspective on participation patterns compares the United States with each of the other established democracies in the ISSP. To simplify the presentation, I constructed two participation indices (Figure 8.5).[21] Electoral participation—voting, campaign activity, and such—is arrayed along the horizontal axis. Americans score third from the bottom among these nineteen democracies (to the far left of the horizontal axis). This is a common pattern, reflecting the low turnout in U.S. elections. The second

| FIGURE 8.4 | Political Participation in the U.S. and Other Democracies |

▶ *Except for voting, Americans are as active as or more active than other democratic publics.*

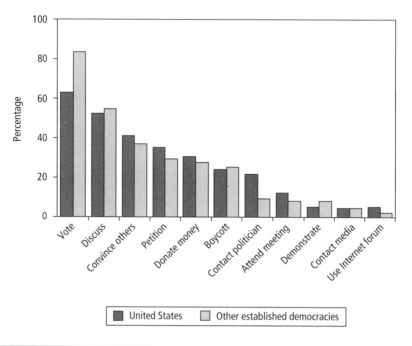

Source: 2004 International Social Survey Program.

Note: Eighteen nations are combined for the established democracies scores.

index of the vertical dimension combines all the forms of nonelectoral participation. Americans score second highest in nonelectoral action, higher than Swedes, Danes, the Dutch, and other publics who typically have high levels of voting. In other words, Americans are politically engaged, but not so much in electoral politics.

Chapter 4 suggested that participation patterns are changing because of changing citizenship norms. In the United States, duty-based citizenship generally encourages participation in elections and party politics but discourages direct action and contentious action. Conversely, engaged citizenship stimulates participation in direct actions and protests while only modestly encouraging electoral participation.

FIGURE 8.5	Political Participation by Nation

▶ *Americans score relatively low on electoral participation but near the top on nonelectoral participation.*

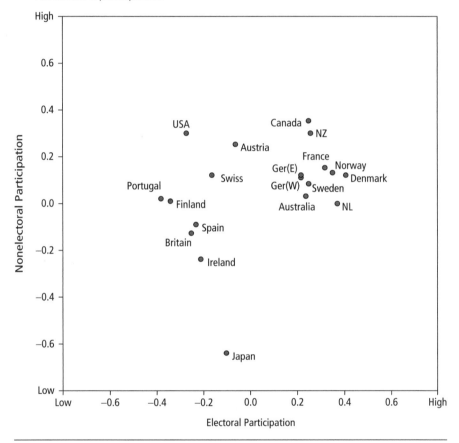

Source: 2004 International Social Survey Program.

Note: Figure entries are national mean scores on electoral and nonelectoral participation indices.

The relationship between norms and participation should not be a distinctly American experience, however, and norms should have similar effects in other democracies. For instance, Swedes who define their citizen role in terms of engaged citizenship should be more likely to protest, pursue methods of direct action, and perhaps vote at a lower rate than duty-oriented citizens.

Figure 8.6 shows the cross-national relationship between citizenship norms and participation for all nineteen nations. The first panel of the figure presents the relationship between citizen duty and the two participation indices in Figure 8.5. As citizen duty increases, so also does participation in electoral politics, since one of the first duties of citizenship is to vote. Simultaneously, citizen duty diminishes nonelectoral forms of action. These contrasting relationships are quite strong and generally apply across the specific activities included in both indices.

Engaged citizenship has a very different influence on participation. As engaged citizenship increases, this modestly stimulates electoral activity. However, as seen in the second panel of the figure, engaged citizenship even more strongly encourages nonelectoral activities, such as boycotts, demonstrations, direct contact with politicians and the media, and Internet activism.

The contrasts in Figure 8.6 graphically illustrate the impact of citizenship norms on participation. As demographic change alters the balance of duty-based and engaged citizenship, a shift in participation patterns should follow. As members of the "Greatest Generation" high in citizen duty leave the electorate and are replaced by Millennials high in engaged citizenship, the repertoire of political action should change. The likelihood of voting may also decrease slightly between these two individuals. In addition, the use of direct and contentious forms of action will markedly increase. This shift has been occurring in most established democracies, even if at different rates and within different institutional settings. Consequently, changing citizenship norms are reshaping how people participate in the democratic process.

Tolerance

Tolerance lies at the very heart of a democratic political culture. Chapter 5 discussed how philosophers and political scientists debate the nature and measurement of political tolerance. Many people say they are committed to tolerance in the abstract but have difficulty applying this to groups that they dislike. Moreover, one might debate what tolerance really means. Is it tolerant to allow free expression to hatred and violence? Germany outlaws Nazi propaganda and paraphernalia; it is illegal to deny the Holocaust, to sell a copy of Hitler's *Mein Kampf*, or to even

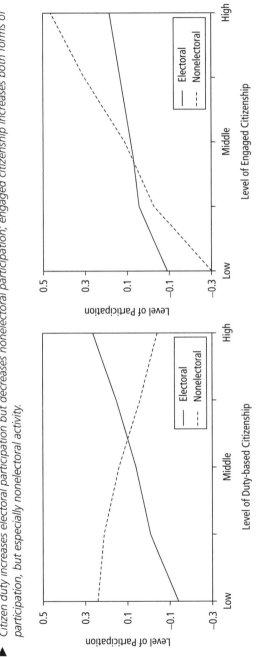

FIGURE 8.6   Citizenship and Electoral Participation

▲ Citizen duty increases electoral participation but decreases nonelectoral participation; engaged citizenship increases both forms of participation, but especially nonelectoral activity.

Source: 2004 International Social Survey Program for all nineteen advanced democracies.

display a swastika (not that you would want to). Would a good democrat prefer that Germany tolerate fascists goose-stepping down their streets wearing swastikas? Is America more democratic because we allow fascist parades, even when they run through Jewish communities? Or does this public action have different meaning for Germans and Americans? Does tolerance really mean we should ignore ideas of right or wrong because we are democrats or because we assume the political correctness logic that all viewpoints are equal?

I raise these difficult questions because the cross-national study of tolerance often evokes such issues. If there are problems in theorizing and measuring the tolerance of Americans, how do we compare American tolerance to that of Swedes or Germans? The best cross-nationally comparable method is probably the "content-controlled" measures of tolerance discussed in Chapter 5. This method asks people which groups they dislike the most and then asks about tolerance toward these groups.[22] Accordingly, it would be more equivalent to compare Germans' tolerance toward their least-liked groups with Americans' tolerance toward their (different) set of least-liked groups.

However, the 2004 ISSP used a simpler measure that asked whether the following three groups should be allowed to hold public meetings: religious extremists, people who want to overthrow the government by force, and people prejudiced against any racial or ethnic group. Without looking at the empirical findings, one might think that this list would severely test the tolerance of Americans. The ISSP survey was completed when memories of the September 11 terrorist attacks by Muslim extremists were still fresh in most people's minds. Racial tensions also have deep roots in the American historical experience.

Figure 8.7 displays the tolerance toward religious extremists and those who want to overthrow the government for our set of ISSP nations. Perhaps surprisingly, Americans are the most tolerant nation on both dimensions (and the same applies to the racial tolerance question). For instance, even in the wake of September 11, a full 73 percent of Americans say a public meeting by religious extremists should be allowed, compared with an average of only 29 percent across the other eighteen nations. In addition, 30 percent of Americans would allow a public meeting by a group trying to overthrow the government, compared with 14 percent

FIGURE 8.7   Political Tolerance by Nation

▶ *Americans score higher than other democratic publics on tolerance toward*
religious extremists and even those who want to overthrow the government.

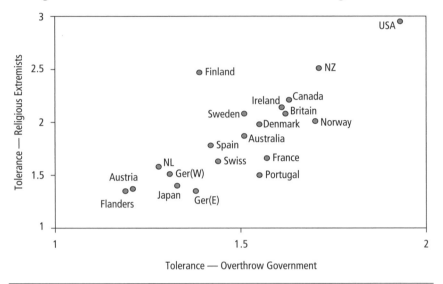

Source: 2004 International Social Survey Program.

Note: Figure entries are national mean scores on willingness to allow public meetings by (a) people who want to overthrow the government by force or (b) religious extremists. The scale was scored: 1 = *should definitely not be allowed,* to 4 = *should definitely be allowed.*

among all these democracies. Moreover, this is not simply an artifact of the groups included in the ISSP survey, since an earlier cross-national comparison of tolerance using a content-controlled method also ranked the American public quite high.[23]

One should interpret such percentages with a dose of skepticism because tolerance is a complex attitude. Yet these results may be surprising because there is so little systematic cross-national evidence of tolerance, and many pundits stake their claims without firm evidence. Or perhaps this is surprising because Americans so quickly accept the often critical comments about this aspect of the American political culture, proffered routinely by pundits both at home and abroad. Certainly there are aspects of the American political culture that deserve criticism. But

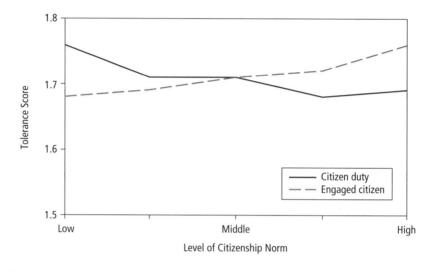

FIGURE 8.8   **Citizenship and Political Tolerance**

▶   *Citizen duty decreases political tolerance, and engaged citizenship increases tolerance.*

Source: 2004 International Social Survey Program for all nineteen advanced democracies.

Note: The figure plots the mean score on the three-item tolerance scale.

far from an example of the erosion of democratic values, Americans express more support for the political rights of negative social groups than do most other democratic publics.

Tolerance is best learned through the experience of living in a democratic society where tolerance is practiced. Tolerance is also linked to the processes of social modernization discussed throughout this book. Consequently, tolerance in the United States and other democracies should be linked to social characteristics and citizenship norms that reflect social modernization.[24] Figure 8.8 shows that across all these nations in the ISSP, strong feelings of citizen duty systematically decrease political tolerance. The relationship in the United States is almost identical to the average of the other eighteen nations. Simultaneously, engaged citizenship increases political tolerance both in general and for each of these three groups.

Citizenship norms do not have equal and strong effects across all democracies, but they work in the expected direction. The variations across nations may be due to the different importance of these challenging groups or specific national conditions.[25] In addition, the levels of tolerance are much higher among the better educated and are distinctly higher among younger generations. Across all Western democracies, for instance, 41 percent of the World War II generation scored at the lowest tolerance level, compared with only 28 percent among Gen X. This suggests that the same general forces of social modernization we described for the United States are also increasing tolerance in other democracies.

Democratic Norms

Perhaps the harshest claims of the crisis-of-American-democracy literature are those asserting that Americans are losing faith in their democratic system. The list of pessimists includes an impressive roster of political scholars.[26] If you want to lose faith in government, you need go no further than the conclusions of these researchers. The sentiments are shared by many political elites, and they have repeated this refrain over the past several decades. For instance, U.S. Supreme Court Justice Stephen Breyer said: "I worry about indifference and cynicism because indifference means nonparticipation and cynicism means a withdrawal of trust . . . without trust and participation, the Constitution cannot work."[27]

Can the state of democracy really be so fragile? Has so much changed since Tocqueville's description of the democratic spirit of America or the early studies extolling America's civic culture? Americans' trust of political elites and key democratic institutions has clearly eroded over the last two generations (see Chapter 7). Yet this pattern is not unique to the United States. Most affluent democracies have experienced the same decline in public support of politicians, political parties, and political institutions.[28] The pundits in Britain, France, Germany, and other democracies are also debating the waning of democracy.

Yet we should not jump to simple conclusions. A thorough analysis of opinion data shows that people today are more skeptical about political elites and even some political institutions. Given the nefarious actions of some elected political officials, such skepticism might seem warranted. However, these people are also committed to democratic ideals and core democratic principles. People have become "critical citizens" or "assertive citizens" who expect more of their government, and they express their dissatisfaction when politics falls short of its democratic ideal.[29] In many ways, commitment to democratic values is more important than trust in the politicians who currently hold office.

Therefore, I compared support for democratic principles across the nations in the International Social Survey Program using the same set of items that were used for the American public in Figure 7.4. Several of the questions tap support for **political rights** identified with democracy: government authorities respect and protect the rights of minorities; government authorities treat everyone equally; politicians take into account the views of the citizens; and people should be given more opportunities to participate. Another item taps a potential dimension of **social rights** that is often stressed in European conceptions of democracy: all citizens should have an adequate standard of living.

Even if people today have doubts about politicians and governments, they remain strongly supportive of democratic principles (Figure 8.9). On a 7-point scale of importance, most people score both political rights and social rights as very important. The horizontal dimension shows that Americans rank fairly high in their support for political rights, which should be reassuring for those who wonder if current political tensions and the strains of battling international terrorism have eroded these democratic values. In fact, several of the nations that score above the United States—East Germany, Spain, and Portugal—might place such emphasis on political rights because they have experienced autocratic governments in their recent past. Americans' commitment to democratic principles is alive and well (although I recognize that further improvements are to be encouraged).

The vertical dimension in the figure measures support for social rights as a democratic principle. One might expect that the individualist orientation of Americans will be most apparent here, since it is linked the limited welfare state policies of the United States. Many European political figures often criticize the United States for being an "elbow society" where people are pushing each other aside in their efforts to gain

FIGURE 8.9	Democratic Values by Nation

▶ *Americans score above average in support for political rights and about average on support for social rights.*

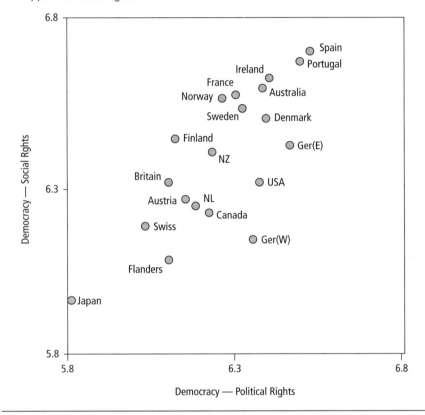

Source: 2004 International Social Survey Program.

Note: Figure entries are national mean scores on four questions of the importance of political rights in a democracy and one question on the importance of an adequate standard of living. The scale was scored: 1 = *not at all important*, to 7 = *very important*.

materialist success and where social protections are limited. Yet even on the social rights dimension, Americans rank near the middle of these other democracies.

I have focused on democratic values to emphasize the positive aspect of the political culture in most democracies—a theme that is often overlooked in the crisis-of-democracy literature. In addition, citizenship norms can reinforce these values. As argued in Chapter 7, good citizenship in a democracy should increase support for democratic principles. Engaged citizenship should very strongly encourage democratic values because these norms emphasize the participatory norms and autonomy underlying democracy. Duty-based citizenship may also encourage support for democratic principles, but these partially conflict with the majoritarian and social order elements of these norms.

Figure 8.10 displays the relationship between citizenship norms and the index of democratic political rights for these democracies. Both citizenship norms strengthen democratic values. However, engaged citizenship has a notably stronger impact than citizen duty.[30] Thus, a shift toward engaged norms reinforces the principles of democracy, a fact which hardly seems a source of political crisis.[31] A good democrat can criticize the government for its failings while remaining committed to democratic principles. Indeed, the democratic principles provide a valuable framework for judging the performance of governments. And in a world where some politicians seem preoccupied with security and order to the detriment of civil liberties, such a commitment to democratic values by the public should be applauded.

CITIZENSHIP IN COMPARATIVE PERSPECTIVE

This chapter represents what might be called a social science version of Einstein's relativity theory. In public opinion there are few absolutes, and we can best understand any single nation by comparing it with other nations. Thus, the political health of the American polity requires either a comparison relative to other time periods (are we getting better or worse?) or a comparison with other nations (how are we doing relative to other democracies?).

In comparing American public opinion with other nations, the implicit logic is that if the opinions of Americans are placing democracy at risk, then the United States should rank poorly in key elements of a democratic political culture. For instance, Americans would be less supportive of democratic values or distinctly less participatory than other established democracies. Such comparisons are often lacking from the

FIGURE 8.10   **Citizenship and Democratic Rights**

▶ *Both norms of citizenship increase support for democratic political rights.*

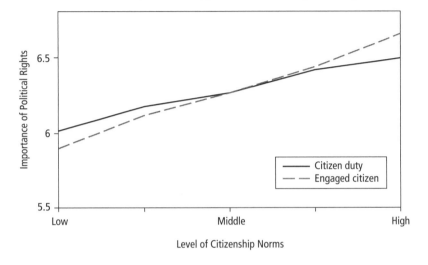

Level of Citizenship Norms

Source: 2004 International Social Survey Program for all nineteen advanced democracies.

Note: Figure entries are national mean scores on four questions of the importance of political rights in a democracy. The scale is scored: 1 = *not at all important*, to 7 = *very important*.

American political science literature, but these comparisons are often made by European scholars who think more comparatively.

Our cross-national comparisons provide little evidence of basic flaws in the American political culture, at least on the dimensions compared here. Americans are less active in elections, but they participate more frequently in many other political activities. American levels of tolerance and democratic values should be a source of reassurance about the vitality of American democracy rather than a cause of concern.

This does not mean that the American political culture is a shining model that all should emulate. There are problems and challenges that face the American public and polity. This applies to any contemporary democracy. For example, French bookstores display titles such as *France on the Brink, France in Freefall,* and *France's Suicide.* "Declinism" has become a school of thought among French intellectuals. The British democracy audit is equally critical of the state of that nation.[32] Over the last decade or more, the Japanese were offered a series of books that explained the decline of the nation. In most democracies, it seems, political analysts clamor to discuss what is wrong with politics in their nation. Such criticism is how governments and democracy improve, to be sure, but accurate criticism is the most valuable of all.

Cross-national comparisons can highlight the strengths and weaknesses of a country while domestic analysts often focus on only the negative side of the scorecard. If one compares the United States with Britain or Germany, for example, one typically sees positive and negative features of both democratic systems. Certainly there are features of the American political culture that represent potential problems for the nation, such as the low levels of voting and rising inequality in who participates. However, only by comparing the United States to other democracies can we develop a reference point for judging political realities. In comparison with other democracies, the American political culture still contains many of the values that make for vibrant democracy, and these may have even increased over the past several decades. Tocqueville would not recognize contemporary American society, but he still might conclude that his observations about the democracy in America generally hold true today.

THE TWO FACES OF CITIZENSHIP

> There is no doubt that democracy has lost a clear conception of
> the type of citizen it wants to create.
>
> Karl Mannheim[1]

Have you seen reruns of those old movie serials (or Saturday morning cartoons) with the heroine tied to the train rails and the threat of death looming on the horizon as the train approaches? Several leading political scientists similarly claim that the vitality of American democracy is at risk, and the risk arises from the public's dwindling civic engagement, declining political participation, and decreasing trust in government.[2] Like the heroine on the train tracks, the vitality of democracy in America is on the line, and the train is rapidly approaching.

Indeed, one can see the speeding train. The American public and American polity have changed in fundamental ways over the past fifty years. We recognize these changes, and a large portion of this book has described, examined, and dissected these trends. But to restate a phrase from the introduction, "the good news is . . . the bad news is wrong." Based on the evidence presented here, I do not believe that American democracy is about to expire. America of today is very different from America of the 1950s. Different does not necessarily mean worse.[3]

A key to understanding the changing nature of the American public are the two faces of citizenship examined in this book. Citizenship in

America, and most other Western democracies, has traditionally emphasized the duties and responsibilities of a good citizen. This meant respect
for the law, paying taxes, and asking not what your country can do for
you but what you can do for your country. A "good citizen" felt a duty to
vote and support the government. Many Americans, especially older
Americans, still embrace this definition of good citizenship. The philosophical literature on citizenship advocates such norms (see Chapter 2).
Indeed, feelings of citizen duty are one of the strengths of American
democracy; they stimulate many people to participate in the political
process, contribute to the nation's needs, and encourage the social capital
that benefits the nation.

Over the past several decades, and now demonstrated over the two
waves of the General Social Survey, the public has shifted toward alternative norms of engaged citizenship. This other face of citizenship stresses
participation, but in a more direct, action-oriented, and collective framework. This other "good citizen" engages in a variety of social and political
activities beyond elections (and often views elections and parties negatively). Engaged citizens put less stress on maintaining the social order,
and they emphasize the need for autonomy and skepticism of government. Engaged citizenship stimulates a concern for the condition of
those who are less well off, both in America and globally.

Many readers will see elements of themselves in both descriptions.
Tom Brokaw's poetic praise of the "Greatest Generation" and their values
reflects many of the positive aspects of citizen duty and its beneficial contributions to the nation.[4] In contrast, engaged citizenship is more common among members of Generation X and the Millennial generation. In
public presentations I humorously suggest social markers for these two
sets of citizenship norms.[5] If you prefer vinyl records, like Frank Sinatra,
don't cross the street when the light is red, pay your taxes promptly and
fully, and answer the letter to serve on a jury, you are probably a duty-
based citizen. If you have all your songs in the cloud, listen to the most
recent Grammy winners, cross streets on the red if there isn't traffic, don't
vote but work as a civic volunteer, and worry as much about the fate of the
world as the fate of your city, then you probably lean toward norms of
engaged citizenship. Neither description is completely accurate nor exclu-
sive, but they tap the essence of these two different faces of citizenship.

The crisis-of-democracy literature misdiagnoses the current situation because it focuses on the negative consequences of the shifting balance of these two norms, without paying sufficient attention to the full pattern of change. The decline in citizen duty will strain certain aspects of our current democratic process, but there are also positive consequences of lower levels of citizen duty. In addition, American society and politics can benefit from a growth of engaged citizenship among the public, but there are also negative consequences of these norms. Perhaps the greatest risk to democracy is missing the full nature of the changes that are transforming the American polity—both positive and negative—and thus advocate reforms to recreate the behaviors of a bygone age that was not as idyllic as some now claim.

BALANCING THE AMERICAN POLITICAL CULTURE

Gabriel Almond described it as the Goldilocks theory of a democratic political culture.[6] A stable democratic society benefits from a civic culture that balances a mix of traits. For instance, good democratic citizenship needs allegiance to the state and obedience to the lawful decisions of government. Good democratic citizenship also requires that people participate in politics and challenge the government to represent their interests and fulfill their democratic responsibilities. Too much of the former pattern of citizenship leads to a deferential and potentially passive citizenry, where government may become unresponsive to its citizens, or worse. Too much of the latter may produce a system where division and political conflict could impede even a well-intentioned government from providing for the collective good. Democracy benefits from a Goldilocks political culture, which is neither too hot nor too cold, too hard nor too soft, too allegiant nor too assertive. Tocqueville said it more poetically: "To love democracy, it is necessary to love it moderately."

Democratic theory and political culture studies recognize this need for balancing diverse elements of a democratic system. In principle, people might accept both value sets and find their own balance—understanding how order has to be balanced against autonomy and how minority and majority interests must be balanced. While individuals do hold a mix of both norms, they tend to emphasize one pattern or another. Almond and Verba, for instance, maintained that some people thought of themselves as fulfilling a subject role and others a more participatory role.[7] Some people think of themselves as centrists, but most people either have a liberal or conservative identity. In other words, the balance in a democratic political culture often arises from different people following distinct sets of norms—and articulating the importance of their views of citizenship—and then society and the polity reflect the relative weight of these distinct groups.

Duty-based Citizenship. If we look back to the electorate of the 1950s, the balance was heavily weighted toward the norms of citizen duty. There are certainly positive consequences of these norms. Citizen duty encourages people to vote and participate in elections as an expression of citizenship and not just an instrumental means to influence government policy. Duty-based citizenship reinforces allegiance to government and the state and features strong feelings of patriotism and national pride. Many of Robert Putnam's examples of the positive aspects of community in America—participating in elections, paying taxes, obeying the law, and supporting the government—reflect these norms of duty.[8] Indeed, when contemporary analysts and politicians decry the decline of citizenship in America, they are often saying that the erosion of duty-based norms is undermining these positive features.

However, these experts sometimes overlook the potential negative consequences of duty-based citizenship, as described in this book. Citizen duty discourages autonomous political action, especially contentious activity such as protests or direct action. Certainly protests challenge the government and disrupt political tranquility. Yet, if one looks back on the past several decades of American politics (or further), there are many examples of our nation benefitting because some citizens were willing to protest against government policy. Democracy requires a citizenry that can be assertive as well as supportive.

Similarly, citizen duty reinforces a majoritarian view of society that sometimes can be carried to excess: individuals should conform, social order is important, dissidence is undesirable, and unconventional groups should not be tolerated. The lower support for democratic values, civil liberties, and political tolerance among individuals high in citizen duty isn't a positive feature of these norms. Majority rights are part of the democratic equation, but an unqualified stress on majority rule can weaken true democracy. In other words, citizen duty may sometimes give elites too much latitude in their actions when they should be challenged and limit minority rights when they should be tolerated or embraced.

Engaged Citizenship. Engaged citizenship counterbalances some of the patterns of duty-based citizenship.[9] Engaged citizens have a broader definition of political participation, and they are especially drawn to civic action and more direct forms of participation. These activities empower the citizenry. Protests by Occupy Wall Street, the Tea Party, and other political movements are signs of the vitality of democracy, even if we disagree with some of their policies. When young people volunteer in a community organization, join Teach for America, or do acts of political consumerism, this is democracy at work.

Often the critics claim that these new patterns of citizenship are examples of individualism and self-centered indulgence. Young engaged citizens, goes this thinking, are too concerned about their rights and their own well-being. Thoughtful social scientists have warned about the decline of duty and the rise of individualism for these reasons. Frances Fukuyama, for instance, cautioned that a "society dedicated to the constant upending of norms and rules in the name of increasing individual freedom of choice will find itself increasingly disorganized, atomized, isolated, and incapable of carrying out common goals and tasks."[10]

However, this stereotype of the self-centered, even selfish new citizen does not jibe with the concern for others that is central to engaged citizenship (see Chapter 2). Engaged citizenship has a broader view of social responsibility than the old norms of citizen duty. This orientation shows in the policy concerns and the behavior of engaged citizens.

Let me offer one final illustration by stepping beyond the political realm to examine examples of civic volunteerism that are nonpolitical in nature. The 2005 CDACS survey asked four questions about volunteerism to test the civic spirit of Americans:

- Are you registered as an organ donor?
- Have you donated blood in the last five years?

- Have you given to charity in the last year?
- Have you picked up someone else's litter in the last year?

These are examples of the positive, social concern that Tocqueville and Putnam would admire, doing good works for the society at large. Figure 9.1 shows that both norms of citizenship encourage such civic virtue. However, duty-based citizenship has a weak impact on volunteerism. One's duty to obey the law and vote in elections does not carry over into broader forms of social engagement. Ironically, then, the renewal of duty-based norms—which is often the message of contemporary pundits—may not produce the civic results they seek. In contrast, those who score high on engaged citizenship are about twice as likely as those at the low end of the scale to do at least three of these volunteer

FIGURE 9.1   Doing "Good Works"

▶ *Citizen duty slightly increases the level of social good works, but engaged citizenship even more strongly encourages these activities.*

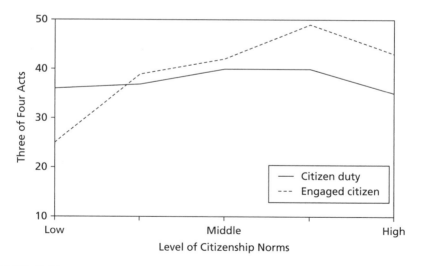

Source: 2005 CDACS Survey.

Note: Figure presents the percentage who have done at least three of the following activities: registered as an organ donor, donated blood, given to charity, or picked up litter in a public place.

activities. This may explain why various studies point to an increase in volunteerism and civic action in America, even while conventional electoral participation is decreasing.[11]

Equally important, engaged citizenship encourages a deeper commitment to democratic values, tolerance toward political groups (of both the left and right), and civil liberties over social order. Engaged citizenship is also more inclusive in attitudes toward minorities and immigrants. These sentiments are joined by strong social concerns, expressed as policies to take care of those at need at home and abroad. Thus, the engaged citizen wants more government spending on a range of social programs. For them, government is a solution to society's problems.

At the same time, engaged citizenship has potential negative effects. A disaffection for political parties and elections leads many otherwise engaged citizens to sit home on Election Day. Since elections determine the make-up of governments and the broad parameters of public policy, absence from the voting booth substantially limits engaged citizens' impact in ways that are inconsistent with the logic of political engagement. If young people and engaged citizens voted at equal rates as duty-based citizens, for example, the outcome of several past elections would have changed, affecting policy as a result.[12] Engaged citizens might not have to protest so frequently or lobby so heavily for policy preferences like environmental protection and health care for the poor if they acted to elect candidates more sympathetic to these causes in the first place.

Similarly, feelings of political distrust and alienation can discourage the activities that are essential for democracy to function as a social contract between citizens and their government. For instance, engaged citizens will often comply less with the government when their own views differ from official government policies.[13] This might be as trivial as crossing a street on a red light, but it also includes paying taxes, filling out census forms, not exploiting government programs, or even taking a job in the public sector. At the same time, these individuals expect the government to pursue a more active policy agenda. Without more acceptance of government, and the compromises required by democratic politics, political dissatisfaction can erode the democratic social contract.

So both aspects of citizenship have positive and negative features. We would not want a polity comprised solely of duty-based citizens any more than we would want only engaged citizens. Democracy functions best when there is a diversity of values within the general framework of democratic citizenship. Many previous writers have stressed this need for balance in various aspects of a democratic civic culture—my argument simply extends this logic to norms of good citizenship.

If we look back to the 1950s, with the hindsight of more than six decades of U.S. history, the balance of citizenship during that period was heavily weighted toward citizen duty. Americans may have been too allegiant, too deferential, too intolerant, and too majoritarian in their citizenship norms. Thus, when the balance of citizenship norms changed, pundits and politicians expressed concern over a perceived risk to democracy—simply because the values identified with an earlier era of American politics were changing.

Despite what these critics say, American political culture has achieved something closer to a Goldilocks balance. The contemporary American public is now more engaged, more tolerant, and more aware of minority rights, and this has strengthened democracy in America.

One might ask if the trend toward engaged citizenship has shifted the balance too much, encouraging Americans to be too critical, too skeptical, and too assertive. This is a valid concern, but it is different from the one raised by critics who insist we should return to a bygone era. Instead we should observe how governments and other political actors respond to these changes in citizenship norms. If we can first correctly understand how norms are changing, then the polity can adapt to accentuate the positive features of norm shift and lessen the negative features. More on this in the last section of this chapter.

UNDERSTANDING MILLENNIALS

One of the most surprising features of writing this book was to see the nearly universal pessimism of older political analysts toward today's youth. Even many young people seem persuaded by the negative characterizations and join this critical bandwagon.[14] Psychologist Jean Twenge has recently written about the psychological tendencies of *Generation Me*.[15] She argues that young Americans are excessively self-indulgent to the point of narcissism, individualistic and oblivious to social rules, materialistic, and sad and depressed by their situation. Twenge sees celebrities like Lindsay Lohan, Justin Bieber, and self-obsessed contestants on *American Idol* as representative of today's youth. Twenge is obviously talking to different people than those interviewed in the surveys presented here.

Citizenship norms are changing, and generations are the vehicle for these changes. The young are different from their elders. But in these differences lay positive potentials as well as negative challenges for the democracy process. It is too easy for older American citizens to complain that younger Americans aren't like them and that democracy will suffer because of it. The evidence presented here offers a corrective to narrow claims that young Americans should be like their parents (or better yet, their grandparents) and suggests that democracy will be strengthened by their very differences.

The Millennial generation is the most educated generation in American history, educated by the best university system in the world, with access to an amazing array of information, a more cosmopolitan life experience, and a standard of living unimaginable by their grandparents at a similar stage in life. And they have benefited from the experiences of their elders (even if they loathe to admit this). Looked at in these terms, we should look forward with hope to the entry of these young people into the American electorate.

Similarly, young Americans subscribe to a range of values and behaviors that should benefit the democratic process. They are more supportive of autonomy and social solidarity as norms of citizenship and more supportive of participation beyond elections. Younger generations are also more politically tolerant and more likely to favor the protection of civil liberties. They are also more likely to endorse strong democratic norms. These traits hardly sound like a threat to the democratic order.

Why, then, is there such widespread negativity toward young Americans? There are three possible reasons. First, the criticism is partially based on the erosion of duty-based citizenship among the young, and analysts' awareness of the positive traits linked to these norms. Since citizen duty is linked to actions such as voting in elections and patriotic behavior, the decline of these behaviors is easily recognized and lamented. And when many young Americans act on their values—such as not voting, using Jon Stewart's *Daily Show* as a political touchstone, and trusting a favorite celebrity more than their elected representatives—this challenges the duty-based sensibilities of their elders. In many ways, young people clearly do not act like their grandparents, and researchers focus on the negative examples that are readily apparent.

Second, the criticism of the young (and the praise of their elders) partially overlooks the positive consequences of engaged citizenship that we find among the young. Part of the corrective of this book is to draw attention to both the positive and negative aspects of generational change. Even when these positive traits are realized, however, they are often discounted as expressions of self-interest or self-indulgence. Yet the measures of volunteerism in Figure 9.1 decrease with age. It isn't that the young are apathetic and unconcerned about politics—they are often involved and they show their concern in different ways than their elders. It isn't that the young are disaffected and cynical about politics—they are cynical about politicians and how the political system currently functions, but supportive of the democratic ideal.

Thus, the current challenge for American democracy isn't to convince young people to act like their grandparents, but to understand their changing values and norms, and respond in ways that integrate them into the political process—and potentially change the process to match this new electorate better.

Third, it may be the way of nature for old people to complain about the young. And then when the Millennial Generation gets older, they may complain about the new youth culture. Old people complain about the young: news at eleven. I say this partially with tongue in cheek, but this pattern is so common throughout history and across societies that one might wonder if this is a normal part of aging and social development. But if the young were exactly like their elders, this might indicate social stagnancy.

TOCQUEVILLE REVISITED

In addition to describing norm shift within America, I also followed Tocqueville's example to compare American norms and behaviors with those of other democratic publics (see Chapter 8).

At one level, these cross-national comparisons show that norm shift isn't unique to America but is occurring in other affluent democracies. Youth in Sweden, Germany, Australia, and other nations also differ from their elders in similar ways. This implies that the unique features of American history aren't the driving force in the process of norm shift because generations are also changing in nations that did not experience the uniquely American experiences of the past fifty years. Instead, norm shift evolves from the broad processes of social modernization that I summarized in Chapter 1. Economic growth, rising educational levels, and the reshaping of life experiences are producing a similar norm shift across the affluent democracies. A large body of research on basic social values argues that citizens are shifting to postmaterial and self-expressive values that are analogous to the norm shift described here.[16] In short, the United States isn't alone in experiencing a shift from duty-based norms to engaged citizenship, and thus the implications of this book's findings broadly apply to other affluent democracies.

Moreover, Welzel and Dalton recently examined the relationship of citizenship with government accountability and effectiveness across more than eighty nations.[17] Allegiant orientations may be related to effective government; deferential, supportive citizens may make it easier for government to make the trains run on time and perform other activities. However, the propensity toward assertive citizenship—similar to our engaged citizens—is more strongly related to accountable and effective government. To be effective and be accountable, citizens have to make demands on their democratic governments. The deferential citizen of the 1950s was ruled by the government, when the relationship should run in the opposite direction.

At another level, these cross-national comparisons allow us to judge the state of the American political culture relative to other democracies. If the political culture indicates the underlying health of a democracy, the United States appears to be relatively well off. I found few signs that the American political culture was noticeably less democratic than other nations. With the exception of elections, Americans remain a highly participatory public, especially in the types of collective action that Tocqueville most admired. Americans are strikingly positive in terms of political tolerance and, much like other democratic nations, strikingly positive in support of democratic values. Even the social concerns of Americans aren't as materialistic and individualistic as are often assumed.

Perhaps the cynics will claim that all democracies are at risk, so comparisons to the other unhealthy cases isn't relevant. I think a more reasonable conclusion is that the American political culture has retained—and even strengthened—many of the democratic elements that Tocqueville once admired. Moreover, most other advanced industrial democracies are also improving. A participatory public of critical citizens who display growing levels of political tolerance and social concern are positive signs, showing us the benefits of changing citizenship norms to the advancement of the democratic ideal.

NORM SHIFT AND AMERICAN DEMOCRACY

I wish I could conclude with a list of reforms to "fix" the American public and the democratic process. But I can't. In part, it isn't clear to me that American public and/or democracy is broken and therefore needs fixing. I am not a Pollyanna when it comes to politics. Certainly we have problems, and there are major challenges to maintaining a democratic order and developing it further. In many ways, however, American democracy is stronger today than during the 1950s and 1960s and undoubtedly over the pre-WWII years. In addition, if we accept that the social modernization processes transformed citizenship norms, then we cannot recreate the norms and behaviors of another age even if we wanted to—nor should we want to recreate them. Calls for renewing traditional norms of citizen duty seem near-sighted and doomed to failure because the changing balance of citizenship norms reflects the restructuring of American society and social relations in a broad scale.

The first step in getting the right answers is to ask the right questions. The current democratic challenge does not arise because Americans are now disinterested in politics or lacking in civic spirit. We should not be asking how we can turn back the clock, restore the norms of citizen duty, and change the underlying values of the American public—although this is the refrain from the democracy-at-risk chorus. Instead, we should be asking a different question: *How does the democratic process adjust to changing norms in order to mitigate the problems and maximize the bene-fits that result?*

If you accept that norm shift is an enduring feature of American politics, then we can outline four examples of how the political process might adapt to the shifting balance of citizenship norms.

A first area of change involves parties and elections. In the United States and most other affluent democracies, participation in elections is decreasing and public trust in parties and government officials is declining. This trend diminishes the democratic process and erodes the political influence of those who forsake electoral politics. However, these analyses are often based on the misdiagnosis that Americans, and especially the young, are politically disengaged and so require a restoration of that sense of civic duty. For instance, one commonly advocated reform is to make voting compulsory—even President Obama has speculated about this idea.[18] Is this really the Jeffersonian vision of the democratic process? Such a regressive enforcement of citizenship duty is unlikely to resonate with those who hold norms of engaged citizenship. The democratic challenge is to think in new ways, to more successfully integrate these new norms into the electoral process.

If we want to increase electoral participation among the young, we should offer reforms that are embedded in a framework of engaged citizenship rather in older models of citizen duty. Just as parties adjust their turnout strategy for minority voters, the elderly, and union workers, they are more likely to involve young Americans through themes and approaches that appeal to youthful interests. For instance, parties could develop campaigns to show how elections can impact issues for which youth now volunteer. Political parties have tended to ignore the youth vote in their programs, campaigns, and even advertising, but these patterns can be reversed.[19] A variety of initiatives from MTV's *Rock the Vote* to the New Voters Project to philanthropic foundations have taken innovative steps to engage the young in elections. Barack Obama forcefully demonstrated the potential of this approach in the 2008 presidential primaries when he spoke to youth about their issues, and youth participation soared. Indeed, since the nadir in 1996, youth turnout has risen more than turnout among the over-30 crowd—so perhaps we have to start debating the poor citizenship of older Americans.

The situation of the young is also often ignored in discussions of electoral reform. For example, a report by the American Political Science Association offered a long list of policy reforms to re-engage Americans in elections process, but it did not mention Internet voting[20] or opening the government to online netizens.[21] Youth live in the digital age; politicians and political parties lag behind.

The burden of voter registration falls most heavily on the young because they must initially register and are more mobile early in life. In March of 2015 Oregon became the first state to institute automatic, universal voter registration for its citizens. This practice is common in European democracies and should have been enacted all over the United States long ago. Instead, some state governments are actively trying to purge voter rolls or limit voter registration, and these initiatives have a disproportionate effect on young people because of their greater mobility. Partisan attacks on the one-person one-vote principle are a real risk to democracy. We should be trying to get more people to vote, rather than just the subset who will vote for one party or the other.

Even more challenging is the need to integrate people with engaged citizenship norms into partisan politics beyond casting a vote. Parties are essential institutions of democratic governance, and it is difficult to imagine how democracy can function without them. However, engaged citizens often see political parties as dinosaurs. For instance, when my former political science department set up a student internship program, students were eager to intern with a public interest group; but there was less interest in working for a political party—even if it was the party they supported.

Political parties have to change if they want to be successful in the new political climate. Political parties have to show that they are as politically relevant and effective as nongovernmental organizations—and as rewarding to their participants. Party leaders and elected officials need to think about how to demonstrate the continuing relevance of parties in new and creative ways. For example, the retired prime ministers of Canada hosted a reality TV show, *The Next Prime Minister*, that selected a young person with the best ideas for improving the nation. In 2009 the ZDF television network aired a similar program on becoming chancellor of

Germany. Each year British youth elect 600 members of a Youth Parliament that meets in the House of Commons and debates a political agenda focused on youth.[22] The winner of the TV programs did not get to be prime minister or chancellor, but these programs help launch careers in public service for many of the participants.

Second, norm shift implies that politics will be more contentious. The pattern of a loyal, passive, and deferential culture is decreasing. There are likely to be tensions between these different norms of citizenship and how they are translated into political action and public policy. For example, is government the solution to policy problems or the source of those problems? This is a basic issue that divides duty-based and engaged citizens. In addition, engaged citizenship encourages a more challenging orientation toward government. They are more likely to use contentious forms of direct action, act less deferential toward elites, and be more assertive in claiming their individual rights. Perhaps it is no wonder why politicians look back longingly to an earlier, more docile American public, but the current question is how to adapt to these new patterns. These shifts may have contributed to the erosion of political comity and impressions of increased polarization. Thus, the second challenge is to define new ways of moderating tensions and contentiousness so that it does not impede democratic decision making.

Third, norm shift also implies that people will connect to their government in new ways, such as through direct action as well as public interest groups. We need to ask how this will happen and what the consequences are. For instance, the increased demands for political access are already prompting governments to open new channels for the public to express their concerns ("interest articulation").[23] These new channels—such as the expansion of referendums and initiatives, public-access administrative hearings, direct contact with policy makers, mini-deliberative publics, and new access through the courts—are perhaps as significant as the populist reforms that transformed American democracy in the early 1900s. Parallel reforms are occurring in other established democracies.[24] This is a beneficial development because voice and access are important elements of a strong democratic process.

But institutional reforms often have unintended consequences. As we experience ongoing institutional reforms, we must consider how these new forms of access alter the democratic process. For example, as interests proliferate and gain greater political voice through new forms of access, it becomes more challenging to reach a collective solution to political questions. We are developing a system of complex governance with multiple access points and decision-making nodes. Thus, the result is increased articulation of interests (more voice) but less aggregation and comparison of interests (the balancing of contending voices). Political parties initially provided such interest aggregation as mass democracy first developed, and groups within the party negotiated on a common governing program. This worked well when electoral democracy was the dominant channel of both voice and interest aggregation. However, as the role of parties has declined within the contemporary political process, and voice and the venues for political articulation have increased, the aggregation process has weakened. Good democratic politics is based on a reasonable judgment among contending voices, not just who can clamor the loudest for their interests. Today, we need new institutional structures to find ways to aggregate interests into coherent public policy.

Finally, changes in the mix of political activity raise new questions about the equality of citizen influence. Voting provides a clear-cut equality: one person, one vote. The new forms of participation (protests, petitions, community activism, and so on) are marked by great variance among individuals based on their education levels, skills, resources, and political sophistication.[25] This has real implications for the voices expressed within the political process. For example, when people organize to prevent polluting industries or to gain government benefits, those with higher education and political skills are likely to have greater voice. The "politically rich" may become even richer using these new forms of action. Simultaneously, those without these same resources may lose influence, and democracy will suffer as a result. Consequently, a change in the mix of political participation can increase the inequality of different sectors of society.[26] Yet in other areas—such as political tolerance—norm shift may decrease social status differences. So the question isn't how to deal with a disinterested and apathetic public, but how to allow for expanding citizen voice while monitoring how norm shift affects inequality in participation, political values, and other political behaviors.

In summary, I do not believe that democracy is at risk in America, unless we reject our own traditions and the positive values represented in the norms of engaged citizenship. This isn't a time for cynicism and retrenchment. It should be a time of democratic reform and expansion. There can be a renewed spirit of our age, and it is reflected not in the rhetoric of most Washington politicians or political scientists, but in those outside Washington who are more sensitive to the changing norms of citizenship.

When he visited the University of California, Irvine, for the 2014 commencement, President Barack Obama spoke of this positive potential of youth for American democracy:

> I think this generation of young people is super underrated. In your young lives, you've seen dizzying change, from terror attacks to economic turmoil; from Twitter to Tumblr. Some of your families have known tough times during the course of the worst economic crisis since the Great Depression. You're graduating into a still-healing job market, and some of you are carrying student loan debt that you're concerned about. And yet, your generation—the most educated, the most diverse, the most tolerant, the most politically independent and the most digitally fluent in our history—is also on record as being the most optimistic about our future. And I'm here to tell you that you are right to be optimistic.
>
> . . . this generation—this 9/11 generation of soldiers; this new generation of scientists and advocates and entrepreneurs and altruists— you're the antidote to cynicism. It doesn't mean you're not going to get down sometimes. You will. You'll know disillusionment. You'll experience doubt. People will disappoint you by their actions. But that can't discourage you. Cynicism has never won a war, or cured a disease, or started a business, or fed a young mind, or sent men into space. Cynicism is a choice. Hope is a better choice.
>
> Hope is what gave young soldiers the courage to storm a beach and liberate people they never met. Hope is what gave young students the strength to sit in and stand up and march for women's

rights, and civil rights, and voting rights, and gay rights, and immigration rights. Hope is the belief, against all evidence to the contrary, that there are better days ahead, and that together we can build up a middle class, and reshape our immigration system, and shield our children from gun violence, and shelter future generations from the ravages of climate change. Hope is the fact that, today, the single largest age group in America is 22 year olds who are all just itching to reshape this country and reshape the world. And I cannot wait to see what you do tomorrow.[27]

If the American polity responds to this generational shift in the norms of citizenship, the democratic ideal can be even stronger.

APPENDIX: STATISTICAL PRIMER

Anyone who reads the news knows that the media regularly report public opinion poll results. Because this information is often displayed in tables and graphs, an informed citizen needs to understand how to read and interpret them.

This book offers similar analyses of public opinion. I often present the relationship between two or more public opinion questions to determine the causes of citizen norms or the effects of these norms on political behavior. For example, what factors influence the levels of citizen duty or engaged citizenship, or how do these two types of citizenship norms affect political participation? We might compare the percentage of people who voted or the average score on opinions of government. These relationships may be shown in graphic terms. Figure 7.5, for example, shows that higher levels of citizen duty increase support for majority rights, but higher levels of engaged citizenship increase support for minority rights.

Implicitly, at least, there is a presumption of causality. For example, when citizen duty is related to higher turnout, we presume that this is because duty-based norms encourage people to vote as part of their civic duty.

Often tables and figures include lots of comparisons, such as many levels of education or many levels of church attendance—and it can become difficult to see the overall pattern amid a blur of numbers. In such cases I use correlation statistics to summarize relationships. Even if you are not numerically inclined, statistics are tools to help you understand relationships. These correlations summarize the extent to which answers on one survey question (such as levels of education) are related to answers on another question (such as whether someone voted).

Statisticians might feel faint after reading the quick summaries that follow and from the limited attention devoted to the assumptions underlying the use of these statistics. Statistics is a complex field, and data analysis can be a very complicated research methodology. Nevertheless, this primer provides a quick reference guide on how to use the statistics presented in the book, with the hope that it helps you understand the presentation of findings.

CORRELATION STATISTICS

I most commonly use three types of correlations:

- **Cramer's *V* correlation.** This correlation measures the relationship between two variables when at least one of them is a "categoric" variable, that is, just a set of categories with no distinct order. An example of a categoric variable would be region, race, religious denomination, or any measure that does not follow a natural order from low to high, agree to disagree, or some other underlying order. Racial differences in citizenship norms in Figure 3.4 is a categoric example.
- **Pearson's *r* or Tau-b correlation.** These correlations measure the relationship between two variables when both have an ordered pattern of categories, such as from low to high or from agree to disagree. This correlation statistic is more powerful and demanding than Cramer's *V* because it does not just see if categories differ on the predicted variable but presumes an ordered pattern to these differences. For example, citizen duty and engaged citizenship have different relationships with various elements of national pride (Figure 7.5).

These correlations also measure the *direction* of a relationship because there is a distinction between higher and lower values. For instance, citizen duty increases voting turnout, but the same norms decrease participation in demonstrations. The first example would produce a positive correlation, and the second a negative correlation.

- **Regression coefficient** (*b*). This statistic is the most complex. Often we want to examine the relationship between two variables, but we think this relationship might partially depend on another variable(s). Multiple regression is a statistical method to simultaneously examine the relationships of several variables with a dependent variable, so that we can assess the separate effects of each predictor variable. The regression coefficient describes the relationship between each predictor and dependent variable, while statistically controlling for the other predictors in the model. For instance, what is the effect of engaged citizenship on protesting while simultaneously controlling for (or statistically removing) the fact that engaged citizens are younger and better educated, which can also influence participation patterns.

This book presents standardized regression coefficients from several such regression analyses (see Figure 3.8 and Table 4.2). These coefficients are comparable to the Pearson *r* and are calculated in a similar way. They signify the direction and strength of a relationship. The regression coefficient indicates how much a predictor variable has an influence *while controlling for the other predictors in the model.*

A simple example shows the logic of regression analysis. We begin with the question of whether engaged citizenship is related to higher participation in protest activity. Figure A.1 shows there is a strong relationship between these two traits.

If we stopped here, we would conclude that engaged citizenship stimulates people to participate in challenging political activities, such as demonstrations. The Pearson correlation between these two variables is a substantial .22. But a skeptic might ask if this result is because of the norms of engaged citizenship or because these individuals also possess other traits—younger age, higher education, and higher cognitive skills—that might be the real source of this relationship.

You already know the answer to this question if you have correctly interpreted Table 4.2. This table presents a regression analysis in which engaged citizenship is used to predict participation in demonstrations while statistically controlling for differences attributable to age, education, cognitive skills, and the other predictors. The regression coefficient

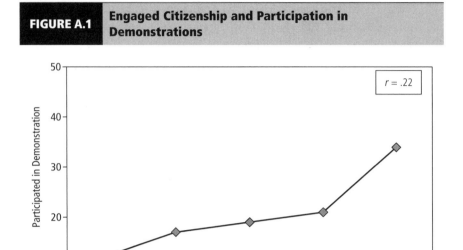

FIGURE A.1   **Engaged Citizenship and Participation in Demonstrations**

Source: 2004 and 2014 General Social Surveys combined.

(β) of .14 indicates that the effect of engaged citizenship is still important even when these other factors are taken into account. In other words, it is citizenship norms, rather than these other predictors, that produced the basic relationship in Figure A.1.

WHAT IS BIG?

Correlations summarize the strength of the relationship between two variables, which raises the question of what a strong relationship is versus a weak relationship. I chose the correlations in this text because they give comparable values for similar relationships, even if they are calculated differently:

• **Cramer's *V* correlation**. This statistic ranges from a value of 0.0 when there are no differences across categories (that is, each group in a table has the same distribution on the dependent variable) to a value of 1.00 when categories in a table differ by a maximum possible 100 percent. Typically, we interpret coefficients of .10 or less as a weak relationship, .10–.20 as a modest relationship, and .20 or larger as a strong relationship.

- **Pearson's *r* or Tau-b correlation.** These statistics measure three properties that are apparent in Figure A.1: (1) how strongly one variable predicts differences in the dependent variable (in Figure A.1 this means how steep is the angle of the line describing this relationship); (2) how individuals within each category cluster around the mean score plotted in the figure, or how well the line represents the overall pattern; and (3) whether a relationship is positive or negative—for instance, citizen duty is linked to support for government security activities (a positive relationship), but engaged citizens are more critical (a negative relationship) (see Figure 5.5).

Thus, these correlations range from a value of −1.0 when there is a perfect negative relationship (a sharp negatively sloped line with all the points clustered on the line) to 0.0 when there are no differences across categories (that is, scores of the predictor variable are unrelated to the dependent variable) to a value of 1.00 when there is a perfect positive correlation. As with Cramer's *V*, we interpret coefficients of .10 or less as a weak relationship, .10–.20 as a modest relationship, and .20 or larger as a strong relationship.

- **Regression coefficient (β).** This statistic is comparable to the Pearson *r*, except that it measures the relationship between two variables while controlling for the effects shared by other variables in the model. Like the Pearson *r*, it ranges from −1.0 for a perfect negative relationship to 1.0 for a perfect positive relationship. As with the other two statistics, we interpret coefficients of .10 or less as a weak relationship, .10–.20 as a modest relationship, and .20 or larger as a strong relationship.

Statistics presented in graphs and tables can sometimes seem complex, but they are simply a shortcut for summarizing a picture like Figure A.1 that describes how much one variable is related to another.

ENDNOTES

CHAPTER 1

1. Stuart Silverstein, "More Freshmen Help Others, Survey Finds," *Los Angeles Times*, January 26, 2006.
2. Kevin Eagin et al., *The American Freshman: National Norms Fall 2013,* UCLA Higher Education Research Institute (www.heri.ucla.edu).
3. Ronald Inglehart, *Culture Shift in Advanced Industrial Society* (Princeton, NJ: Princeton University Press, 1990); Christian Welzel, *Freedom Rising: Human Empowerment and the Quest for Emancipation* (New York: Cambridge University Press, 2013); Russell Dalton, *Citizen Politics*, 6th ed. (Washington, DC: CQ Press, 2013).
4. "What's Gone Wrong with Democracy?" *The Economist,* March 1, 2014, 47.
5. Some of the most prominent examples are Alan Wolfe, *Does American Democracy Still Work?* (New Haven, CT: Yale University Press, 2006); Stephen Macedo et al., *Democracy at Risk* (Washington, DC: Brookings Institution Press, 2005); Fareed Zakaria, *The Future of Freedom: Illiberal Democracy at Home and Abroad* (New York: Norton, 2003); John Hibbing and Elizabeth Theiss-Morse, *Stealth Democracy: Americans' Beliefs about How Government Should Work* (New York: Cambridge University Press, 2002); and perhaps the most well-reasoned project, Robert Putnam, *Bowling Alone: The Collapse and Renewal of American Community* (New York: Simon and Schuster, 2000).
6. Putnam, *Bowling Alone*; Tom Brokaw, *The Greatest Generation* (New York: Random House, 1998).
7. Putnam, *Bowling Alone*, 283.
8. William Damon, "To Not Fade Away: Restoring Civil Identity among the Young," in *Making Good Citizens: Education and Civil Society,* ed. Diane Ravitch and Joseph Viteritti (New Haven, CT: Yale University Press, 2001). Also see Mark Bauerlein, *The Dumbest Generation: How the Digital Age Stupefies Young Americans and Jeopardizes Our Future (or, Don't Trust Anyone under 30)* (New York: Penguin, 2008); Martin Wattenberg, *Is Voting for the Young?* (New York: Longman, 2006); Jean Twenge, *Generation Me: Why Today's Young Americans Are More Confident, Assertive, Entitled—and More Miserable Than Ever Before* (New York: Free Press, 2006).
9. Josh Sanburn "Millennials, The Next Greatest Generation?" *Time,* May 9, 2013.
10. Inglehart, *Culture Shift in Advanced Industrial Society*; Ronald Inglehart, "Changing Values among Western Publics from 1970 to 2006," *West European Politics* 31 (2008): 130–146.
11. Cliff Zukin, Scott Keeter, Moly Andolina, Krista Jenkins, and Michael X. Delli Carpini, *A New Engagement? Political Participation, Civic Life, and the Changing American Citizen* (New York: Oxford University Press, 2006); Russell Dalton, *The Good Citizen*, rev. ed. (Washington, DC: CQ Press, 2009).
12. "The Staid Young: Oh! You Pretty Things" *Economist,* July 12, 2014.
13. Ronald Inglehart, *Culture Shift in Advanced Industrial Society*; Welzel, *Freedom Rising.*

14. Gregg Easterbrook, *The Progress Paradox: How Life Gets Better While People Feel Worse* (New York: Random House, 2003); Matt Ridley, *The Rational Optimist: How Prosperity Evolves* (New York: Harper Collins, 2010); Robert Collins, *More: The Politics of Economic Growth in Postwar America* (New York: Oxford University Press, 2002).

15. Richard Florida, *The Rise of the Creative Class—Revisited*, 2nd ed. (New York: Basic Books, 2012), 1–3.

16. Angus Campbell et al., *The American Voter* (New York: Wiley, 1960); Angus Campbell et al., *Elections and the Political Order* (New York: Wiley, 1966).

17. Morley Winograd and Michael Hais, *Millennial Momentum: How a New Generation Is Remaking America* (New Brunswick, NJ: Rutgers University Press, 2011); Paul Taylor, *The Next America: Boomers, Millennials, and the Looming Generational Showdown* (New York: Public Affairs, 2014).

18. Neil Nevitte, *The Decline of Deference* (Petersborough, Canada: Broadview Press, 1996).

19. Robert Putnam, *Our Kids: The American Dream in Crisis* (New York: Simon and Schuster, 2015), discusses a widening opportunity gap between affluent and disadvantaged youth.

20. Norman Nie, Jane Junn, and Kenneth Stehlik-Barry, *Education and Democratic Citizenship in America* (Chicago: Chicago University Press, 1996).

21. Samuel Popkin, *The Reasoning Voter* (Chicago: University of Chicago Press, 1991).

22. James Flynn, *What Is Intelligence?* (Cambridge, UK: Cambridge University Press, 2007); Steven Pinker, *The Better Angels of Our Nature: Why Violence Has Declined* (New York: Viking, 2011), 650–660.

23. Benjamin I. Page and Lawrence R. Jacobs, *Class War? What Americans Really Think about Economic Inequality* (Chicago: University of Chicago Press, 2009); Peter Drucker, *Post-Capitalist Society* (New York: Harper Business, 1993). The comparative politics literature notes a similar development in most other Western democracies, labeling this group as the "new middle class" or the "salatariat." Oddbjørn Knutsen, *Class Voting in Western Europe* (Lanham, MD: Lexington Books, 2006).

24. Florida, *The Rise of the Creative Class*, 77–80.

25. Florida, *The Rise of the Creative Class*, ch. 3.

26. The ANES is a major election study project that I use throughout this book (http://www.election studies.org/). I did not include retirees in this figure because their prior employment status was often ambiguous, and the number choosing this retirement category rises significantly over this five-decade span. If retirement is meant to imply previous employment, then the trends in Figure 1.4 are even sharper.

27. The Center for American Women and Politics (www.cawp.rutgers.edu) reports that only twenty-six women were members of the 83rd U.S. Congress in 1953, and by the 113th Congress (elected in 2012) this had increased to ninety-nine women. Twenty-three women held statewide elective offices in 1969; this increased to seventy-three in 2013. In 1971, there were 244 women in all the state legislatures combined, and by 2014 this increased to 1,789—a seven-fold increase.

28. Katherine Tate, *From Protest to Politics: The New Black Voters in American Elections* (Cambridge, MA: Harvard University Press, 1993).

29. Daniel Bell, *Postindustrial Society* (New York: Free Press, 1973); Ronald Inglehart, *The Silent Revolution* (Princeton, NJ: Princeton University Press, 1977); Inglehart, *Culture Shift in Advanced Industrial Society*.

30. Michael Shermer, "Life Has Never Been So Good for Our Species," *Los Angeles Times*, April 30, 2010; see also Easterbrook, *The Progress Paradox*.

31. There is a tendency, however, to idealize the past, implying that Americans had access to more and better information in the past, when newspaper readership was higher and television was still uncommon; Putnam, *Bowling Alone*; Wattenberg, *Is Voting for Young People?* Certainly access to information is much greater today than in the 1950s; this seems indisputable.

32. The citizenship battery was included in the 2004 and 2014 General Social Survey (GSS) as part of the ISSP module on Citizenship. We use the 2004 International Social Survey for the cross-national comparisons; the 2014 ISSP module should be available sometime in 2016. I thank the principal investigators and the ICPSR and GESIS archives for providing these data; all the interpretations and analyses are my responsibility.

33.   I appreciate the Center for Democracy and Civil Society and Marc Howard for sharing these data. The CDACS survey replicated a battery of citizenship questions asked in the 2002 European Social survey. In-person interviews were conducted with 1,001 American respondents between May 16 and July 19, 2005. For additional information see http://www.icpsr.umich.edu/icpsrweb/ICPSR/studies/4607.

CHAPTER 2

1.   See, for example, Hein-Anton van der Heijden, ed., *Handbook of Political Citizenship and Social Movements* (London: Elgar, 2014); Derek Heater, *A Brief History of Citizenship* (New York: New York University Press, 2004); Derek Heater, *Citizenship: The Civic Ideal in World History, Politics and Education*, 3rd ed. (Manchester, UK: Manchester University Press, 2004).

2.   Jennifer McKnight-Trontz, *The Good Citizen's Handbook: A Guide to Proper Behavior* (San Francisco: Chronicle Books, 2001).

3.   I began my research with the rich philosophical literature on citizenship. Unfortunately, much of the recent literature is of uncertain value because it offers abstract normative arguments rather than describing reality. Few of these authors look for objective evidence to support their theorizing.

4.   Gabriel Almond and Sidney Verba, *The Civic Culture: Political Attitudes and Democracy in Five Nations* (Princeton, NJ: Princeton University Press, 1963).

5.   Aristotle, *Politics*, trans. E. Barker (Oxford: Clarendon Press, 1946), 1283b, italics added.

6.   Robert Dahl, *Democracy and Its Critics* (New Haven, CT: Yale University Press, 1989); Robert Dahl, *On Democracy* (New Haven, CT: Yale University Press, 1998); Sidney Verba, Kay Schlozman, and Henry Brady, *Voice and Equality: Civic Voluntarism in American Politics* (Cambridge, MA: Harvard University Press, 1995); Carole Pateman, *Participation and Democratic Theory* (Cambridge: Cambridge University Press, 1970).

       Even with the near universal acceptance of the mass franchise, many analysts still prescribe a narrow role for the citizen. The elitist critique of democracy typically argues that too many citizens lack the knowledge or interests to make informed decisions, and thus limited participation is desirable; Almond and Verba, *The Civic Culture*; Samuel Huntington, *American Politics: The Promise of Disharmony* (Cambridge, MA: Harvard University Press, 1981); Michael Delli Carpini and Scott Keeter, *What Americans Know about Politics and Why It Matters* (New Haven, CT: Yale University Press, 1996).

7.   Robert Putnam, *Bowling Alone: The Collapse and Renewal of American Community* (New York: Simon and Schuster, 2000); National Conference on Citizenship, *2009 Civic Health Index: Civic Health in Hard Times* (Washington, DC: National Conference on Citizenship, 2009) (www.ncoc.net); Stephen Macedo et al., *Democracy at Risk: How Political Choices Undermine Citizen Participation, and What We Can Do about It* (Washington, DC: Brookings Institution Press, 2005).

8.   Ronald Inglehart, *Culture Shift in Advanced Industrial Society* (Princeton, NJ: Princeton University Press, 1990); Wayne Baker, *America's Crisis of Values: Reality and Perception* (Princeton, NJ: Princeton University Press, 2004); Christian Welzel, *Freedom Rising* (Cambridge: Cambridge University Press, 2013).

9.   Cliff Zukin, Scott Keeter, Moly Andolina, Krista Jenkins, and Michael X. Delli Carpini, *A New Engagement? Political Participation, Civic Life, and the Changing American Citizen* (New York: Oxford University Press, 2006).

10.   U.S. Citizenship and Immigration Service, *Learn about the United States: Quick Civics Lessons for the Naturalization Test* (Washington, DC: U.S. Government Printing Office, 2014), 4.

11.   U.S. Citizenship and Immigration Service, *Learn about the United States*, 12–13. To point out a small irony, the Prussian government of the nineteenth century also stressed three norms for a "good citizen": pay your taxes, serve in the army, and keep your mouth shut. This example suggests that citizenship norms in authoritarian and democratic governments share state sovereignty as a core principle.

12.   T. H. Marshall, *Citizenship and Social Class*, ed. T. Bottomore (London: Pluto Press, 1992; originally published 1950).

13. Although this book emphasizes the modern roots of social citizenship, these concepts were part of the discussion of citizenship beginning with Aristotle. See Heater, *Citizenship*, 270–284.

14. Judith Shklar, *American Citizenship* (Cambridge, MA: Harvard University Press, 1991); D. Harris, *Justifying State Welfare* (Oxford: Blackwell, 1987); Michael Walzer, *Spheres of Justice: A Defense of Pluralism and Equality* (Oxford: Blackwell, 1983).

15. John Keene, *Global Civil Society?* (Cambridge: Cambridge University Press, 2003); Michael Walzer, ed., *Toward a Global Civil Society* (Providence, RI: Berghahn Books, 1995).

16. For example, see Putnam, *Bowling Alone*; Macedo et al., *Democracy at Risk*; Martin Wattenberg, *Where Have All the Voters Gone?* (Cambridge, MA: Harvard University Press, 2002); Tom Tyler, *Why People Obey the Law* (New Haven, CT: Yale University Press, 1990); Robert Bellah et al., *Habits of the Heart* (Berkeley: University of California Press, 1985).

17. The 1984 General Social Survey and the 1987 Swedish Citizenship Survey included some initial questions on the duties of citizenship. The 1998 Swedish Democracy Audit was the first systematic attempt to measure these norms. For additional information see Linda Bennett and Stephen Bennett, *Living with Leviathan: Americans Coming to Terms with Big Government* (Lawrence: University Press of Kansas, 1990); Olof Petersson, Anders Westholm, and Göran Blomberg, *Medborgarnas makt* (Citizen Power) (Stockholm: Carlssons, 1989), ch. 8; Olof Petersson, J. Hermansson, Michelle Micheletti, J. Teorell, and Anders Westholm, *Demokrati och Medborgarskap: Demokratiradets Rapport 1998* (Stockholm: SNS Förlag, 1998).

 The "Citizens, Involvement and Democracy" (CID) project replicated several of these items across a set of European nations in the late 1990s; and the European Social Survey (ESS) asked a subset of these items for twenty-two European nations in 2002. See Sigrid Rossteutscher, "Die Rückkehr der Tugend?" in *Deutschland in Europa*, ed. Jan van Deth (Wiesbaden: VS-Verlag, 2005); Bas Denters, Oscar Gabriel, and Mariano Torcal, "Norms of Good Citizenship," in *Citizenship and Involvement in Europe*, ed. Jan van Deth, J. Ramón Montero, and Anders Westholm (London: Routledge, 2006). The 2005 CDACS survey conducted by Georgetown University replicated parts of the 2002 ESS survey in a study of American public opinion. For additional information on the CDACS survey see Russell Dalton, *The Good Citizen*, rev. ed. (Washington, DC: CQ Press, 2009).

18. For additional information visit the ISSP website (www.issp.org).

19. The GSS asked this citizenship battery in the United States, and the same items were asked in the International Social Survey Program survey (see Chapter 8). For more information visit www.gss.norc.org.

20. Petersson et al., *Demokrati och Medborgarskap*.

21. Denters et al., "Norms of Good Citizenship."

22. The deletion of this item on military service is a major theoretical and empirical loss. Obeying the law and paying taxes are widely endorsed, providing little variance on these items. Military service received less support (see Figure 2.1) and is especially salient to the prewar "Greatest Generation." The military service item displayed the strongest relationship with age of any of the citizenship items in the 2004 survey. Either the item on military service or a question on jury duty (used in the 2005 CDACS survey) might have better captured a duty-based definition of citizenship.

23. Marshall, *Citizenship and Social Class*.

24. Raymond Wolfinger and Stephen Rosenstone, *Who Votes?* (New Haven, CT: Yale University Press, 1980), 7–8; Andre Blais, *To Vote or Not to Vote? The Merits and Limits of Rational Choice Theory* (Pittsburgh: University of Pittsburgh Press, 2000), 92.

25. U.S. Immigration and Naturalization Service, *Citizenship Education and Naturalization Information*, 11.

26. Bennett and Bennett, *Living with Leviathan*, ch. 5; Neil Nevitte, *The Decline of Deference* (Petersborough, Canada: Broadview Press, 1996); Neil Nevitte, "The Decline of Deference Revisited: Evidence after 25 Years," in *The Civic Culture Transformed*, ed. Russell Dalton and Christian Welzel (Cambridge: Cambridge University Press, 2014).

27. Wattenberg, *Where Have All the Voters Gone?*; Martin Wattenberg, *Is Voting for the Young?* (New York: Longman, 2006).

28. Benjamin Barber, *Strong Democracy: Participatory Politics for a New Age* (Berkeley: University of California Press, 1984).

29. W. Lance Bennett, Chris Wells, and Allison Rank, "Young Citizens and Civic Learning: Two Paradigms of Citizenship in the Digital Age," *Citizenship Studies* 13 (2009): 105–120; W. Lance Bennett, "Changing Citizenship in the Digital Age," in *Civic Life Online,* ed. W. Lance Bennett (Cambridge, MA: MIT Press, 2008).

30. Inglehart, *Culture Shift in Advanced Industrial Society*; Welzel, *Freedom Rising.*

31. The eta correlations of time with each item ranged from .00 to .06, with an average of .03.

32. Nevitte, *The Decline of Deference*; Nevitte, "The Decline of Deference Revisited."

33. Almond and Verba, *The Civic Culture,* 24–26.

34. Charles Merriam and Robert Merriam, *American Government* (Boston: Ginn, 1954), 805.

35. Dalton and Welzel, *The Civic Culture Transformed.*

36. I explored several principal component analyses before deciding on the results in Table 2.A. In Dalton, *The Good Citizen,* I used the 2004 survey to test for the four categories in Table 2.1. The standard cutting point based on eigenvalues greater than 1.0 yielded three dimensions, and the third dimension barely passed the normal cutting point of 1.0 (3.01, 1.32, 1.16). The second and third dimensions also had several overlapping variables. Therefore, I decided on a two-dimensional solution of the GSS items. I used a varimax rotated solution to distinguish between different aspects of citizenship. I replicated this methodology with the 2014 GSS data. Table 2.A presents the results based on combining both surveys into a single analysis. I used this principal components analysis to create component scores that are the two indices of citizenship norms used throughout this book.

37. Dalton, *The Good Citizen,* ch. 2.

CHAPTER 3

1.   In 2014 Jolie continued this unusual coupling when Queen Elizabeth of England named her as an honorary dame—the female version of a knight—for her UN work in combating sexual violence in war zones. A similar odd couple was Bono's collaboration with President George Bush on programs to address the AIDS crisis in Africa.

2.   Tom Brokaw, *The Greatest Generation* (New York: Random House, 1998); Robert Putnam, *Bowling Alone: The Collapse and Renewal of American Community* (New York: Simon and Schuster, 2000).

3.   Brokaw, *The Greatest Generation,* xix–xx.

4.   Linda Bennett and Stephen Bennett, *Living with Leviathan: Americans Coming to Terms with Big Government* (Lawrence: University Press of Kansas, 1990), 126–130.

5.   Jonathan Cohn, "A Lost Political Generation?" *The American Prospect* 3, no. 9 (March 1992).

6.   For instance, Mark Bauerlein, *The Dumbest Generation: How the Digital Age Stupefies Young Americans and Jeopardizes Our Future* (New York: Tarcher, 2008); Jean Twenge and W. Keith Campbell, *The Narcissism Epidemic: Living in the Age of Entitlement* (New York: Atria Books, 2010); William Damon, *The Moral Child* (New York: Free Press, 1990).

7.   National Conference on Citizenship, *America's Civic Health Index: Broken Engagement* (Washington, DC: National Conference on Citizenship, 2006), 8.

8.   See Ronald Inglehart, *Culture Shift in Advanced Industrial Society* (Princeton, NJ: Princeton University Press, 1990); W. Lance Bennett, Chris Wells, and Allison Rank, "Young Citizens and Civic Learning: Two Paradigms of Citizenship in the Digital Age," *Citizenship Studies* 13 (2009): 105–120.

9.   Wayne Baker, *America's Crisis of Values: Reality and Perception* (Princeton, NJ: Princeton University Press, 2004).

10. Citizenship norms are measured by component scores computed from the analyses in the appendix to Chapter 2. Because of the construction method, a value of zero equals the position of the average American. The construction method also produces two indices that are statistically unrelated to each other.

11. I coded generation in two steps. The first step defined five historical periods: Prewar (until 1945), Boomer generation (1946–1960), Sixties generation (1961–1975), Eighties generation (1976–1990),

Gen X (1991–2000), and Millennials (2000 or later). Then I assigned respondents to a generation based on the period in which they turned eighteen years of age.

12. See Dalton, *The Good Citizen*, ch. 3.

13. There are too few of the prewar generation in 2014 ($N = 14$) and too few Millennials in 2004 ($N = 58$) to yield reasonable estimates for these generations. In addition, we should be cautious about too fine a comparison because the natural variability in survey samples adds some imprecision to estimates at both times. A further caveat is that changes in the national condition may occur between surveys, moving all generations in a specific direction. Indeed, the Great Recession is such an experience, and it might have stimulated duty norms across generations compared with the 2004 GSS findings.

14. A similar figure for engaged citizenship shows the prewar generation is an outlier in the 2004 survey, but otherwise there is a similar trend toward engaged citizenship among younger generations. For contrasting evidence see M. Kent Jennings, "The Dynamics of Good *Citizenship Norms*," in *Citizenship and Democracy in an Era of Crisis*, ed. Thomas Poguntke et al. (London: Routledge, 2015).

15. Gabriel Almond and Sidney Verba, *The Civic Culture* (Princeton, NJ: Princeton University Press, 1963), 163.

16. Philip Converse, "Change in the American Electorate," in *The Human Meaning of Social Change*, ed. Angus Campbell and Philip Converse (New York: Russell Sage Foundation, 1972); Henry Milner, *Civic Literacy: How Informed Citizens Make Democracy Work* (Hanover, NH: Tufts University Press, 2002); Almond and Verba, *The Civic Culture*, ch. 6.

17. Norman Nie, Jane Junn, and Kenneth Stehlik-Barry, *Education and Democratic Citizenship in America* (Chicago: University of Chicago Press, 1996), ch. 2.

18. Almond and Verba, *The Civic Culture*, chs. 6 and 9.

19. Nie et al., *Education and Democratic Citizenship in America*, ch. 4.

20. Russell Dalton and Christian Welzel, eds., *The Civic Culture Transformed: From Allegiant to Assertive Citizens* (Cambridge: Cambridge University Press, 2014).

21. The original 2004 GSS found a weak positive correlation (+.07) between education and citizen duty; Russell Dalton, *The Good Citizen*, ch. 3. The 2005 CDACS survey found a weak negative correlation (−.05).

22. Pippa Norris and Ronald Inglehart, *A Rising Tide* (New York: Cambridge University Press, 2004).

23. Catherine Bolzendahl and Hilde Coffe, "Citizenship beyond Politics: The Importance of Political, Civil and Social Rights and Responsibilities among Women and Men," *British Journal of Sociology* 60 (2009): 764–791.

24. Bolzendahl and Coffe, "Citizenship beyond Politics"; also Norris and Inglehart, *A Rising Tide*.

25. However, women who have never married are least supportive of duty-based norms, and housekeepers score highest on citizen duty. This implies that shifts in the employment status of women (Figure 1.4) may have also changed citizenship norms. Another indication of changing gender patterns comes from generational comparisons. Women score significantly higher than average in citizen duty among older generations, but this above average score decreases and then reverses among Millennials.

26. Hilde Coffe and Catherine Bolzendahl, "Racial Group Differences in Support for Citizenship Duties and Rights in the US: Racial Differences in Citizenship Duties and Rights," *Acta Politica* 48 (2013): 47–67.

27. The "other" category is difficult to interpret because it combines racial and ethnic groups that are too small a share of the overall population to be reliably compared in separate analyses.

28. Bas Denters, Oscar Gabriel, and Mariano Torcal, "Norms of Good Citizenship," in *Citizenship and Involvement in Europe*, ed. Jan van Deth, José Ramón Montero, and Anders Westholm (London: Routledge, 2006).

29. For religious denominations, the eta correlation for citizen duty increased from .16 to .20; for engaged citizenship the eta correlation was .07 in both years.

30. The question asked: "Would you consider yourself a very strong (denomination) or a not very strong (denomination)?" The responses were (1) very strong, (2) not very strong, (3) somewhat strong, and (4) no religion.

31. This is broadly similar to the patterns that exists among European publics: Denters et al., "Norms of Good Citizenship."

32. For instance, Laver and Budge included measures of social order, morality, and social welfare in defining the Left/Right orientation of political parties in Western democracies. Michael Laver and Ian Budge, *Party Policy and Government Coalitions* (New York: St. Martin's Press, 1992).

33. Charles Merriam, *American Political Ideas, 1865–1917* (New York: MacMillan, 1923), 28.

34. For example, see David Campbell, Meira Levinson, and Frederick Hess, eds., *Making Civics Count: Citizenship Education for a New Generation* (Cambridge, MA: Harvard Education Press, 2012); James Youniss, Peter Levine, and Lee Hamilton, eds., *Engaging Young People in Civic Life* (Nashville: Vanderbilt University Press, 2009); Bennett et al., "Young Citizens and Civic Learning."

35. These analyses use a multivariate regression analyses (OLS). The model estimates the independent influence of each predictor as a beta coefficient. A positive beta coefficient indicates the predictor increases the citizenship norm, and a negative beta coefficient indicates a decrease in the norm. Coefficients significant at the .05 level are noted by an asterisk in Figure 3.8.

36. Inglehart, *Culture Shift in Advanced Industrial Society;* Christian Welzel, *Freedom Rising: Human Empowerment and the Quest for Emancipation* (Cambridge: Cambridge University Press, 2013).

37. The major measurement problem is the decline in the number of items that reflect a duty-based notion of citizenship and the overrepresentation of engaged citizenship items. The 2004 survey with the inclusion of military duty, and the 2005 CDACS survey with the inclusion of jury duty, produced a clearer structure contrasting citizen duty and engaged citizenship, and hence often stronger relationship with the correlates of citizenship norms. Nevertheless, I tried to present analyses similar to the first edition of this book so that interested readers can directly see the stability of the empirical results.

CHAPTER 4

1. Alexis de Tocqueville, *Democracy in America* (New York: Knopf, 1966), 249.

2. Sidney Verba and Norman Nie, *Participation in America* (New York: Harper and Row, 1972), 3.

3. Gabriel Almond and Sidney Verba, *The Civic Culture* (Princeton, NJ: Princeton University Press, 1963). Also see Samuel Barnes, Max Kaase, et al., *Political Action* (Beverly Hills, CA: Sage, 1979).

4. Robert Putnam, *Bowling Alone: The Collapse and Renewal of American Community* (New York: Simon and Schuster, 2000), ch. 2; Martin Wattenberg, *Where Have All the Voters Gone?* (Cambridge, MA: Harvard University Press, 2002); Janet Leighley and Jonathan Nagler, *Who Votes Now?* (Princeton, NJ: Princeton University Press, 2014); Martin Wattenberg, *Is Voting for the Young?* (New York: Longman, 2006); National Conference on Citizenship, *America's Civic Health Index: Broken Engagement* (Washington, DC: National Conference on Citizenship, 2006) (www.ncoc.net).

5. Putnam, *Bowling Alone,* 35.

6. John Hibbing and Elizabeth Theiss-Morse, *Stealth Democracy: Americans' Beliefs about How Government Should Work* (New York: Cambridge University Press, 2002), 1.

7. Wattenberg, *Is Voting for the Young?*; Jean Twenge, Elise Freeman, and W. Keith Campbell, "Generational Differences in Young Adults' Life Goals, Concern for Others, and Civic Orientation, 1966–2009)," *Journal of Personality and Social Psychology* 102 (2012): 1045–1062; Mark Bauerlein, *The Dumbest Generation: How the Digital Age Stupefies Young Americans and Jeopardizes Our Future (Or, Don't Trust Anyone under 30)* (New York: Tarcher, 2008).

8. Russell Dalton, *Citizen Politics: Public Opinion and Political Parties in Advanced Industrial Democracies,* 6th ed. (Washington, DC: CQ Press, 2013), chs. 2–4; Cliff Zukin, Scott Keeter, Moly Andolina, Krista Jenkins, and Michael X. Delli Carpini, *A New Engagement? Political Participation, Civic Life, and the Changing American Citizen* (New York: Oxford University Press, 2006); Pippa Norris, *Democratic Phoenix: Reinventing Political Activism* (Cambridge: Cambridge University Press, 2002), ch. 10; Eva Anduiza, Michael Jensen, and Laia Jorba, eds., *Digital Media and Political Engagement Worldwide* (Cambridge: Cambridge University Press, 2012); Dietlind Stolle and Michele Micheletti, *Political Consumerism* (Cambridge: Cambridge University Press, 2013).

9. Ronald Inglehart, *Modernization and Post-Modernization* (Princeton, NJ: Princeton University Press, 1997), 307.

10. Russell Dalton, *The Good Citizen*, rev. ed. (Washington, DC: CQ Press, 2009), 58.

11. Putnam, *Bowling Alone*, and Macedo et al., *Democracy at Risk*, present trends in participation in a wide variety of activities, but many of these trends are from commercial marketing polls of uncertain quality (for more recent evidence, see the last page of this chapter and note 60).

12. For example, surveys often change the time reference of the question; asking whether individuals have done an activity over the past year, two years, or longer. More common, there are subtle but significant changes in how the various forms of participation are described in different surveys or variations in the methodology of surveys.

13. Jan van Deth, "A Conceptual Map of Political Participation," *Acta Politica* 49 (2014): 349–367.

14. Wattenberg, *Where Have All the Voters Gone?*; Aina Gallego, *Unequal Political Participation Worldwide* (New York: Cambridge University Press, 2015).

15. Michael McDonald and Samuel Popkin, "The Myth of the Vanishing Voter," *American Political Science Review* 95, no. 4 (2001): 963–974. Also see McDonald's website on voting turnout: http://elections .gmu.edu.

16. Turnout is decreasing for many reasons; see Leighley and Nagler, *Who Votes Now?* The content of the election and the candidates affects turnout. In addition, presidential campaigns now focus their turnout efforts in the battleground states. Overall turnout dropped 3.5 percent from 2008 to 2012, but in the ten battleground states turnout declined by about half that amount.

17. Gallego, *Unequal Political Participation Worldwide*.

18. Rosenstone and Hansen, *Mobilization, Participation and Democracy in America*; Putnam, *Bowling Alone*, ch. 2.

19. More information is available on the project website: http://www.electionstudies.org. The ANES is an extremely high-quality survey based on in-person interviews of people selected by random probability models. There is also extensive quality control, including efforts to maximize response rates.

20. Changes in campaign finance laws have altered the way that people give money to campaigns. Table 4.1 presents those who have given money to a party in the campaign. However, other funds go directly to candidates or to political action groups. In 2004, for instance, 15 percent of the public gave to at least one of these sources, so the percentage in the table is a conservative estimate.

21. Andrew Chadwick and Philip Howard, eds., *Routledge Handbook of Internet Politics* (London: Routledge, 2008); Bruce Bimber, *Information and American Democracy* (New York: Cambridge University Press, 2003).

22. Jason Gainous and Kevin Wagner, *Rebooting American Politics: The Internet Revolution* (Lanham, MD: Rowman & Littlefield, 2011); Eva Anduiza, Michael Jensen, and Laia Jorba, eds., *Digital Media and Political Engagement Worldwide* (Cambridge: Cambridge University Press, 2012).

23. A similar question in the 2004 Comparative Study of Electoral Systems (CSES) reported that 28 percent had contacted a government official in the previous twelve months.

24. The 2004 CSES found 36 percent had taken part in a community activity during the last five years. The 2000 and 2006 Social Capital Surveys asked about community activity in the last twelve months: 38 percent had participated in 2000 and 37 percent in 2006.

25. Barnes, Kaase et al., *Political Action*; Inglehart, *Culture Shift in Advanced Industrial Society*.

26. Stolle and Micheletti, *Political Consumerism*.

27. Using slightly different questions, the 2000 and 2006 Social Capital Surveys found that 7 percent claimed to have participated in a demonstration, boycott, or march during the past year; the 2004 Comparative Study of Electoral Systems reported that 7 percent participated in a protest in the past five years.

28. Chadwick and Howard, *Routledge Handbook of Internet Politics*; Bimber, *Information and American Democracy*.

29. Jeffrey H. Birnbaum, "On Capitol Hill, the Inboxes Are Overflowing," *Washington Post*, July 11, 2005.

30. Sasha Issenberg, *The Victory Lab: The Secret Science of Winning Campaigns* (New York: Crown, 2012); John Sides and Lynn Vavreck, *The Gamble: Choice and Chance in the 2012 Presidential Election* (Princeton, NJ: Princeton University Press, 2014).

31. Gainous and Wagner, *Rebooting American Politics*; Anduiza et al., *Digital Media and Political Engagement Worldwide*.

32. Aaron Smith, Civic Engagement in the Digital Age, April 25, 2013, http://www.pewinternet.org/2013/04/25/civic-engagement-in-the-digital-age/.

33. Lee Rainie, "Social Media and Voting," Pew Center's Internet and the American Life Project, November 6, 2012, http://www.pewinternet.org/2012/11/06/social-media-and-voting/; Aaron Smith and Maeve Duggan, "Online Political Videos and Campaign 2012," Pew Center's Internet and the American Life Project, November 3, 2012, http://www.pewinternet.org/2012/11/02/online-political-videos-and-campaign-2012.

34. Norman Nie, Jane Junn, and Kenneth Stehlik-Barry, *Education and Democratic Citizenship in America* (Chicago: University of Chicago Press, 1996). They argue that education primarily marks the social stratification of the public, and thus the rise in education does not translate directly into an increase in participation. However, their analyses also show that education is related to democratic norms, much as we find in Chapter 7. This combination of education's resources component and norm component shifts the patterns of action.

35. Wattenberg, *Is Voting for the Young?*; Mark Franklin, *Voter Turnout and the Dynamics of Electoral Competition in Established Democracies since 1945* (New York: Cambridge University Press, 2004).

36. Verba and Nie, *Participation in America*.

37. William Damon, "To Not Fade Away: Restoring Civil Identity among the Young," in *Making Good Citizens*, ed. Diane Ravitch and Joseph Viteritti (New Haven, CT: Yale University Press, 2001), 123. In less polemic terms, the same sentiments have been expressed by Putnam in *Bowling Alone* and Macedo and his colleagues in *Democracy at Risk*.

38. Dalton, *Citizen Politics,* chs. 2–4; Zukin et al., *A New Engagement?*

39. Zukin et al., *A New Engagement?* 189.

40. Better educated was coded as more than twelve years of schooling. The advantage of combining both GSS surveys is that it provided enough respondents to include both the prewar generation and Millennials, as well as have more reliable estimates for each generational unit.

41. For the youngest age cohort, many are still in school or will complete additional years of schooling. Therefore, I estimated the eventual size of better/lesser educated within this cohort, rather than their present size in the survey.

42. Even the castigation of youth for their declining turnout is overstated. The turnout among the voting eligible electorate under age thirty has varied within a narrow band since 1976 (discounting the first youth enfranchisement election of 1972). Thomas Patterson, "Young Voters and the 2004 Election," www.ksg.harvard.edu/presspol/vanishvoter/.

43. Dalton, *The Good Citizen*, rev. ed., epilogue.

44. See Elizabeth Theiss-Morse, "Conceptualizations of Good Citizenship and Political Participation," *Political Behavior* 15 (1993): 355–380.

45. Raymond Wolfinger and Stephen Rosenstone, *Who Votes?* (New Haven, CT: Yale University Press, 1980), 7–8.

46. Blais, *To Vote or Not to Vote* (Pittsburgh: University of Pittsburgh Press, 2000), 92.

47. Catherine Bolzendahl and Hilde Coffe, "Are 'Good' Citizens 'Good Participants'?" *Political Studies* 61 (2013): 45–65; also Dalton, *The Good Citizen*, ch. 4.

48. The GSS asked respondents to identify the meaning of ten words; the index counts the number of right answers. Also see Nie et al., *Education and Democratic Citizenship in America*.

49. Bolzendahl and Coffe, "Are 'Good' Citizens 'Good Participants'?"

50. This measure included the two autonomy items and the two social citizenship items into a simple additive index.

51. The 2004 GSS included questions on parties encouraging activism and support for referendums. Engaged citizens are slightly disapproving of the former and approving of the latter. Also see Chapter 7.

52. Verba and Nie, *Participation in America,* 52.

53. Bruce Cain, Russell Dalton, and Susan Scarrow, eds., *Democracy Transformed? Expanding Political Access in Advanced Industrial Democracies* (Oxford: Oxford University Press, 2003).

54. Verba and Nie, *Participation in America*.

55. Sidney Verba, Kay Schlozman, and Henry Brady, *Voice and Equality* (Cambridge, MA: Harvard University Press, 1995), 72.

56. Several recent publications have used trend data from the Roper polls or the DDB surveys, most notably Putnam's *Bowling Alone*. The Roper surveys used a mix of area probability sampling and quota or random-walk selection of respondents at the last stage; so these are not fully random samples. The sampling methods also changed during the time series collection. In addition, the short fieldwork time span and commercial orientation of the Roper polls would imply less accuracy of these data. The DDB surveys used by Putnam and the National Conference on Citizenship were mail surveys. The initial lists of names are not generated on a systematic random sampling basis, interviews are sent and returned by mail, and the response rates are substantially below the GSS or the ANES.

57. There is an anomaly with the 1967 data. The data distribution (which has only three categories) does not match the codebook (which has four response categories). In addition, it appears that some 200+ cases that are very low in political interest were mistakenly coded as missing data. After discussion with the principal investigator and analysis of these data, I recoded these missing data cases to the "no interest" category and recoded the other categories to regain the distribution of four categories. This is my best assumption on the actual distribution of responses in the 1967 survey. This reconstructed distribution is used in the table, although the results cannot be verified against the original survey findings.

58. Similarly, the American National Election Study finds a slight increase in general political interest since the early 1960s. See Dalton, *Citizen Politics*, rev. ed., ch. 2. The percentage that follows "what's going on in government and public affairs" trends slightly upward over time. In contrast, a different question about interest in the specific election campaign trends downward since 1952. This reinforces my assertion that fewer Americans are engaged in elections, but general interest is increasing.

59. Gallup asked the question between 1952 and 1984; the Pew Center repeated the question in September/October 1996 and October 2000. The question asks about general political interest, not tied to campaigns: "Generally speaking, how much interest would you say you have about politics—a great deal, a fair amount, only a little, or no interest at all?" There are eleven monthly time points between 1952 and 2000. Interest fluctuates within a fairly narrow band, and it tends to increase around elections. Political interest generally increases over time ($r = .26$). The source of these data is the IPOLL database at the Roper Center.

60. For preliminary results of the 1967/1987/2014 trends, see Russell Dalton, "DeTocqueville Revisited," Center for the Study of Democracy, UC Irvine, http://www.socsci.uci.edu/~rdalton/archive/tocqueville.pdf. These data are available at http://www3.norc.org/GSS+Website/Download. They were released as this book was being completed.

CHAPTER 5

1. Richard M. Fried, *Nightmare in Red: The McCarthy Era in Perspective* (New York: Oxford University Press, 1991).

2. David K. Johnson, *The Lavender Scare: The Cold War Persecution of Gays and Lesbians in the Federal Government* (Chicago: University of Illinois Press, 2004).

3. James Gibson, "Political Intolerance and Political Repression during the McCarthy Red Scare," *American Political Science Review* 82 (June 1988): 511–529.

4. The University of California and California State Universities still require a loyalty oath from employees. As late as 2008 a Quaker was rejected for a CSU faculty position because she insisted on adding "non-violent" to the oath's wording to "defend the Constitution."

5. Reynold Humphries, *Hollywood's Blacklists: A Political and Cultural History* (Edinburgh: Edinburgh University Press, 2009). The Motion Picture Producers and Distributors of America (MPPDA) required that all films produced and distributed by its members have the seal of approval of its Production Code Administration (PCA). The PCA had detailed guidelines to protect moral standards and reinforce "correct" standards of life. If you look at old movies from the era, many still display their PCA number.

6. Jerome Karabel, *The Chosen: The Hidden History of Admission and Exclusion at Harvard, Yale, and Princeton* (New York: Houghton Mifflin, 2005).

7. Jim Gibson, "Enigmas of Intolerance: Fifty Years after Stouffer's *Communism, Conformity, and Civil Liberties*," *Perspectives on Politics* 4 (2005): 21–34; Samuel Stouffer, *Communism, Conformity and Civil Liberties* (New York: Doubleday, 1955).

8. Clyde Nunn, Harry Crockett, and J. Williams, *Tolerance for Non-Conformity* (San Francisco: Jossey-Bass, 1978), 7.

9. Norman Nie, Jane Junn, and Kenneth Stehlik-Barry, *Education and Democratic Citizenship in America* (Chicago: University of Chicago Press, 1996), 64.

10. Herbert McClosky and Alida Brill, *Dimensions of Tolerance: What Americans Believe about Civil Liberties* (New York: Russell Sage Foundation, 1983); and Nie, Junn, and Stehlik-Barry, *Education and Democratic Citizenship in America*. Others have questioned the evidence of increasing tolerance, and I discuss this critique below. See John Sullivan, James Piereson, and George Marcus, *Political Tolerance and American Democracy* (Chicago: University of Chicago Press, 1982); Gibson, "Enigmas of Intolerance."

11. Stouffer, *Communism, Conformity and Civil Liberties*.

12. James Davis, "Communism, Conformity, Cohorts and Categories: American Tolerance in 1954 and 1972–73," *American Journal of Sociology* 81 (1975): 491–513; also see Nunn et al., *Tolerance for Non-Conformity*.

13. Nunn et al., *Tolerance for Non-Conformity*, 51.

14. Sullivan et al., *Political Tolerance and American Democracy*.

15. Paul Sniderman et al., "Principled Tolerance and the American Mass Public," *British Journal of Political Science* 19 (1989): 25–45.

16. James Gibson, "Alternative Measures of Political Tolerance: Must Tolerance Be 'Least-Liked'?" *American Journal of Political Science* 36 (1992): 560–577.

17. To underscore this chapter's theme of the rising political tolerance of Americans, in the wake of September 11, 2001, the 2004 General Social Survey asked whether religious extremists should be allowed to hold a public meeting: 74 percent said they should be allowed. Even though the specific reference of this question is not clear, this extent of tolerance in the wake of September 11 is noteworthy.

18. I separated the respondents in the 1974–2012 cumulative file into self-identified liberals, centrists, and conservatives. Using tolerance of speech as an example, there are comparable negative trends over time among all three ideological groups (the Pearson r correlation of speech tolerance and year of study):

	Communist	Atheist	Homosexual	Militarist	Racist
Liberal	−.06	−.09	−.16	−.09	.02
Center	−.0	−.12	−.18	−.11	−.01
Conservative	−.10	−.10	−.17	−.11	.00

19. Russell Dalton, *Citizen Politics: Public Opinion and Political Parties in Advanced Industrial Democracies*, 6th ed. (Washington, DC: CQ Press, 2013), ch. 6.

20. Robert Putnam, *Bowling Alone: The Collapse and Renewal of American Community* (New York: Simon and Schuster, 2000), 352.

21. The 2014 GSS included a new question on tolerance of anti-American Muslim clergy. Tolerance was lower for that group than for any of the groups in Table 5.1: make a public speech (44%), teach (33%), and don't remove a book from the library (49%). For the European experience, see Paul Sniderman and Louk Hagendoorn, *When Ways of Life Collide: Multiculturalism and Its Discontents in the Netherlands* (Princeton, NJ: Princeton University Press, 2007).

22. Philip Schwadel and Christopher Garneau, "An Age–Period–Cohort Analysis of Political Tolerance in the United States," *The Sociological Quarterly* 55 (2014): 421–452.

23. Nie et al., *Education and Democratic Citizenship in America*, ch. 7; also Paul Sniderman, Richard Brody, and Philip Tetlock, *Reasoning and Choice* (New York: Cambridge University Press, 1991); Nunn et al., *Tolerance for Non-Conformity*, ch. 4.

24. Nunn et al., *Tolerance for Non-Conformity*, ch. 5; McClosky and Brill, *Dimensions of Tolerance*, 387–403; Bobo and Licari, "Education and Political Tolerance," *Public Opinion Quarterly* 53 (1989): 285–308.

25. Christian Welzel, *Freedom Rising: Human Empowerment and the Quest for Emancipation* (Cambridge: Cambridge University Press, 2013).

26. Putnam, *Bowling Alone*, 357; see also James Davis, "Changeable Weather in a Cooling Climate atop the Liberal Plateau," *Public Opinion Quarterly* 56 (1992): 261–306.

27. Tocqueville discusses the potential tyranny of an omnipotent majority that leaves little space for dissident views. He cites examples of political opposition to the War of 1812 or racial prejudice in America and concludes: "what I find most repulsive in America is not the extreme freedom reigning there, but the shortage of guarantees against tyranny [of the majority]" (*Democracy in America*, vol. I, ch. 7). Similarly, McClosky and Brill are equally critical of the historical absence of tolerance in American political practices, quoting Levy: "The persistent image of colonial America as a society that cherished freedom of expression is a sentimental hallucination that ignores history. . . . The American people and their representatives simply did not understand that freedom of thought and expression for the other fellows, particularly the fellow with the hated ideas." Leonard Levy, ed., *Legacy of Suppression: Freedom of Speech and Press in Early American History* (Cambridge, MA: Harvard University Press, 1960), 9.

28. Herbert McClosky and John Schaar, "Psychological Dimensions of Anomie," *American Sociological Review* 30 (1965): 14–40.

29. McClosky and Brill, *Dimensions of Tolerance*, ch. 8.

30. Ewa Golebiowska, "Individual Value Priorities, Education, and Political Tolerance," *Political Behavior* 17 (1995): 23–48; also see Mark Peffley and Robert Rohrschneider, "Democratization and Political Tolerance in Seventeen Countries: A Multi-Level Model of Democratic Learning," *Political Research Quarterly* 56 (2003): 243–257.   •

31. The 2004 citizenship module only included three questions on tolerance toward religious extremists, those who wish to overthrow the government, and racists. These results are presented in the previous edition of this book. To use the broadest measure of tolerance, this figure uses only the 2014 data where all five groups are included as part of the citizenship module.

32. Russell Dalton, *The Good Citizen*, rev. ed. (Washington, DC: CQ Press, 2009).

33. The 2004 survey included five items; the Pearson *r* correlations between engaged citizenship and citizen-duty follow:

	Engaged Citizenship	Citizen Duty
Immigrants improve society	.21	−.04
Government does not spend too much on immigrants	.26	−.09
Parents of children born in the U.S. should receive citizenship	.20	−.07
Children of U.S. parents born outside country should be citizens	.12	−.03
Legal immigrants should have same rights as native born	.14	−.08

34. The Center for Democracy and Civil Society at Georgetown University conducted the survey. The list included thirteen groups and an option to mention another disliked group that did not appear on the list. For this list and other information on the CDACS survey, see http://www.icpsr.umich.edu/icpsr web/ICPSR/studies/4607. The CDACS measure of citizenship norms is essentially the same as the GSS and is described in the previous edition of this book.

35. The items were developed by Jim Gibson, and I appreciate his willingness to share these data. This classification of items is based on a factor analysis that identified two dimensions in the responses to the civil liberties battery.

36. If you like movies, see *Mona Lisa Smile* for a portrayal of life at a women's college in the 1950s; the recent film *Selma* is an emotional story of the life of African Americans in the South during the civil rights movement of the 1960s.

37. Putnam, *Bowling Alone*, ch. 22.

CHAPTER 6

1. Derek Heater, *Citizenship: The Civic Ideal in World History, Politics and Education*, 3rd ed. (Manchester, UK: Manchester University Press, 2004), 274.

2. F. A. Hayak, *The Road to Serfdom* (Chicago: University of Chicago Press, 1944); F. A. Hayak, *The Constitution of Liberty* (Chicago: University of Chicago Press, 1960); Robert Nozick, *Anarchy, State and Utopia* (New York: Basic Books, 1977); Lawrence Mead, *Beyond Entitlement: Obligations of Citizenship* (New York: Free Press, 1986).

3. Ronald Reagan, Inaugural Address, 1981, http://www.reagan.utexas.edu/archives/speeches/1981/12081a .htm.

4. T. H. Marshall, *Citizenship and Social Class*, ed. T. Bottomore (London: Pluto Press, 1992; originally published 1950).

5. John Gray, *Men Are from Mars, Women Are from Venus: A Practical Guide for Improving Communication and Getting What You Want in Your Relationships* (New York: HarperCollins, 2005).

6. Linda Bennett and Stephen Bennett, *Living with Leviathan: Americans Coming to Terms with Big Government* (Lawrence: University Press of Kansas, 1990); Russell Dalton, *Citizen Politics: Public Opinion and Political Parties in Advanced Industrial Democracies*, 6th ed. (Washington, DC: CQ Press, 2012), ch. 6.

7. The question wording reads: "We are faced with many problems in this country, none of which can be solved easily or inexpensively. I'm going to name some of these problems, and for each one I'd like you to tell me whether you *think* we're spending too much money on it, too little money, or about the right amount. First (READ ITEM A) . . . are we spending too much, too little, or about the right amount on (ITEM)?"

8. Stuart Soroka, and Christopher Wlezien. *Degrees of Democracy: Politics, Public Opinion and Policy* (New York: Cambridge University Press, 2010).

9. Bennett and Bennett, *Living with Leviathan*.

10. Bennett and Bennett, *Living with Leviathan*, 137.

11. The wording of the spending choices can strongly impact the responses. The term "welfare," for instance, produces less support for social spending than a question about "helping the poor." Therefore, I focus on the broad trends in Table 6.1 rather than specific support for any single policy option.

12. Soroka and Wlezien, *Degrees of Democracy*.

13. The citizenship norms question was not asked on the same section of the GSS as the traditional spending items, so instead I use the alternate spending question. This asks about the same policy areas but with slightly different question wording.

14. Russell Dalton, *The Good Citizen: How a Younger Generation Is Reshaping American Politics*, rev. ed. (Washington, DC: CQ Press, 2009), ch. 6.

15. Soroka and Wlezien, *Degrees of Democracy*; Benjamin Page and Robert Shapiro, *The Rational Public: Fifty Years of Trends in Americans' Policy Preferences* (Chicago: University of Chicago Press, 1992).

16. This classification of items is based on principal components analyses that produced three components. The social dimension has the highest loadings for assisting the poor, health care, and education. The security dimension was defined by spending on national defense and law enforcement. The third component combined space exploration, aid to other countries, and aid to big cities. I constructed scores for each component and these are used in the regression analyses in Table 6.2.

17. See Dalton, *The Good Citizen*, epilogue.

18. Russell Dalton, *The Apartisan American* (Washington, DC: CQ Press, 2012).

19. Ronald Inglehart, *Culture Shift in Advanced Industrial Societies* (Princeton, NJ: Princeton University Press, 1990); Ronald Inglehart, *Modernization and Postmodernization* (Princeton, NJ: Princeton University Press, 1997).

CHAPTER 7

1. Hans-Dieter Klingemann, "Mapping Political Support in the 1990s," in *Critical Citizens,* ed. Pippa Norris (Oxford: Oxford University Press, 1999); Pippa Norris, "Introduction," in Norris, *Critical Citizens*; Russell Dalton and Christian Welzel, eds., *The Civic Culture Transformed: From Allegiant to Assertive Citizens* (Cambridge: Cambridge University Press, 2014).

2. Gabriel Almond and Sidney Verba, *The Civic Culture* (Boston: Little Brown, 1965), 313–314.

3. At the same time, American political thought and history often highlight antigovernment traditions in the United States. The nation was founded by those who opposed British government, and these sentiments are supposedly enshrined in the political culture. One approach stresses this antigovernment element of American culture: Seymour Martin Lipset, *Continental Divide: The Values and Institutions of the United States and Canada* (New York: Routledge, 1990); Samuel Huntington, *American Politics: The Promise of Disharmony* (Cambridge, MA: Harvard University Press, 1981). When early empirical studies found high levels of political support in the United States, most political scientists argued that these patterns were an essential part of a democratic civic culture.

4. Seymour Martin Lipset and William Schneider, *The Confidence Gap* (New York: Free Press, 1983); E. J. Dionne, *Why Americans Hate Politics* (New York: Simon & Schuster, 1991); John Hibbing and Elizabeth Theiss-Morse, *Congress as Public Enemy: Public Attitudes toward American Political Institutions* (New York: Cambridge University Press, 1995); Joseph Nye, Philip Zelikow, and David King, eds., *Why Americans Mistrust Government* (Cambridge, MA: Harvard University Press, 1997).

5. For example, see the discussions in Russell Dalton, *Democratic Challenges, Democratic Choices* (Oxford: Oxford University Press, 2004), ch. 1; Stephen Macedo et al., *Democracy at Risk* (Washington, DC: Brookings Institution, 2005), ch. 1.

6. David Easton, *A Systems Analysis of Political Life* (New York: Wiley, 1965); David Easton, "A Reassessment of the Concept of Political Support," *British Journal of Political Science* 5 (1975): 435–457.

7. Ridicule of government is as American as apple pie. Mark Twain, for example, asked "Suppose you were an idiot. And suppose you were a member of Congress," and then he added, "But I repeat myself." Similarly, Will Rogers wrote that Americans feel the same way when Congress is in session as when the baby gets hold of a hammer: "It's just a question of how much damage he can do before we take it away from him." For a contemporary study of political humor see Jody Baumgartner and Jonathan Morris, *Laughing Matters: Humor and American Politics in the Media Age* (London: Routledge, 2007).

8. Pew Center for People and the Press, *Distrust, Discontent, Anger and Partisan Rancor: The People and Their Government*. (2010). http://www.people-press.org/2010/04/18/distrust-discontent-anger-and-partisan-rancor/.

9. Hibbing and Theiss-Morse, *Congress as Public Enemy*; Joseph Cooper, ed., *Congress and the Decline of Public Trust* (Boulder, CO: Westview, 1999); Jonathan Rauch, *Government's End: Why Washington Stopped Working* (New York: Public Affairs, 1999).

10. Thomas Patterson, *Out of Order* (New York: Knopf, 1993); Thomas Patterson, *Doing Well and Doing Good: How Soft News and Critical Journalism Are Shrinking the News Audience and Weakening Democracy and What News Outlets Can Do about It* (Cambridge, MA: Shorenstein Center, Harvard University, 2001).

11. John Hibbing and Elizabeth Theiss-Morse, *Stealth Democracy: Americans' Beliefs about How Government Should Work* (New York: Cambridge University Press, 2002).

12. Nye, *Why Americans Distrust Government*, ch. 12.

13. Dalton, *Democratic Challenges, Democratic Choices*.

14. Ronald Inglehart, "Postmodernization, Authority and Democracy," in Norris, *Critical Citizens*; Dalton and Welzel, *The Civic Culture Transformed*.

15. I used factor analyses to determine the items that tap each dimension of political support. I relied on these analyses to group and interpret items in this chapter as well as providing the basis for the multivariate analyses in the chapter appendix.

16. The question asks: "On the whole, on a scale of 0 to 10 where 0 is very poorly and 10 is very well, how well does democracy work in America today? And how about ten years ago? How well did democracy work in America then? And how about ten years from now? How well do you think democracy will work in America then?"

17. Dalton and Welzel, *The Civic Culture Transformed*.

18. Marc Hetherington, *Why Trust Matters: Declining Political Trust and the Demise of American Liberalism* (Princeton, NJ: Princeton University Press, 2005).

19. I should note that this chapter is not a paid advertisement for Starbucks. In fact, I routinely hold "office hours" at the Panera near the UC Irvine campus and not the Starbucks.

20. Dahl, *On Democracy*, 37–38. In addition, these four categories clearly overlap with the ideas of citizenship discussed in Chapter 2. The degree of overlap is the point of the analyses here.

21. The question reads: "There are different opinions about people's rights in a democracy. On a scale of 1 to 7, where 1 is not at all important and 7 is very important, how important is it to . . ."

22. The index is a factor score from principal components analyses. Because some of the items were not asked in 2014, this index is based only on the 2004 survey. The 2004 analysis finds that all six items are positively loaded on a first dimension: treat everyone equally (.75), politicians consider citizens (.73), protect minority rights (.70), adequate standard of living (.65), participate in decisions (.62), and civil disobedience (.18).

23. This clustering is based on a factor analysis of Q85 that yields two dimensions. The listing of items in the text reflects the size of their factor loadings. The second dimension deals with equality and participation, and this is not significantly related to either citizen duty (–.03) or engaged citizenship (–.04).

24. Such patterns also appear in analyses that compare democratic values and trust in government as a function of postmaterial values. Dalton and Welzel, *The Civic Culture Transformed*.

25. Dalton, *Citizen Politics*, ch. 12.

26. Huntington, *Who Are We?*; Elizabeth Theiss-Morse, *Who Counts as an American? The Boundaries of National Identity* (New York: Cambridge University Press, 2009).

27. Hetherington, *Why Trust Matters*.

28. See Klingemann, "Mapping Political Support in the 1990s"; Dalton and Welzel, *The Civic Culture Transformed*. In contrast, Huntington in *American Politics* viewed such "creedal passion" as a negative feature of American political history; but in the conclusion we will argue this is one of the positive driving forces of democratic growth.

CHAPTER 8

1. Alexis de Tocqueville, *Democracy in America* (New York: Knopf, 1960).

2. See the examples cited in Seymour Martin Lipset, *The First New Nation: The United States in Historical and Comparative Perspective* (New York: Basic Books, 1963); Seymour Martin Lipset, *American Exceptionalism: A Double-edged Sword* (New York: Norton, 1997).

3. Seymour Martin Lipset, *Continental Divide* (New York: Routledge, 1990); Anthony King, "Distrust of Government: Explaining American Exceptionalism," in *Disaffected Democracies*, ed. Susan Pharr and Robert Putnam (Princeton, NJ: Princeton University Press, 2000).

4. These points are discussed extensively in Chapter 4 in this book.

5. Bas Denters, Oscar Gabriel, and Mariano Torcal, "Norms of Good Citizenship," in *Citizenship and Involvement in Europe*, ed. Jan van Deth, J. Ramón Montero, and Anders Westholm (London: Routledge, 2006); Robert Putnam, *Democracies in Flux* (Oxford: Oxford University Press, 2002); Pattie Charles, Patrick Seyd, and Paul Whiteley, *Citizenship in Britain: Values, Participation, and Democracy* (New York: Cambridge University Press, 2004).

6. Liam Fay, "Young Voters Are Right to Smell a Rate in Presidential Age Frivolity," *Independent*, May 4, 2015.

7. Lipset, *American Exceptionalism*, 17; Rudyard Kipling perhaps stated it more eloquently when he said "And what should they know of England, who only England know?" from "The English Flag," in *Barrack-room Ballads and Other Verses* (London: Methuen, 1892), stanza 1.

8. Robert Kagan, *Of Paradise and Power: America and Europe in the New World Order* (New York: Knopf, 2003).

9. Lipset, *American Exceptionalism*; Deborah Madsen, *American Exceptionalism* (Edinburgh: Edinburgh University Press, 1998); Charles Lockhart, *The Roots of American Exceptionalism: Institutions, Culture and Policies* (New York: Palgrave Macmillan, 2011).

10. Lipset, *American Exceptionalism*, ch. 1; Lipset, *Continental Divide*, ch. 2.

11. Ronald Inglehart et al., *Human Beliefs and Values* (Madrid: Siglo XXI Editores, 2004).

12. Gabriel Almond and Sidney Verba, *The Civic Culture* (Princeton, NJ: Princeton University Press, 1963); Sidney Verba, Norman Nie, and Jae-on Kim, *Participation and Political Equality* (New York: Cambridge University Press, 1978); Samuel Barnes, Max Kaase, et al., *Political Action* (Beverly Hills, CA: Sage, 1979); Pippa Norris, *The Democratic Phoenix* (New York: Cambridge University Press, 1999); Russell Dalton, *Citizen Politics*, 6th ed. (Washington, DC: CQ Press, 2013).

13. T. H. Marshall, *Citizenship and Social Class*, ed. T. Bottomore (London: Pluto Press, 1992; originally published 1950).

14. The GESIS archive at the University of Cologne provided these data (ZA 3950). The 2004 ISSP includes the following established democracies: the United States, Australia, Austria, Britain, Canada, Denmark, Finland, Flanders, France, Germany, Ireland, Japan, New Zealand, Netherlands, Norway, Portugal, Spain, Sweden, and Switzerland. I do not examine the new democracies in the ISSP because of the focus on how citizenship has evolved in affluent, established democracies. Different causal processes are likely at work in new democracies as people first learn democratic citizenship.

15. I replicated the two-dimensional factor structure described in Chapter 2 using the additional military service items from 2004. Engaged citizenship was the first dimension, explaining 25.9 percent of the variance in these ten items; citizen duty was the second dimension (21.7 percent variance). In general terms, the factor analysis for these nineteen nations produced the same general structure as for the U.S. analyses. I then computed factor scores for the two dimensions, and the average scores for each nation locate nations in Figure 8.2.

16. The U.S. patterns in Figure 8.1 are slightly different in absolute values from the generational comparisons of Figure 3.1 because the citizenship scores were recalculated based on the pooled factor analysis of all nineteen nations and included the military service question. Generation groups are defined in the same way as in Figure 3.1: the pre-WWII generation came of age before 1946; Boomers came of age between 1946 and 1960; the Sixties generation was between 1961 and 1975; the Eighties generation was between 1976 and 1990; and Generation X was after 1990. There were too few Millennials in the 2004 survey to analyze them separately.

17. National Conference on Citizenship, *America's Civic Health Index: Broken Engagement* (Washington, DC: National Conference on Citizenship, 2006), 4 (www.ncoc.org). The report also presents a measure of America's civic health, which shows an improvement since 2000; but then the report drops "three controversial measures" to produce a continuing decline since 2000 (8).

18. Aina Gallego, *Unequal Political Participation Worldwide* (New York: Cambridge University Press, 2015); Dalton, *Citizen Politics*, ch. 3.

19. The question asked: "Here are some different forms of political and social action that people can take. Please indicate, for each one, whether you have done any of these things in the past year."

20. Norris, *Democratic Phoenix*; Steve Weldon and Russell Dalton, "Democratic Structures and Democratic Participation: The Limits of Consociational Theory," in *Elections and Democracy: Representation and Accountability*, ed. Jacques Thomassen (Oxford: Oxford University Press, 2014).

21. Factor analyses identified two dimensions. The electoral dimension includes voting, discussing politics, and trying to convince others. The remaining items are strongly related to a second, nonelectoral dimension. I computed factor scores on both dimensions and compared national mean scores in Figure 8.5.

22. Mark Peffley and Robert Rohrschneider, "Democratization and Political Tolerance in Seventeen Countries: A Multi-level Model of Democratic Learning," *Political Research Quarterly* 56 (2003): 243–257.

23. Peffley and Rohrschneider, "Democratization and Political Tolerance in Seventeen Countries."

24. Peffley and Rohrschneider, "Democratization and Political Tolerance in Seventeen Countries." Also see Chapter 5.

25. Spain, for instance, does not follow the general pattern. First, both dimensions of citizenship are negatively related to tolerance in Spain. On further examination, I found that the general dimensions of citizenship are not configured in the same way among the Spanish sample, which may explain some of the divergence.

26. Philip Coggan, *The Last Vote: The Threats to Western Democracy* (New York: Penguin, 2013); Alan Wolfe, *Does American Democracy Still Work?* (New Haven, CT: Yale University Press, 2006); Fareed Zakaria, *The Future of Freedom: Illiberal Democracy at Home and Abroad* (New York: Norton, 2003).

27. Stephen Breyer, "Americans Cynical about Government," Associated Press, May 4, 1999.

28. Pippa Norris, *Democratic Deficit: Critical Citizens Revisited* (Cambridge: Cambridge University Press, 2011); Russell Dalton, *Democratic Challenges, Democratic Choices* (Oxford: Oxford University Press, 2004).

29. Russell Dalton and Christian Welzel, eds., *The Civic Culture Transformed: From Allegiant to Assertive Citizens* (Cambridge: Cambridge University Press, 2014).

30. Similarly, social rights are positively related to engaged citizenship ($r = .26$) and citizen duty ($r = .17$).

31. In separate analyses replicating those in Figure 7.2, citizen duty is more strongly related to trust in government ($r = .17$) than is engaged citizenship ($r = .10$). This implies that changing citizenship norms are increasing the percentage of critical citizens who are dissatisfied with government but more committed to democratic values.

32. Stuart Weir and David Beetham, *Political Power and Democratic Control in Britain: The Democratic Audit of the United Kingdom* (London: Routledge, 2000); also Coggan, *The Last Vote*.

CHAPTER 9

1. Karl Mannheim, *Freedom, Power and Democratic Planning*, quoted in T. Brennan, *Political Education and Democracy* (Cambridge: Cambridge University Press, 1981), 106.

2. Philip Coggan, *The Last Vote: The Threats to Western Democracy* (New York: Allen Lane, 2013); Alan Wolfe, *Does American Democracy Still Work?* (New Haven, CT: Yale University Press, 2006); Stephen Macedo et al., *Democracy at Risk: How Political Choices Undermine Citizen Participation, and What We Can Do about It* (Washington, DC: Brookings Institution Press, 2005); John Hibbing and Elizabeth Theiss-Morse, *Stealth Democracy: Americans' Beliefs about How Government Should Work* (New York: Cambridge University Press, 2002); Robert Putnam, *Bowling Alone: The Collapse and Renewal of American Community* (New York: Simon and Schuster, 2000).

3. Seymour Martin Lipset, *American Exceptionalism: A Double-edged Sword* (New York: Norton, 1997), 267, offered a refreshingly balanced statement that summarizes our view: "The critics [of America] have exaggerated many of the problems in the quest to demonstrate decay. There is, however, no denying that the impression of a change in basic values exists, and to dismiss public perception [of crisis] as somehow wrong or misinformed is to deny the reality of individual experience."

4. Tom Brokaw, *The Greatest Generation* (New York: Random House, 1998). See also Chapters 2 and 3.

5. The Pew Center has developed a fun an informative online quiz that judges whether your views and life conditions make you part of the Millennial generation: http://www.pewresearch.org/quiz/how-millennial-are-you/.

6. Gabriel Almond, *The Civic Culture: Prehistory, Retrospect, and Prospect*, paper published by the Center for the Study of Democracy, http://repositories.cdlib.org/csd/96-01/.

7. Gabriel Almond and Sidney Verba, *The Civic Culture* (Princeton, NJ: Princeton University Press, 1963).

8. Putnam, *Bowling Alone*.

9. For a cross-national discussion of this change in norms, see Russell Dalton and Christian Welzel, eds., *The Civic Culture Transformed: From Allegiant to Assertive Citizens* (Cambridge: Cambridge University Press, 2014).

10. Frances Fukuyama, *The Great Disruption* (New York: Touchstone, 2000), 15.

11. For example, John Bridgeland, *Heart of the Nation: Volunteering and America's Civic Spirit* (Lanham, MD: Rowman & Littlefield, 2013); Shirley Sagawa, *The American Way to Change: How National Service and Volunteers Are Transforming America* (New York: Jossey-Bass 2010).

12. Martin Wattenberg, *Is Voting for Young People?* (New York: Longman, 2006).

13. This is based on analyses of the impact of distrust in government: Marc Hetherington, *Why Trust Matters: Declining Political Trust and the Demise of American Liberalism* (Princeton, NJ: Princeton University Press, 2005); Russell Dalton, *Democratic Challenges, Democratic Choices* (Oxford: Oxford University Press, 2004), ch. 9.

14. For example, Jonathan Cohn, "A Lost Political Generation?" *The American Prospect,* 9, no. 3 (1992); Ted Halstead, "A Politics for Generation X," *The Atlantic Monthly,* August 1999.

15. Jean Twenge, *Generation Me,* rev. ed. (New York: Atria, 2014); also see Lynne Lancaster and David Stillman, *When Generations Collide: Who They Are. Why They Clash. How to Solve the Generational Puzzle at Work* (New York: Harper, 2002).

16. Ronald Inglehart, *Culture Shift in Advanced Industrial Society* (Princeton, NJ: Princeton University Press, 1990); Christian Welzel, *Freedom Rising* (Cambridge: Cambridge University Press, 2013); Dalton and Welzel, *The Civic Culture Transformed.*

17. Christian Welzel and Russell J. Dalton, "From Allegiant to Assertive Citizens," in Dalton and Welzel, *The Civic Culture Transformed;* also see Bettina Geissel, "Do Critical Citizens Foster Better Governance? A Comparative Study," *West European Politics* 31 (2008): 855–873.

18. Obama discussed this idea during a speech in March 2015; also see Wattenberg, *Is Voting for Young People?* ch. 7; Arend Lijphart, "Unequal Participation: Democracy's Unresolved Dilemma," *American Political Science Review* 91 (1997): 1–14.

19. Alison Fields, *The Youth Challenge: Participating in Democracy* (New York: Carnegie Corporation of New York, 2003).

20. For a discussion of the potential for Internet voting, see Michael Alvarez and Thad Hall, *Electronic Elections: The Perils and Promises of Digital Democracy* (Princeton, NJ: Princeton University Press, 2010).

21. Aneesh Chopra, *Innovative State: How New Technologies Can Transform Government* (New York: Atlantic Monthly Press, 2014); Gavin Newsom and Lisa Dickey, *Citizenville: How to Take the Town Square Digital and Reinvent Government* (New York: Penguin, 2013).

22. http://www.ukyouthparliament.org.uk/.

23. Bruce Cain, Russell Dalton, and Susan Scarrow, eds., *Democracy Transformed? Expanding Citizen Access in Advanced Industrial Democracies* (Oxford: Oxford University Press, 2003).

24. Graham Smith, *Democratic Innovations: Designing Institutions for Citizen Participation* (Cambridge: Cambridge University Press, 2009); Kimmo Grönlund, André Bächtiger, and Maija Setälä, *Deliberative Mini-Publics Involving Citizens in the Democratic Process* (Colchester, UK: ECPR Press, 2014).

25. Caroline Lee et al., eds., *Democratizing Inequalities: Dilemmas of the New Public Participation* (New York: New York University Press, 2015); Robert Putnam, *Our Kids: The American Dream in Crisis.* (New York: Simon and Schuster, 2015); Cain et al., *Democracy Transformed?* ch. 13; also Sidney Verba, Kay Schlozman, and Henry Brady, *Voice and Equality* (Cambridge, MA: Harvard University Press, 1985).

26. The patterns over time are unclear. It appears that the decline in election turnout is greater among individuals with lower social status: Jan Leighley and Jonathan Nagler, *Who Votes Now? Demographics, Issues, Inequality and Turnout in the United States* (Princeton, NJ: Princeton University Press, 2014). However, research does not show a growth in political inequality for other forms of political participation: Henry Brady et al., "Who Bowls? The (Un)Changing Stratification of Participation," in *Understanding Public Opinion,* ed. Barbara Norrander and Clyde Wilcox (Washington, DC: CQ Press, 2002). Thus, the major patterns of inequality appear to be across different forms of action rather than trends over time.

27. https://www.whitehouse.gov/the-press-office/2014/06/13/remarks-president-university-california-irvine-commencement-ceremony.

INDEX